# HISTORY'S GREATEST DECEPTIONS

and the People Who Planned Them

# HISTORY'S GREATEST DECEPTIONS

and the People Who Planned Them

Eric Chaline

First published in the United Kingdom in 2010
by The History Press
The Mill, Brimscombe Port
Stroud GL5 2QG
www.thehistorypress.co.uk

Printed in Hong Kong

9 8 7 6 5 4 3 2 1

Digit on the right indicates the number of this printing

ISBN: 978-0-7524-5771-0

Conceived, designed, and produced by
Quid Publishing
Level 4, Sheridan House
114 Western Road
Hove BN3 1DD
England
www.quidpublishing.com

To the Angels in my life

# CONTENTS

# INTRODUCTION

According to Holy Writ, the history of humankind begins with two deceptions: that of Eve by the Serpent, immediately followed by Eve's deception of Adam. From these dishonest beginnings, we may have to face up to the unhappy realisation that humans might be predestined to connive, cheat and deceive their way through life.

Nature herself is no stranger to subterfuge. In the world of plants and animals, we find many impostors and con-artists who fight the battle for survival with guile and trickery rather than brute strength: butterflies use the colourful wing markings that we find so pretty to frighten predators; other insects mimic poisonous or stinging species while being quite harmless themselves. Pitcher plants and Venus Flytraps lure insects to their deaths with the promise of food or mates, while anglerfish dangle lures like human fishermen to attract their prey. The cuckoo famously lays her eggs in the nests of other birds, letting surrogate parents do all the hard work of raising her young. Where deceit is concerned, however, there are notable differences between the motivations of plants and animals and those of humans. While the former deceive to survive and occasionally to procreate, humans have 'higher' motives for their deceptions: the pursuit of wealth, power and fame.

The deceptions included in this book are listed under seven main headings. We begin with an evergreen favourite: religious deceits. For most of history, life – as the great political philosopher Thomas Hobbes (1588–1679) pointed out – has been 'poor, nasty, brutish, and short'. Therefore it is easy to imagine the attraction of knowing what the future will hold (Ancient Oracles, pp. 10–14), or of being able to buy a place in Heaven (Fake Relics and Indulgences, pp. 41–7). Military subterfuges are also well represented, from the stratagem that sealed the fate of Troy (Odysseus, pp. 15–19), to the extraordinary efforts of the Allies to hide their plans for the D-Day landings from the Germans during World War Two (Operation Fortitude, pp. 139–44).

Although one might think that the world of science, with its exacting standards of evidence and proof, might be immune from deceit, there have been several outrageous scientific deceptions in this and the last century, including the hoax 'missing link' (Piltdown Man, pp. 85–90) and the claims for an inexhaustible, cheap, non-polluting power source by two deluded scientists (Cold Fusion, pp. 222–6). Impostors ancient and modern are also well represented in these pages, including two fake British princes (Lambert Simnel and Perkin Warbeck, pp. 35–40), a trio of bogus tsars (The False Dimitrys, pp. 48–53), as well as a Russian royal impostor of more recent vintage, Anna Anderson, who claimed to be the sole surviving scion of the Russian Imperial family (Anna Anderson, pp. 102–6). Another rich seam of imposture is that of people claiming to be something that they are not: the British-born Tibetan lama (Cyril Hoskin, pp. 163–7), for example, or the serial impostor who claimed in turn to be a doctor, a lawyer and an airline pilot (Frank W. Abagnale, Jr., pp. 179–83).

Impostures are not just concerned with identity, qualifications or status, but can also involve the pretence of being of the opposite gender. Before the emancipation of women, females who wished to pursue their own course in the world had no option but to cross-dress. Such was the case of China's female warrior, Hua Mulan (pp. 31–4). A more intriguing case is that of the only woman said to have sat on the papal throne ('Pope' Joan, pp. 27–30). Three more recent examples of male-to-female cross-dressing are a French spy (The Chevalière d'Éon, pp. 63–7), an Olympic athlete (Stanisława Walasiewicz, pp. 121–3) and an academic (Charlotte Bach, pp. 195–8).

In the lucrative world of the fine arts and literature, forgeries also abound. Some are created for financial gain (Elmyr de Hory, pp. 151–5), others by disappointed artists who wish to prove that they can equal the great masters, or as hoaxes to deceive the experts. Take the cases of the fake Shakespeare plays (William Ireland, pp. 58–62) and the fake Mozart piano concerto (Marius Casadesus, pp. 129–32). Forged documents, films and photographs can be used for political ends (*The Donation of Constantine*, pp. 23–6 and the Zinoviev Letter, pp. 112–6), or to prove the existence of everything from mythical creatures (The Patterson –Gimlin film, pp. 190–4, and the Loch Ness Monster Hoaxes, pp. 133–8) to UFOs (George Adamski, pp. 145–50). Finally, the reader will discover a fair number of financial frauds and confidence tricks scattered among these pages, including my personal favourite, Miami's Brassiere Brigade (pp. 156–9), and the recent $65-billion-dollar Ponzi schemer, Bernard Madoff (pp. 246–51).

**DECEPTION**

**Religious deceit**

Military subterfuge

Financial fraud

Fake or counterfeit

Imposture or cross-dressing

Confidence trick

Scientific deception

# VOICES OF THE GODS: ANCIENT ORACLES

**Main Culprits:** Priests and diviners

**Motivation:** Power and financial gain

**Damage Done:** Misled the credulous into making wrong decisions, leading to loss, death and destruction on an epic scale

*So [Croesus] sent his messengers in different directions, some to Delphi, some to Abae in Phocis, and some to Dodona [....] To Libya he sent another embassy, to consult the oracle of Ammon. These messengers were sent to test the knowledge of the oracles, that, if they were found really to return true answers, he might send a second time, and inquire if he ought to attack the Persians.*

**From *The Histories* by Herodotus (484–425 BCE)**

Divination and prophecy were integral parts of the religious practices of Antiquity. In a time when life could be extremely short, uncertain and violent, an inside track on the future was often a matter of life or death. Each ancient civilisation used different methods to obtain foreknowledge of the future. The ancient Chinese, creators of one of the earliest literate cultures on earth, inscribed questions on animal bones, to which they applied a heated iron to create patterns of cracks that the diviner interpreted for the questioner. The Babylonians, who lived in what is now Iraq, gave us one of the few divinatory systems that have survived in the present-day West: astrology. The Romans sacrificed animals to the gods, sliced them open, and tried to read the future in the position, shape and size of internal organs, and also interpreted the flight of birds. But perhaps to us the strangest and most fascinating of ancient religious practices was the belief in oracles – direct verbal communications from a god or goddess.

**GOD'S MOUTHPIECE**

Two cultures of Antiquity are particularly associated with oracular divination: Egypt and Greece. The link is not accidental, as legend holds that the tradition was transmitted directly from Egypt to Greece. Ancient Egypt and Greece shared a belief in a multitude of gods and goddesses, each in charge of his or her own domain. After Alexander the Great (356–323 BCE) conquered Egypt in 332–331 BCE, the pantheons of both cultures began to merge. Hence, Amun (Ammon to the Greeks), the principal Egyptian divinity, was associated with Zeus, father of the Olympian gods, and became Zeus-Ammon. Divinities, as a rule, are not known for their conversational skills, hence they need intermediaries to convey their words. In rituals that depended on the interpretation of natural phenomena – such as the movement of birds or of the stars, or the analysis of a particularly interesting liver or gall bladder – the diviner or augur themselves may well have believed what they were saying. Engaging a divinity in a one-to-one conversation, however, required a lot more creative input from the attendants of the god.

There were many oracles in Egypt, but the best-known was the oracle of Amun at the vast city-sized temple complex of Karnak. The first sanctuary of Amun was established at Karnak in the middle of the second millennium BCE, and continued to function for over one thousand years. Karnak was not only the largest temple complex in Egypt, it was also the richest and politically most influential. The crowned pharaoh might be a living god and therefore an intermediary between his human subjects and the gods, but he or she had to be crowned first, and it was at the succession that the priesthood of Amun could exercise considerable political influence. When the succession was disputed, the candidate with the backing of the priesthood had a considerable advantage over his or her rivals. For example, Queen Hatshepsut (d. 1458 BCE), one of the few women to reign in pre-Hellenic Egypt in her own right, was confirmed as pharaoh by the oracle of Amun. She was appropriately grateful to the god and built lavishly at Karnak.

It is not known exactly how Egyptian oracles communicated with their questioners. In one well-documented practice, however, the statue of the god, borne aloft on the shoulders of his priests, was paraded in front of the faithful. The movements of the statue and where it stopped were the means that conveyed the answer to a question. In the oracle

**SON OF ZEUS**
Alexander the Great visited the oracle of Siwa, where the god declared him to be his 'son'. He either believed it himself or used it to inspire his troops.

of Zeus-Ammon in the oasis of Siwa, the oracle room had a false ceiling, indicating that it could have been the hiding place for priests to overhear what petitioners asked the god. Siwa is 560 km (350 miles) east of Cairo, deep in the Libyan Desert. Alexander the Great visited the oracle just before embarking on his epic world conquest. He entered the sanctuary alone, and refused to reveal what the god had said to him. But he clearly liked what he heard as he went on to conquer Egypt, and then the rest of the vast Persian Empire, and reached northern India, where even his overweening ambition and self-confidence failed him, and he was forced to return to Babylon, where he died.

It was after his visit to Siwa that he began to style himself the 'son of Zeus-Ammon' and depict himself on his coins with the ram's-horn helmet that was the symbol of the god. As his arrival in Egypt was not unexpected, and he made his intention clear to visit Siwa, it is very likely that the answer to Alexander's question had been carefully crafted by the priests of Amun in the Egyptian capital of Memphis days before he himself reached the oracle. The priests were politically astute enough to see that Alexander had a good chance of liberating Egypt from the Persians, so the oracle must have encouraged him to persevere and declared him to be the rightful pharaoh. Whether Alexander himself believed in the oracle, or he merely used its fame to strengthen the morale of his Macedonian and Greek troops and obtain the support of the local population, we shall never know. However, ever the astute politician, Alexander, too, built lavishly in Egypt.

Alongside the Egyptians, the ancient Greeks had one of the strongest oracular traditions of Antiquity. The Greek world, consisting of the Greek mainland and Aegean Islands, Crete and Cyprus, the eastern part of Turkey (Asian Ionia), and the Greek colonies of Spain, France, Sicily and Italy, was never a single unified empire but a shifting web of alliances between squabbling city-states, the most famous of which were Athens, Sparta, Corinth and Thebes. Each city looked to a patron deity or sometimes a deified hero, such as Herakles (Hercules), who spoke to his faithful through oracles; but one of the Olympian gods, Apollo, was particularly renowned for bestowing the gift of prophecy to his devotees.

**A MIGHTY EMPIRE SHALL FALL**

Apollo had several oracles, but the most famous was located in mainland Greece in the city of Delphi on the flanks of Mount Parnassus. In piecing together the history of the oracle of Delphi, we have to combine the evidence of archeology with ancient stories and legends. Historians still debate when the oracle was established, giving dates ranging from the eighth to the sixth century BCE. Legend tells us that a giant snake-like monster, the Python, guarded the sacred spot, and that Apollo slew the beast, giving humans access to the oracle. Another less fantastic story asserts that it was a shepherd or goatherd who discovered the oracle. He noticed that his flock behaved strangely when it approached a natural fissure in the mountainside. After investigating this geographic phenomenon, he discovered that he had been granted the gift of prophecy. A sanctuary was built over the spot, and in time, a priestess, known as the 'Pythia', was appointed to convey the messages of the god. She sat in a small chamber, seated on a three-legged stool, and gave the answers to questions in verses that were so cryptic or vague that they themselves needed interpretation. One theory put forward argues that the shrine of the oracle was built over a natural fissure in the earth's crust, and that a gas emanating from the ground inspired the Pythia's prophetic utterances.

The accuracy of oracles was the subject of controversy even in ancient times. Questioners who had the ready cash, because consulting an oracle did not come cheap, could ask the same question of several oracles and see which of them got the right answer. One such man was King Croesus of Lydia (595–547 BCE). Lydia was sandwiched between the Greek cities of Asian Ionia and the growing might of the Persian Empire. Concerned for the survival of his kingdom, Croesus decided to consult the oracles as to the likely outcome of a war with the Persians. He first tested the principle oracles of the day (see quote). From the replies he received, the king decided that only two oracles, including Apollo's at Delphi, were trustworthy. He sent them a further question about the outcome of an attack on Persia. The answer he obtained from Delphi was: 'When Croesus fords the river Halys, a mighty empire shall fall.' Around 547 BCE, encouraged by this reply, and believing that the oracle foretold the fall of the Persian Empire, Croesus assembled his troops and crossed the Halys that was the boundary between his realm and the Persian Empire. He met with a crushing defeat, and was burned alive by the Persian king, Cyrus the Great (c. 600–530 BCE), who was curious to see if Apollo would intervene to save Croesus' life.

KING CROESUS MET WITH A CRUSHING DEFEAT, AND WAS BURNED ALIVE BY THE PERSIAN KING, CYRUS THE GREAT (C. 600–530 BCE).

Despite this and other spectacular failures, the oracle at Delphi continued to operate until the fourth century CE, when the Christian emperor Theodosius the Great (347–395 CE) decreed the closure of all pagan temples in the Roman Empire. The Church banned all kinds of divination as remnants of paganism and later as Satanic witchcraft, but the lure of future knowledge was too strong even for the leaders of the Catholic Church, the popes, who employed their own astrologers during the Middle Ages.

The continuing popularity of fortune-telling techniques, including astrology, the tarot and the I-Ching, is a testament to the desperate need that drives humans to believe that inanimate objects – be they heavenly bodies, pieces of brightly coloured cardboard or bits of wood – are capable of predicting the future. Give me a human oracle any time; in my experience, stars, cardboard and bits of wood aren't all that bright.

# BEWARE GREEKS BEARING GIFTS: ODYSSEUS

**DECEPTION**

Religious deceit

**Military subterfuge**

Financial fraud

Fake or counterfeit

Imposture or cross-dressing

Confidence trick

Scientific deception

**Main Culprit:** Odysseus

**Motivation:** Power and glory

**Damage Done:** Destruction of Troy

*If doomed it be indeed that Priam's burg*
*By guile must fall before the war-worn Greeks,*
*A great Horse let us fashion, in which*
*Our mightiest shall take ambush.*

**From *The Fall of Troy* by Quintus Smyrnaeus (fl. c. 350 CE)**

There is no more famous military stratagem than the story of the Trojan Horse. The Greeks, stalemated after their ten-year siege of the city of Troy, seek a means to bring the war to a swift and decisive end. Odysseus, King of Ithaca, who is famed for his cunning, suggests that they build a giant wooden horse, an animal held to be sacred to Poseidon, the god of the sea, who is also the patron of Troy. In the second part of their plan, Odysseus tells the Greeks to board their ships and sail to the lea of a neighbouring island, to make it look as if they have abandoned the siege and returned home.

When they see the great horse on the beach, the Trojans think that the Greeks have left it as an offering to Poseidon to ensure their safe return. Even when one of the Trojans, Laocoön, warns his countrymen, saying 'I fear the Greeks, even when they bring gifts,' and begs them not to bring the horse into the city, the Trojans cannot escape the doom that the gods have decreed for them. They ignore Laocoön's perfectly justified warning and drag the horse to the main square of the city as a victory trophy. As Laocoön had foreseen, Odysseus and 29 other Greek warriors are hidden inside the hollow belly of the horse. During the early hours, as the Trojans celebrate the lifting of the siege, Odysseus and his companions climb out of the horse and open the gates to their army, which has returned under cover of darkness. The city of the topless towers is sacked and burned, and the Trojans are all killed, enslaved or forced to flee into exile.

**TROY BURNS**
Historians have speculated that the 'Trojan Horse' was in reality a type of siege engine or a natural disaster, such as an earthquake.

**STRANGER THAN FICTION**

The tale, retold countless times since Antiquity (see quote), latterly in the Hollywood film, *Troy* (2004), has fascinated the public and historians alike, but how much historical truth is there in the story? In the 1870s, the German archeologist Henrich Schliemann (1822–90) excavated the site of Hisarlik in northeastern Turkey, which he identified as the site of the legendary Troy, described in Homer's *Iliad*. The site had been first occupied in 3000 BCE (Troy I), but Schliemann identified a later stage of the city, Troy VII (c. 1300–1190 BCE), as the town destroyed by the Greeks in the Trojan War. It is now certain that a large city with a population of about 10,000 existed at the site and was destroyed in war in the late Bronze Age, but without written documents from the period, there is no evidence as to how the city was taken or by whom.

Several theories have been put forward to explain the story of the horse. The first suggests that it was a metaphor for an earthquake, which the ancients believed were caused by the god Poseidon, that destroyed the city. Evidence suggests that a seismic event destroyed the previous stage of the city, Troy VI (1600–1300 BCE), but there is no evidence of war during this period. Another theory holds that the horse was actually a type of siege engine that the attackers built to breech the city walls or gates.

Before the Trojan War begins, so the story goes, the wily Odysseus is an unwilling warrior. An oracle has predicted that he will have a difficult journey home, and when he is summoned by King Agamemnon of Mycenae, the leader of the Greeks, to join the campaign, he hopes to escape the draft by pretending to be insane. To prove his madness, he hitches an ox and a donkey to his plough, and sows salt in the uneven furrows. On this occasion, it is Odysseus who is outwitted, as the messenger, Palamedes, sent to test his madness, places Odysseus' baby son, Telemachus, in the path of the plough to see if the father will kill his own child. Thwarted, Odysseus nurses a grudge against Palamedes, and he is able to take his revenge during the siege of Troy. He frames the unfortunate Palamedes by forging a letter to him from the Trojans and hiding gold in his tent. Palamedes is condemned to be stoned to death as a traitor.

Homer's second epic poem, the *Odyssey*, recounts Odysseus' ten-year journey home to Ithaca. It is not the distance that causes the journey to be so long, as Ithaca, an island on the western side of mainland Greece, is only 500 km (300 miles) from the site of Troy-Hisarlik. However, the gods have decided that Odysseus is much too clever for his own good and needs to be taught a lesson. Like that other great Greek hero, Herakles (Hercules), he must be tested to prove himself worthy. He will need all his ingenuity to survive the many obstacles and tests that the gods place in his way. Two of his adventures demonstrate his cunning.

When Odysseus and his crew land on an island populated by man-eating, one-eyed giants called the Cyclopes, they are trapped inside a cave by one of their number, Polyphemus, who plans to have them for lunch. He seals the cave with a giant boulder, thus preventing any hope of escape. The giant, however, opens the cave to let his flock of sheep in and out to graze. Odysseus manages to get the Cyclops drunk, and tells him that his name is 'Nobody'. When Polyphemus has fallen asleep, Odysseus and his men blind him with a wooden stake that they have sharpened to a point and hardened in the fire. The injured blind Polyphemus calls on his brothers to help him. When they ask him what has happened, he replies, 'Nobody has hurt me!' Thinking that his injury must be a punishment from the gods, the other giants do not come to his aid. In the morning, Polyphemus opens the cave to let out his sheep. Odysseus escapes from the cave by tying himself and his men to the underside of the sheep, thus fooling the Cyclops, who can only feel the back of his sheep with his hands.

Later on in the journey, Odysseus has to sail past the island of the Sirens. In Greek mythology, the Sirens were not mermaids that were half-human, half-fish, but monsters with the head of a woman and the body of a bird of prey. Cruel creatures sent to torment humanity, the Sirens lured sailors to their deaths on the rocks of their island by attracting them with their 'Siren songs'. Odysseus is determined to hear the song, and to avoid wrecking his ship, he stops the ears of his crewmates with wax and has himself tied to the mast of his ship. He gives strict orders that he must not be untied, no matter what he says.

**SIREN SONG**
Odysseus ordered his crew to tie him to the mast so that, even if driven mad by the song of the sirens, he would not throw himself overboard.

Driven mad by the Sirens' irresistible song, Odysseus pleads with his men to untie him and row towards the island, but deaf to his pleas they row past to safety.

After his arduous ten-year journey, Odysseus finally makes it back home to Ithaca, to be reunited with his wife Penelope and son Telemachus. However, he has one final trial to overcome. During his absence, a group of suitors has gathered in the palace, each determined to marry Penelope, whom they believe to be a widow, and become king of Ithaca. Penelope, who easily matches her husband in cunning, avoids making a decision by saying that she will pick a husband as soon as she has finished weaving a shroud for Odysseus' father. In reality, each night she undoes part of the weave so that the shroud is never finished. Just as Odysseus arrives on the island, however, her trick is betrayed by a maidservant. Forced to choose one of the suitors, Penelope says she will marry the man who can string her husband's great hunting bow and shoot a single arrow through a line of twelve axe shafts.

Meanwhile, Odysseus, assisted by his son, lays his plan to punish the suitors and reclaim his rightful place as king of Ithaca and husband of Penelope. With the help of the goddess Athena, he disguises himself as an old man, who comes to the palace to beg for alms and a place to sleep. He is only recognised by his old nurse from a scar on his leg, and he swears her to secrecy. On the day of the contest, not one of the suitors has the strength to string the bow. At this point, the disguised Odysseus asks if he can try, to the derision of the suitors. Not only does he string the bow but he also shoots an arrow through the axe shafts. Suddenly revealed as Odysseus the king, he turns his bow on the suitors, whom he kills to a man.

**NOT ONLY DOES HE STRING THE BOW BUT HE ALSO SHOOTS AN ARROW THROUGH THE AXE SHAFTS.**

The stories recounted in the *Iliad* and the *Odyssey* were ancient oral traditions that were compiled into poems in the eighth century BCE. It is probable that the *Odyssey* is a compilation of stories from different periods and cultures, and about several different folk heroes. Parallels have been made between the story of Odysseus and that of the third millennium BCE culture hero Gilgamesh, one of the mythical early kings of the Sumerian city of Uruk (now in southern Iraq). As for the fall of Troy, there is good historical evidence of the sacking of Troy VII at the hands of an invading army. At a time when there existed no weapons that could breech a city's walls, it is more than probable that a military subterfuge, such as the infiltration of soldiers by cover of night, was the cause of the city's downfall.

**DECEPTION**

Religious deceit

Military subterfuge

**Financial fraud**

Fake or counterfeit

Imposture or cross-dressing

Confidence trick

Scientific deception

# THE QUANTITATIVE EMPEROR: NERO

**Main Culprit:** Nero

**Motivation:** Greed

**Damage Done:** Loss of confidence in the economic system; inflation; social upheaval; overthrow and murder of Nero

*The Roman emperors learned to make debasement a routine procedure. One might argue that the Romans had no choice, given the dynamics of their society and their empire. Even though they succeeded in developing abundant supplies of gold throughout their empire – and, in fact, expanded their empire in some directions primarily to acquire new sources of gold – their financial requirements and insatiable demand for adornment in gold grew so rapidly that they simply never had enough gold to satisfy their needs.*

**From *The Power of Gold* by P. Bernstein (2000)**

© Dreamstime

The first true coinage minted in the western world originated in the mid-seventh century BCE in the kingdom of Lydia, which occupied an important position on East–West trade routes. The innovation quickly spread to Lydia's immediate neighbours, the Greeks to the west and the Persians to the east, and in the next few centuries came into use in most parts of Europe and the Middle East. The Greeks took coinage westward with them to their colonies of Italy, France and Spain. One early problem with currency was counterfeiting. As there was no reliable means of measuring the purity of a gold or silver coin, base metals could be mixed with them to the same weight. In the mid-third century BCE, however, the Greek scientist and inventor Archimedes of Syracuse (287–212 BCE) discovered a method of measuring the density of metals by immersing them in water.

Although this may have begun to tackle the problem of counterfeit coins, it could do nothing to prevent the debasement of the currency by the state itself. One early example was the tyrant Dionysius of Syracuse (405–367 BCE), who, upon finding himself short of money to pay his debts, recalled all the coinage in the kingdom and had all one-*drachma* coins re-stamped to a value of two drachmas. Having paid off his debts at a discount of fifty per cent, he reissued the coins at their original value. The Roman Republic began to issue its own coinage in the third century BCE, minting both gold (*aureus*) and silver (*denarius*) coins.

© iStockphoto

**FIDDLING NERO**
Obsessed by gold, Nero begged, stole and borrowed until he was forced to debase Rome's currency to obtain more.

Nero (37–68 CE) was the fifth and last emperor in the line of the great Julius Caesar (100–44 BCE). Reigning for six years, his rule has gone down as an exemplar of tyranny, waste and corruption. He is blamed for starting the Great Fire of Rome (64 CE) and for many excesses, personal and governmental, that led to his overthrow and forced suicide (see *History's Worst Decisions*, pp. 32–6). Economic historians, however, hold him guilty of a much more heinous crime – that of destabilising the Roman world's economic system through his 'reform' of the Roman coinage.

Governments, ancient and modern, are perpetually short of funds. They have three principal means to meet any financial shortfalls: raise taxes – never a popular option with the people; borrow – if someone is willing to lend to them; or increase the money supply by issuing more currency. When currency is inexpensive, such as unsecured paper, for example, a government can try to print its way out of a tight financial corner. This is what the leading Western economies did in response to the Credit Crunch of 2007–9, through a policy euphemistically known as 'quantitative easing' – which actually means printing money you haven't earned. Currency in Roman times, however, was not made with paper but minted from gold or silver, so the only way the state could increase the money supply was to reduce the size of the coins or their gold and silver content by alloying them with other metals. The results of this financial sleight of hand, however, are the same whether the currency is paper or metal: a loss in confidence in the soundness of the economic system, rising interest rates and inflation.

**THE MAN WITH THE GOLDEN TOUCH**

In the wake of the Great Fire, Nero needed considerable sums to carry out his ambitious plans to rebuild Rome as a suitable stage for the divinely inspired artist he believed himself to be. He planned a vast new palace, the *Domus Aurea* (the Golden House), which would occupy a 300-acre site in what had been the centre of the city before the fire. Nero was obsessed by gold, which he saw as an attribute of the divine Nero, the human incarnation of the god Apollo on earth. Having failed to raise enough through taxation, the confiscation of property and borrowing, Nero resorted to debasing the empire's coinage. In his reform of the currency of 64–65 CE, he reduced the weight of the gold aureus by four per cent, allowing 45 coins to be struck from a pound (454 g) of gold instead of the previous 40. At the same time, he lowered the silver content of the denarius and alloyed it with copper, reducing its value by between five and ten per cent.

Although Nero was able to complete the building of the Domus Aurea, he did not live very long to enjoy its splendid accoutrements. Challenged by repeated rebellions among the army and aristocracy, and beset with economic woes triggered by his debasement of the currency that obliged him to raise ever-higher taxes, Nero was forced to flee Rome, and finally to commit suicide rather than be captured and put to death by his enemies.

# RENDER UNTO GOD: *THE DONATION OF CONSTANTINE*

**Main Culprits:** The pope and the king of the Franks

**Motivation:** Power and legitimacy

**Damage Done:** Was used to legitimise the doctrine of papal supremacy that contributed to the schism between the Catholic and Greek Orthodox churches and to the disputes between church and state that led to the Protestant Reformation

*[Constantine] placed a tiara on the Pope's head and held the reins of his horse. He left to [Pope] Sylvester and his successors Rome and all the provinces, districts and cities of Italy and the West to be subject to the Roman Church forever; he then moved East because, where the princedom of bishops and the head of the Christian religion has been established by the heavenly Emperor it is not just that an earthly Emperor should have power.*

**From *The Coronation of Charlemagne: What Did it Signify?* by C. Delisle Burns (1959)**

© Dreamstime

The document known as *The Donation of Constantine* (*Donatio Constantini*) is one of the most famous forgeries of the early Middle Ages. Our best guess is that it was written in the second half of the eighth century CE, some time between 750 and 775. But it is the purported aim of the *Donation* that is quite breathtaking: nothing less than a claim by the head of the Catholic Church, the pope, to have both spiritual and temporal authority over the lands that once comprised the western half of the Roman Empire – that is, the former imperial provinces of Italy, Gaul (France and Belgium), Hispania (Spain and Portugal) and Illyricum (western Balkans). Before we explore who might have written it and to what end, we have to go back 450 years to the purported date of the *Donation* in the fourth century CE.

In the year 300 CE, the Roman domination of the Mediterranean basin was already more than four centuries old. Roman power extended north to Britain, west to Spain, south to Egypt and east as far as Mesopotamia (modern-day Iraq). What the Romans found, however, is that the empire had become far too large to be governed by one man. In order to try to remedy the situation, in 293 CE the Emperor Diocletian (244–311 CE) devised the system known as the tetrarchy (rule of four), with

**HOLY ALLIANCE**
The forged *Donation* looked back to the greatest triumph of the early Church, when the emperor Constantine adopted Christianity.

two Caesars and two junior Augusti, who would succeed them in due course. The Caesars divided the empire roughly into two: the Latin-speaking West and the Hellenised Greek-speaking East, with the border somewhere in the Balkans. The emperors were meant to rule in concert, and enact one another's decrees in their respective halves of the empire. Imagine that the United States were governed by two parallel administrations, one in the North and one in the South, with two presidents and Houses of Congress – as was indeed the case during the American Civil War (1861–5). The results in the Roman Empire were very similar. The Caesars and Augusti not surprisingly fell out, and the empire was torn apart by a series of devastating civil wars that lasted until 313 CE.

Enter Constantine (272–337 CE), known to history as 'the Great'. Having won the emperorship of the western half of the empire, he now coveted the eastern half, ruled by his former ally Licinius (c. 250–325 CE). The empire had, until this point, been officially pagan. The gods and deified emperors were worshipped in temples, and the growing minority of Christians was sometimes tolerated and sometimes persecuted. Constantine, legend has it, turned his back on the Roman gods and supported the Christian cause because of a vision of the Cross before a key battle in 312 CE.

When he became undisputed emperor of the Roman world, Constantine legalised Christianity and actively promoted it by building and endowing churches. His second major accomplishment was to found the city of Constantinople (now Istanbul), as the New Rome in the East, on the site of the old Greek city of Byzantium. This strategic decision ensured that the Roman Empire would endure in the East for another eleven centuries, but it also formalised the division of the empire into its eastern and western halves. From that time on, the destinies of the eastern and western empires and of their respective churches began to diverge.

By the fifth century, the Western Roman Empire was in a parlous state. The barbarians were not only at the door, they had invited themselves in for dinner and were hogging the best of the food. In 476 CE, the last Roman emperor in the West was deposed and the former Roman provinces became barbarian kingdoms. The Catholic Church alone remained the guardian of Roman law, language and culture. It looked for support to Constantinople and made what accommodations it could with the new barbarian rulers of Europe. In the east the former Roman, now Byzantine, Empire prospered and grew in wealth and power, until, in the sixth century, the Emperor Justinian (483–565 CE) felt powerful enough to launch an invasion of Italy and North Africa. The Byzantines held out in Italy until 571, when they were expelled by another Germanic semi-pagan people, the Lombards.

When the *Donation* was written, the former Roman, now Byzantine, Empire survived in the East despite the meteoric rise of Islam, to which it had lost much of its former territory in the Middle East and North

**THE KEYS OF THE KINGDOM**

Africa, and it had also been expelled from the Italian mainland by the Lombards. The Christian church, though in theory universal and united, was in practice divided between the Greek Orthodox Church, headed by the patriarch and the emperor of Constantinople, and the Catholic Church, led by the pope in Rome. The growing power in the West was that of the Franks, under their kings, Pepin the Short (714–768) and his son Charlemagne (742–814), whom the pope would crown 'Emperor of the Romans' in the year 800 CE.

For the pope, the *Donation* did two things: it confirmed the supremacy of the Church of Rome and the See of Saint Peter over its main rival, the Patriarchate of Constantinople; and it gave legal standing to Rome's claim to the former Byzantine provinces that would later become the Papal States, ruled by the pope as an independent ruler. For the Franks it legitimised the transfer of the title of 'Emperor of the Romans' from the emperor in Constantinople to Charlemagne, by providing evidence that Constantine the Great had given Pope (later Saint) Sylvester (fl. mid-fourth c.; see quote) power over the western half of the empire. The document was invoked on several occasions during the Middle Ages in order to protect the interests of the papacy and assert its supremacy over temporal rulers.

**FOR THE FRANKS IT LEGITIMISED THE TRANSFER OF THE TITLE OF 'EMPEROR OF THE ROMANS' FROM THE EMPEROR IN CONSTANTINOPLE TO CHARLEMAGNE.**

The *Donation* was denounced as a forgery in the fifteenth century by a Catholic cardinal, Nicholas of Kues (1401–64), and at the same time, by the eminent scholar Lorenzo Valla (1406–57). Both had political motives for their actions: Nicholas wanted to reform the relationship between the Church and the Holy Roman Empire and to improve relations with the then beleaguered Byzantine Empire; Valla was working for the king of Spain, who was fighting a war with the pope over territorial claims in Italy. A century later the Protestant reformers in Germany and England also accused the Catholic Church of forging the *Donation* to further its own political interests. Finally, some eight hundred years after it had been written, this strange document that had inverted Christ's call to 'Render therefore unto Caesar the things which be Caesar's, and unto God the things which be God's' (Matthew: 25) was finally put to rest and declared by the pope to be a forgery.

# THE WOMAN WHO SAT ON THE THRONE OF SAINT PETER: POPE JOAN

**DECEPTION**

Religious deceit

Military subterfuge

Financial fraud

Fake or counterfeit

**Imposture or cross-dressing**

Confidence trick

Scientific deception

**Main Culprit:** Pope Joan

**Motivation:** To live as freely as a man

**Damage Done:** Her death by public stoning

*Concerning a certain pope or rather female pope, who is not set down in the lists of popes or bishops of Rome, because she was a woman who disguised herself as a man and became, by her character and talents, a curial secretary, then a cardinal and finally pope. One day, while mounting a horse, she gave birth to a child. Immediately, by Roman justice, she was bound by the feet to a horse's tail and stoned by the people for half a league.*

**From the *Chronica Universalis Mettensis* (*Universal Chronicle of Metz*) by Jean de Mailly**

As we shall see, impostures come in many forms. People can pretend to have a different identity, social status or professional qualification, or can claim to be of the opposite gender. The first of many impostors to grace these pages combines two of these: a female who not only pretended to be male but also to be an ordained priest of the Church when that office was open only to men. A century after the *Donation of Constantine* had been forged (see pp. 23–6), so legend has it, a woman called Joan changed her name to John and rose through the Church hierarchy until she reached the papal throne. Having climbed to such heights, her fall would prove to be fatal.

With an average life expectancy of 30–35 years, the early Middle Ages were not the best time to be alive. After the relative comfort and security of Antiquity, the human condition had sunk back into poverty, ignorance and squalor, and many succumbed to epidemics, famines and wars. The lives of women were if anything worse than those of men. Women had no civil rights to speak of, and were little more than chattels to be transferred from father to husband. They received little or no education, and were prisoners in their own homes. Their only escape from endless domestic servitude was to enter the service of the Church as nuns, where they would be spared the attentions of a husband but would live under the strict discipline of the convent. Little wonder then that many women sought escape from the condition imposed on them by the luck of the chromosomal lottery.

**SUBVERSIVE**
An engraving from a seventeenth-century book criticising the Catholic Church, written by "a lover of truth."

We will never know how many medieval women cut their hair and donned men's clothes, but tales such as the one about the woman who became pope are echoes of the many true stories of women who defied convention and took on the male world as soldiers, priests or merchants. The choice of an ecclesiastical career, however, would not be such a strange one. At a time when eunuchs served in the Church, women would have found it easier to pass as clerics than other professions. However, if discovered, the penalty would have been grave, as the crime was not just one of fraud, but also one of blasphemy against the teachings of the Church.

The two earliest accounts of the story (though the Catholic Church prefers the term 'legend') of Pope Joan date from the thirteenth century, therefore several hundred years after the event. One dates Joan's papacy to the year 1099 and the other to 850. The first version was penned by the Dominican friar, Jean de Mailly (fl. 13th c.; see quote). He places Joan at the close of the eleventh century, but gives few details about her life, and his account does not even name her. After her execution at the hands of the enraged mob of Romans who had witnessed their pontiff giving birth, she was buried at the spot where she died. The place was marked, de Mailly explains, by the Latin inscription: *'Petre, Pater Patrum, Papisse Prodito Partum'* (Peter, father of fathers, reveal the female pope's childbirth).

A more complete biography is given by the second source for the story, the monkish chronicler Martin of Troppau (or Martin of Opava; d. 1278). The tale appears in his *Chronicon Pontificum et Imperatorum* (*Chronicles of the Popes and Emperors*). In this version, Joan was born in the German town of Mainz. She travelled disguised as a man to the city of Athens with a lover, where she studied the arts and sciences and outshone her male contemporaries. She went to Italy where she lectured and taught in the most famous academies of Rome. At the time, those pursuing an academic career were also ordained priests of the Church. She served in the Curia, the Church's civil service, and such was her reputation as a scholar that she was elected pope after the death of Leo IV (r. 847–55). She sat on the papal throne under the name of John VIII. Two years and seven months into her papacy, Joan was riding in procession from St Peter's Basilica to the Church of the Lateran when she went into labour and gave birth in full view of the populace as she was passing between the Church of Saint Clement and the ruins of the Colosseum. A later tradition asserted that subsequent popes avoided the direct route between Saint Peter's and the Lateran to avoid passing the scene of Joan's unmasking and death.

Martin's *Chronicon* predates the invention of the printing press and began life as a handwritten manuscript. As it was the practice of the time for readers to add footnotes and comments in the margins, which were sometimes incorporated by copyists into the text, the book now exists in several versions. In one edition, the fate of Pope Joan is the

**OF POPES AND EMPERORS**

same as in de Mailly's account, whereby Joan is killed and buried where she dies. In another account, however, she and her child survive – she is immediately deposed and retires to a convent to do years of penance for her sins. Her son becomes bishop of the port city of Ostia near Rome. Upon her death, he has her buried in the cathedral and her tomb becomes a shrine where miracles are performed.

Once the story had entered the historical canon, it grew and developed, finding its way into other histories of the Church and the papacy, including those written by historians commissioned by the Vatican itself. An early fifteenth-century chronicle gives her name as Agnes, not Joan, and tells of a statue of her in Rome. A pilgrim's guidebook to Rome written in the same century explains that her remains were interred in St Peter's Basilica. Pope Joan appeared in medieval fiction, and her likeness graced the front of the Cathedral of Siena among other incumbents of the See of Saint Peter. Another legend connected to Pope Joan is the story of two ancient Roman marble chairs in the Lateran Church, which were used during the enthronement ceremonies. The chairs had holes in their seats, and the story grew that the newly elected pope was sat on the seats to allow the cardinals, looking through the holes, to check that he was indeed of the male gender.

POPE JOAN APPEARED IN MEDIEVAL FICTION, AND HER LIKENESS GRACED THE FRONT OF THE CATHEDRAL OF SIENA AMONG OTHER INCUMBENTS OF THE SEE OF SAINT PETER.

For several centuries the Church itself accepted the tradition of a female pope as true. The enemies of the Church, heretics and reformers alike, used the story to discredit the papacy and its claims of infallibility and supremacy. In 1601, Pope Clement VIII (r. 1592–1605) declared that the story was apocryphal. He ordered the image of Pope Joan on Siena Cathedral to be re-carved into the more fitting image of the undoubtedly male and genuine Pope Zachary (r. 741–52). The story, however, continues to fascinate the public and has been the inspiration for many fictional retellings, including the 1972 and 2009 films, both entitled *Pope Joan*.

# CHINA'S ALL-ACTION FEMALE HERO: HUA MULAN

**DECEPTION**

Religious deceit

Military subterfuge

Financial fraud

Fake or counterfeit

**Imposture or cross-dressing**

Confidence trick

Scientific deception

**Main Culprit:** Hua Mulan

**Motivation:** To save her father from conscription

**Damage Done:** Loss of the man she loved

'My father has no older son,
I have no older brother.
I wish to buy a horse and gear
And march to war in father's stead.'
In the eastern market she bought a fine steed,
In the western market she bought blanket and saddle.
In the southern market she bought bit and bridle.
In the northern market she bought a long whip,
At dawn she bade her parents farewell.
By the Yellow River she camped at dusk.
She did not hear her parents' calls,
But only the horses' sad whinnying.

**From the popular Chinese song 'The Ballad of Mulan'**

© Dreamstime

If a woman might be able to pass as a male cleric, even as pope (see previous entry) in the relatively placid and above all chaste world of the Church, it would have been a much greater challenge for one to pretend to be a man in the macho world of an all-male army, but such is the tale told by the popular Chinese song, 'The Ballad of Mulan'. The earliest reliably dated version of the story is found in a collection of songs and poems compiled in the twelfth century, but several sources place the story as far back as the Northern Wei Dynasty (386–534 CE), and others in the later Tang Dynasty (618–907 CE). The story has become an established favourite among the Chinese public, and during the Ming Dynasty (1368–1644), it became the subject of a novel and a play. In the modern period, the story of Mulan has been filmed for TV and the big screen more than half a dozen times, and the tale received the ultimate accolade when Disney chose it as the subject for a full-length animated feature (*Mulan*, 1998).

Roughly contemporaneous with the fall of the Western Roman Empire (476 CE), the Northern Wei period of Chinese history is one of sweeping political, cultural and social change. In contrast to Europe, which was experiencing the break-up of the Roman world into dozens of small states with different languages, religions and cultures, China was slowly being moulded into a vast culturally unified, Chinese-speaking empire. During the Northern Wei period, the greater part of northern China was unified, the imperial government underwent an important process of reform, and Buddhism was firmly established as China's principal religion. The process, however, was an extremely violent one, punctuated by constant wars between rival Chinese states, raids by barbarian tribes from Central Asia, and civil wars between rival claimants to the throne. Such is the historical background to 'The Ballad of Mulan'.

**GREATER LOVE HATH NO DAUGHTER**

One morning Mulan is washing clothes at the river with the other girls. The peaceful scene is disturbed by the sound of gongs announcing the arrival of a recruiting party to the town. Although her father is old and frail, he has been drafted to serve in the emperor's army in a campaign against invading nomadic tribesmen. When the recruiting sergeant arrives at Mulan's house, however, he is greeted by the 'son' of the house, who volunteers to take his father's place. Mulan leaves on horseback with her fellow recruits, disguised as a man and carrying the family's ancestral sword.

Anxious to keep her true identity a secret lest her family is punished for her imposture, Mulan keeps herself to herself and volunteers for guard duty at night rather than sleep in a tent with the other soldiers. She becomes the target of a fellow soldier, Zhang Shazi, who bullies her for her strange behaviour. A young officer called Jin Yong rescues her from Zhang and invites her to share his tent. The two become fond friends, and over the next ten years they share the trials and tribulations of life in the field. Such is Mulan's bravery and martial skill that she is promoted to the rank of general.

During a surprise night attack Mulan is wounded. She goes to convalesce at the house of Han Mei, a girl whose life she had once saved from the enemy. Han Mei is in love with the gallant 'general', and confesses her love to 'him'. She asks Mulan to take her as 'his' wife. At this point, Mulan is forced to reveal her true identity to Han Mei and Jin Yong. Jin Yong, realising that his faithful companion at arms is actually a woman, can finally give full expression to the feelings of love he has been harbouring for her. One night Mulan is troubled by a nightmare in which she marries Jin Yong but is rejected by her husband's family for not being a 'real' woman because she is a warrior and a general. Soon after, Jin Yong confesses that he is deeply in love with her, and she promises that as soon as the war is over, they will be married.

In the best traditions of the Peking opera, tragedy strikes the lovers. During an enemy attack, when Mulan is about to be killed, Jin Yong saves her but at the cost of his own life. Mulan defeats the enemy but she is heartbroken at the loss of Jin Yong and so many other brave men under her command. She returns to the battlefield to offer a sacrifice to the souls of the fallen, but she does so dressed as a woman. Finally the soldiers whom she had led for ten years realise that their general is a woman. Instead of condemning her, the soldiers are overcome with a feeling of awe and respect for a woman who has faced so many hardships and accomplished so much.

Hearing the story, even the emperor himself is moved. He offers her a position at court, but she turns him down, saying: 'I have no use

ANXIOUS TO KEEP HER TRUE IDENTITY A SECRET, LEST HER FAMILY IS PUNISHED FOR HER IMPOSTURE, MULAN KEEPS HERSELF TO HERSELF AND VOLUNTEERS FOR GUARD DUTY AT NIGHT RATHER THAN SLEEP IN A TENT WITH THE OTHER SOLDIERS.

to be a grand secretary. Just loan me a camel with fast-running feet to carry me back home.' The 'Ballad of Mulan' concludes with the following lines:

> *The male hare's legs have a nervous spring,*
>
> *The female hare's eye wanders.*
>
> *But when two hares run together,*
>
> *Who can tell which is the boy and which the girl?*

**MULAN ADAPTED**

In its many retellings, the story of Mulan has morphed from a short ballad (see quotes above) to a long and involved narrative full of incident, and a morality tailored to the sensibility of each age. In the Ming period, the tale was held to be an exemplar of filial piety and of service to the emperor. In a later version she writes to the emperor after he has offered her many rewards and distinctions: 'Honours and disgrace, gains and losses are all external things; all that matters is utter dedication and loyalty to serve the country.'

**FAR PAVILIONS**
The fortified capital of the Northern Wei bears witness to the constant strife that marks this period of Chinese history.

For centuries, the shock value of the story of Hua Mulan was based on the impossibility of a female becoming a warrior in China's male-dominated culture, but to the modern reader, who has seen women soldiers take combat roles in Afghanistan and Iraq, the story does not seem quite so improbable. As to whether Hua Mulan was a historical figure, the reader will have to make up his or her own mind. Like the story of Pope Joan told above, it must be based on a real incident, but it has been so transformed and embellished over the centuries that we are unlikely ever to discover the truth behind the legend.

# THE MISSING PRINCES: LAMBERT SIMNEL AND PERKIN WARBECK

**DECEPTION**

Religious deceit

Military subterfuge

Financial fraud

Fake or counterfeit

**Imposture or cross-dressing**

Confidence trick

Scientific deception

**Main Culprits:** Lambert Simnel and Perkin Warbeck

**Motivation:** Power

**Damage Done:** Civil war; executions of Warbeck and of the Earl of Warwick

*Stay, yet look back with me unto the Tower.*
*Pity, you ancient stones, those tender babes*
*Whom envy hath immured within your walls!*
*Rough cradle for such little pretty ones!*
*Rude ragged nurse, old sullen playfellow*
*For tender Princes use my babies well!*
*So foolish sorrow bids your stones farewell.*

**Richard III, Act 4, Scene 1 (c. 1591) by William Shakespeare**

Before we can fully understand the royal impostures of Lambert Simnel (c. 1477–1525) and Perkin Warbeck (c. 1474–99), we need to revisit one of the darkest footnotes of English history, the murder of the two 'Princes in the Tower' at the very end of the long-drawn-out dynastic feud known as the Wars of the Roses (1455–85). I apologise in advance to my readers for the lack of imagination shown by the English aristocracy in naming their sons and would ask them to concentrate when they read the following paragraphs because all the main players in the story, apart from the two impostors, are called Richard, Edward or Henry.

**ROYAL REFUGE**
The defeated Perkin Warbeck hid in Beaulieu Abbey in the vain hope of escaping capture by Henry VII.

Although the actual fighting started in the mid-fifteenth century, the enmity between the great houses of York and Lancaster had been brewing since 1399, when Henry IV of Lancaster (1367–1413) deposed Richard II of York (1367–1400). The throne changed hands with the fortunes of war, and Edward IV of York (1442–83) became king after Henry V (1386–1422) and VI (1421–71), both of Lancaster. Edward secretly married Elizabeth Woodville (1437–92) with whom he fathered ten children, including Edward, Prince of Wales (1470–83), and Richard, 1st Duke of York (1473–83).

When Edward IV died unexpectedly in 1483, his eldest son, the 13-year-old Edward, succeeded as Edward V. However, Edward IV's scheming brother Richard of Gloucester, the future Richard III (1452–85), and also the young king's uncle, had other ideas. He had Parliament declare his brother's marriage to Elizabeth invalid. This meant that his children by her were illegitimate and therefore could not succeed him on the throne. He then claimed the crown for himself. The history of the English succession was by then so convoluted that there were several other claimants to the throne, including yet another Edward, Edward Plantagenet, Earl of Warwick (1475–1499), who had briefly been made Richard III's heir after his own son's death.

Edward IV's two sons vanished into the Tower of London never to be heard of or seen again. Their exact fate is still unknown, though the skeletons of two children were discovered in the Tower in the seventeenth century. Similarly, historians still argue about who murdered them. The two main suspects are their uncle Richard III and the man who defeated him in 1485 and ascended the English throne as Henry VII (1457–1509), the first king of the Tudor dynasty (1485–1603), whose descendants included Henry VIII (1491–1547) and Elizabeth I (1533–1603). The survival of Edward IV's two sons would have been a threat to either Richard or Henry, so both had good motives for murder. As for Edward Plantagenet, Earl of Warwick, he too, remained imprisoned in the Tower on the orders of Henry VII. No doubt thoroughly confused, the reader may now proceed to the strangely intertwined tales of the Princes in the Tower, Perkin Warbeck, Lambert Simnel and Edward Plantagenet, Earl of Warwick.

For many, especially the Yorkists, but for many Lancastrians, too, Henry VII, a distant Welsh relation of the Lancastrian line, was an upstart who had interposed himself just as the feud was getting interesting and had stolen the crown from both sides. Unlike his son, Henry VIII (he of the many wives), he was an unattractive character who committed the cardinal sins in the eyes of the English nobility of being an able if harsh administrator, a successful soldier, and a ruthless and effective politician. However, he is unique in English history in having had to deal with two impostors claiming his throne: Lambert Simnel and Perkin Warbeck.

Lambert Simnel was born around 1477. He was a commoner by birth. Aged around ten, he met Roger Simon (fl. 1470s), a priest, who noticed his striking resemblance to Richard, Duke of York, the youngest of the Princes in the Tower. Simon trained Lambert in the role of an English prince, and but he changed the boy's identity when he heard rumours of the death of Edward Plantagenet, Earl of Warwick, in the Tower, thinking that the latter would have stronger support among the dissident nobles. Claiming that Edward had escaped from imprisonment, Simon took Simnel to Ireland where he was welcomed by Yorkist sympathisers, who had the boy crowned as Edward VI in Dublin Cathedral in 1487.

Although Henry had brought the real Earl of Warwick out of the Tower to prove that Simnel was a fake, various nobles, including John de la Pole, Earl of Lincoln (1462–87), who himself had a tenuous claim to the throne, and the Earl of Warwick's aunt, Margaret of York and

**THE EARL AND THE PAUPER**

Burgundy (1446–1503), joined the rebellion and backed the young impostor. Margaret provided 2,000 Flemish mercenaries, who sailed to Ireland to join Simnel's Irish forces. Simnel and his army landed on the west coast of England in 1487 and were immediately defeated by Henry at the Battle of Stoke Field. The ringleaders of the conspiracy were executed, imprisoned or fled into exile, but Henry, in an unusual act of clemency, pardoned the ten-year-old Simnel, who became a spit-turner in the royal kitchens and then a falconer. He died in 1525 during the reign of Henry VIII, having outlived Henry VII by 16 years.

The second impostor to claim Henry VII's throne, Perkin Warbeck, was by far the greater threat. His imposture lasted far longer than Simnel's, starting in 1490 and ending with his death on the gallows in 1499, and it cost Henry a great deal of money. Although Perkin claimed to be Richard of Shrewsbury, Duke of York (see above), Edward IV's second son, he was probably not English by birth. Historians believe that he was either of French or Flemish extraction and was born in the town of Tournai (now in Belgium). Nevertheless, he seems to have persuaded many of the crowned heads of Europe that he was the missing English prince.

ALTHOUGH PERKIN CLAIMED TO BE RICHARD OF SHREWSBURY, DUKE OF YORK, EDWARD IV'S SECOND SON, HE WAS PROBABLY NOT ENGLISH BY BIRTH.

Warbeck made his first appearance as Richard, Duke of York, at the court of his 'aunt', Margaret of York and Burgundy, who had been involved in backing the imposture of Lambert Simnel. She was an implacable foe of Henry VII and never missed an opportunity to harass him. In 1491 he followed Simnel's example and sailed to Ireland, hoping to gather support for his claim. On this occasion, maybe still bruised by their defeat in 1487, the Irish did not rally to his side, and he was forced to return to Europe. After his return, he visited France where he was welcomed by Charles VIII of France (1470–98), and was officially recognised as Edward's son by Margaret of Burgundy. Henry tried to outmanoeuvre Warbeck by having him ejected from France and Burgundy. Although France acquiesced, Burgundy defied him and continued to back the young pretender. In 1493, Warbeck travelled to Vienna, the capital of the Holy Roman Empire, to attend the funeral of the Emperor Frederick III (1415–93). Frederick's son Emperor Maximilian I (1459–1519) recognised him as Richard IV of England,

and in return, Warbeck promised that his claim to the English throne would pass to the emperor if he died before becoming king.

Having won what support he could in Europe, in 1495 the 21-year-old 'King Richard IV' landed in Kent, in southeast England, with a small force funded once more by Margaret of Burgundy. Henry VII was never a popular monarch, and Warbeck and his backers must have hoped that the populace would rise up against him and carry the pretender in triumph all the way to London. However, just as in 1487, Henry easily defeated the small invading force. Warbeck escaped to Ireland, where he tried unsuccessfully to besiege the English stronghold of Waterford. Despite the support of some prominent Irish noblemen, he was forced to flee once more, this time to England's long-standing enemy, the independent kingdom of Scotland.

**A GRISLY END**
While Henry had pardoned the young Simnel, he was not so merciful to Warbeck, who was hung at Tyburn in London.

James IV of Scotland (1473–1513), who rejoiced in this opportunity to embarrass the hated English, welcomed Warbeck and even married him to one of his cousins. In 1496, James and Warbeck led an invasion of England, hoping for a popular uprising among the Yorkist nobility against Henry. Once again the rebellion failed to materialise, and the invaders were forced to withdraw. James was now disenchanted with his guest and asked him to leave. Warbeck sailed back to Ireland, where he tried and failed again to capture Waterford. The English chased him back to the Continent, which he reached with just two ships and a handful of men remaining.

Warbeck was to attempt one more throw of the dice. In 1497, he landed in England's westernmost county of Cornwall, which had recently risen in rebellion against Henry's taxation policies. He promised to lower taxes and to declare war on his former ally, James IV of Scotland – always a popular policy with the English. He was acclaimed as King Richard IV by his Cornish army, and marched east, taking the cities of Exeter and Taunton. Henry's much larger army headed west to intercept him. Warbeck lost his nerve and deserted his army, which immediately surrendered to the king. The pretender was hunted down and arrested at Beaulieu Abbey in Hampshire. His adventure was now over. He was taken to London in chains and paraded around the city to be mocked by the populace. However, he was not immediately tried and executed. He was imprisoned in the Tower together with Edward Plantagenet, Earl of Warwick, the last genuine Yorkist claimant to the English throne.

Henry had proved himself to be remarkably magnanimous to the young Lambert Simnel, whom he had pardoned and even employed in his own palace. Nor had he executed Edward Plantagenet, because the young nobleman is thought to have suffered from what we now call 'serious learning disabilities'. Neither Simnel nor Warwick had really been responsible for their actions, and Henry had spared them. In 1499, however, Warwick and Warbeck were accused of plotting to escape from the Tower. They were tried and found guilty of treason in short order. Warwick, as befitted a true royal prince, was beheaded, but Warbeck was taken to Tyburn in London, where he read out a confession of his crimes before being hanged, as befitted his lowly commoner status.

Although the English, and after the 1701 Act of Union with Scotland, the British, succession continued to be the cause of considerable civil and foreign strife through the next three centuries, there was never again a case of royal imposture. The last two claimants to the British throne were the genuine descendants of the deposed Stuart dynasty, the 'old' and the 'young' pretenders, James Stuart (1688–1766) and Charles Stuart (1720–88), who led invasions of England in 1715 and 1745, but never truly challenged the hold of the German-born dynasty that continues to rule the United Kingdom to this day.

WARWICK, AS BEFITTED A TRUE ROYAL PRINCE, WAS BEHEADED, BUT WARBECK WAS TAKEN TO TYBURN IN LONDON, WHERE HE WAS HANGED.

# STAIRWAY TO HEAVEN: FAKE RELICS AND INDULGENCES

**DECEPTION**

**Religious deceit**

Military subterfuge

Financial fraud

Fake or counterfeit

Imposture or cross-dressing

Confidence trick

Scientific deception

**Main Culprit:** The Catholic Church

**Motivation:** Power and financial gain

**Damage Done:** Abused the credulousness of the faithful; were factors leading to the Protestant Reformation, the schism of the Christian Church, and the religious wars of the sixteenth and seventeenth centuries

*If the clothes, the kerchiefs, and the very shadows of the saints, whilst yet on earth banished disease and restored health and vigour, who will have the hardihood to deny that God can still work the same wonders by the holy ashes, the bones, and other relics of his saints who are in glory?*

**From the *Roman Catechism* of the Council of Trent (1566)**

In 1453, when the Ottoman Turks finally took the city of Constantinople (now Istanbul, Turkey), and the remnants of the Byzantine Empire in Europe and Asia came under Muslim rule, the Catholic Church's major rival, the Greek Orthodox Church, lost most of its territory and political influence. For the pope, it must have been a moment of secret exultation, as the only other contender as undisputed leader of the Christian world for over a thousand years – the Byzantine emperor – was finally no more. The Catholic Church had survived the fall of Rome to the barbarians in 476 CE and the onslaughts of heresy and Islam, and now reigned supreme in Western Europe. Unfortunately for the pope, his triumph was to be short-lived: within a century a new and far more dangerous threat to Church unity emerged from within its own ranks.

During the Dark and Middle Ages, the Church had developed practices that were at odds with the ideas of sixteenth-century reformers, in

particular the doctrine of the veneration of the saints that many critics equated with pagan idolatry, and the sale of pardons for the remission of penance, known as indulgences, which was little more than 'buying a ticket to Paradise'. In 1517, Luther famously nailed the *Disputatio pro declaratione virtutis indulgentiarum* (*Ninety-Five Theses on the Power and Efficacy of Indulgences*) to the doors of the church of Wittenberg Castle. The document, which admittedly does not have the snappiest title

**TAKE YOUR PICK**
One of the four 'Holy Lances' that the faithful believe pierced the side of Christ at his crucifixion.

in the world, initiated the religious revolution known as the Protestant Reformation. In the *Ninety-Five Theses*, Luther specifically attacked the practices of selling indulgences and the worship of relics that had become widespread throughout the Catholic world. Fifty years later, when a great many words had been written and not a little blood had flowed, the pope convened the marathon eighteen-year Council of Trent (1545–63), which restated Roman Catholic doctrine and clarified the thorny issues of indulgences and relics in the *Roman Catechism* (see quote). Although the council reformed the worst abuses of the medieval church, it confirmed the efficacy of both relics and indulgences, making it impossible for Protestants and Anglicans to return to the papal fold.

Quite apart from the debate between Protestants and Catholics as to whether relics and indulgences were in themselves efficacious in obtaining salvation was the issue of fakes and forgeries. The unscrupulous, many of them monks and priests, smelled a way of making money out of the credulity of the masses. Not only were dubious relics paraded before the faithful, but there was also a huge international trade in relics, both real and fake, as royal collectors vied to have the largest and most meritorious collections. Among the oddities collected and exhibited, which we shall examine in more detail below, were vials of the milk of the Virgin Mary, and boards from the manger in Bethlehem, the latter still being a precious relic in the possession of the Roman Catholic Church.

## HOLY RELICS AND PROFANE FORGERIES

Christianity is not unique in showing respect to the remains of particularly holy or great men, or of the artifacts associated with them. In Antiquity the bones of great heroes, kings and emperors were accorded special honours and buried in shrines and temples. Objects were also venerated, such as the armour and shield of Achilles, which were kept in a temple in the city of Troy (see pp. 15–19). Relics of the historical Buddha (c. 563–483 BCE) were placed in pagodas all over the Buddhist world. Christians were unique, however, in their belief in the miraculous powers associated with the mortal remains of saints and of objects that they had owned or even merely touched.

One possible explanation for this is the difference between pagan religion and Christianity. The Greeks and Romans worshipped hundreds of gods and other supernatural folk, such as demi-gods, nymphs and satyrs. As the divine was an integral part of their lives, pagans felt a close connection to their gods – especially as they could pop into a temple to have a chat with them (see Ancient Oracles, pp. 10–14). Early Christianity, in contrast, was an abstract religion that did not use images until comparatively late in Antiquity.

God was a remote almighty creator who dwelt far from humanity in Heaven. Even his son Jesus Christ had been taken up to sit by God's right hand. The humble man and woman needed intermediaries with the Almighty, and they found them in fellow humans who had been particularly holy, and had usually been martyred for their holiness. Another link between the cult of the saints and of the pagan gods was that churches were often been built on the sites of pagan shrines and temples. As a result, the saints to whom the churches were dedicated often took over some of the powers of the gods that they had superseded.

From the earliest days of the Church, there was no shortage of men and women who qualified for sainthood because they had been martyred for the faith. The Roman authorities persecuted the Christians periodically from the reign of Nero (37–68 CE; see pp. 20–22) until the reign of Constantine the Great (272–337 CE). The remains of martyrs were associated with miraculous events, cures, and even the raising of the dead, hence the cult of their relics quickly grew. The Church never condemned the practice outright, although opinions varied among theologians as to whether the miracles were performed by the relics themselves, or by God 'in the presence' of the relics.

Some of Christendom's most sacred relics emerged in the fourth century. They were objects associated with Jesus Christ (c. 4 BCE–c. 30 CE). As he had risen and been taken up to Heaven, there could be no physical remains of his body. However, there was no shortage of objects associated with Jesus' life and death. The first and most important of these was the cross on which he had been crucified, known as the 'True Cross'. The problem, however, was finding the exact whereabouts of the cross. The Romans had destroyed Jerusalem after the Jewish uprising of 70 CE. It remained a deserted ruin until the 130s, when the Emperor Hadrian (76–138 CE) rebuilt Jerusalem as a pagan Roman city, renaming it Aelia Capitolina. The new foundation obliterated the site of Jesus' passion, and Hadrian dedicated a temple to Venus over the site of Jesus' tomb.

**PIOUS PIUS**
Pope Pius V abolished the sale of indulgences that had brought the Church into disrepute and started the Protestant Reformation.

Some time after Constantine had become emperor, his elderly mother the Empress (later Saint) Helena (c. 246–c. 330) went on a pilgrimage to Jerusalem. She ordered the temple over Jesus' tomb to be demolished. It was during this work that the True Cross was unearthed, along with the nails used in the crucifixion. Helena sent a fragment of the cross and the nails to Constantinople, and entrusted the rest to the Church of the Holy Sepulchre, which was built over the site. Fragments of the True Cross soon found their way across the Roman Empire and beyond.

Today, there are wooden fragments claiming to be parts of the True Cross in Italy, France, Spain, Belgium, Greece and Ethiopia. Contradicting the later gibes that if reunited the fragments would amount to a forest of crosses, a Catholic prelate has calculated that all the pieces now extant account for only a portion of the type of cross used in crucifixion in Jesus' time. However, this is slightly missing the point. What the reader should consider is the likelihood of anyone finding the one True Cross, three centuries after the event, in a country where crucifixion was routinely practised as a punishment, and where there would be crosses aplenty to be found.

In addition to the True Cross, relics of Jesus' life and death include the Crown of Thorns, the post he was tied to when he was flagellated, the Holy Sponge, the Holy Lance that pierced his side (of which there are at least four), and the boards of the manger from Bethlehem. According to the French, the complete crown of thorns is kept in Notre Dame Cathedral in Paris, which raises concern about the genuineness of the other fragments in Belgium, Italy, Spain and the United Kingdom. The boards from Jesus' manger are preserved in a splendid chapel in the Basilica of Santa Maria Maggiore in Rome. The Church claims that refugees from the Muslim conquest of Jerusalem in 637 brought the boards with them to Rome, but more sceptical scholars have argued that there is no evidence of the relic before the eleventh century. The date is significant as it coincides with the date of the First Crusade (1096–9), after which western crusaders brought back many 'relics' from the Holy Land.

One of the most controversial Christian relics is the Turin Shroud, preserved in a shrine in Turin Cathedral, Italy. The shroud is a large piece of linen cloth, in which, according to believers, Jesus was buried, and onto which his image was miraculously imprinted at the moment of his resurrection; or, according to scientists who carbon-dated the shroud in 1988, it is a clever medieval forgery. Real or fake, relics became a serious point of contention during the Reformation. Protestant critics alleged that the veneration of relics and the belief in their miraculous powers amounted to the sin of idolatry – the worship of images and objects that is strictly forbidden by the Ten Commandments. The second practice that led to the rupture between the Catholic Church and the Protestant

**THE BOARDS FROM JESUS' MANGER ARE PRESERVED IN A SPLENDID CHAPEL IN THE BASILICA OF SANTA MARIA MAGGIORE IN ROME.**

## THE PRICE OF INDULGENCE

reformers, especially Luther (see above), was the abuse of the system of pardons known as indulgences. The Church holds that there are two types of sins, 'mortal sins' that result in eternal damnation, and less serious 'venial sins' that will earn the sinner temporary (or temporal) punishment, and can be atoned for by acts of penance and good works, or remitted by the granting of indulgences. The indulgence does not actually forgive the sin, which still has to be absolved in confession, but it releases the sinner from temporal punishment, which in medieval times was believed to be the length of time (counted in days) a person would spend in Purgatory before being allowed to go up to Paradise. The Church, theologians argued, had the power to grant indulgences because of the abundance of merit to be found in the persons of Jesus Christ and the saints.

The pope could issue a 'plenary' indulgence – a full remission of penance – for especially meritorious service to the Church, like the one granted by Pope Urban II (1042–99) to those taking part in the First Crusade; or the Church could grant 'partial' indulgences – remissions of punishment that would sometimes be counted in the number of days in Purgatory the grantee would be spared. When the practice of almsgiving was recognised as a means to earn an indulgence – in other words, when they could be bought for hard cash – the system became widely abused by both the religious and civil authorities.

In 'The Pardoner's Tale' in *The Canterbury Tales*, Geoffrey Chaucer (c. 1343–1400) gives a portrait of a 'pardoner', a professional seller of indulgences. Chaucer's fictional pardoner is an avaricious rogue who peddles false relics and extorts money from the poor and credulous by selling them indulgences and pocketing the money. The caricature, however, was not far from the truth. In the late Middle Ages, there were many cases of clerics and pardoners selling forged indulgences that promised not only the remission of temporal penance, but the release of the damned from Hell or absolution for future sins. Despite repeated attempts at reform by the papal authorities, the practice was far too lucrative to abolish altogether.

The immediate cause of Martin Luther's denunciation of the Church in 1517 was not the existence of forged indulgences but the sale of indulgences by the Church itself. In 1517, the Dominican friar Johann Tetzel (1465–1519) sold indulgences in Germany to raise funds for the reconstruction of Saint Peter's Basilica in Rome, promising not just the remission of temporal punishment but forgiveness for sins yet to be committed. This was too much even for the pope. The Council of Trent abolished the office of pardoner, and in 1567, Pope Pius V (1504–72) cancelled all indulgences that had been bought and sold. Further reform established that only the pope himself could issue indulgences.

Although for all intents and purposes the papacy abolished indulgences in the late Middle Ages, and these eventually ceased to be a bone of contention between the Catholic and Protestant churches, the Catholic veneration of the relics of the saints, Jesus Christ, and members of the Holy Family continues to this day. Churches in Catholic countries such as France, Italy and Spain display elaborate gold and silver reliquaries decorated with precious stones, and many of the faithful continue to believe that they have the power to perform miracles.

In addition to such ancient relics as the True Cross, the Crown of Thorns, the Turin Shroud and the bones of the apostles, more recent relics are also believed to have miraculous powers. The mortal remains of the nineteenth-century French Carmelite nun and doctor of the Church, Saint Thérèse of Lisieux (1873–97), are much better travelled than the reclusive Thérèse herself ever was. In 1999–2000, they toured the United States; in 2002, they travelled to the Republic of Ireland and then to Iraq in the vain hope of preventing the outbreak of war. In 2009, the relics toured the UK, stopping at over a dozen destinations, including the chapel of Wormwood Scrubs prison in London.

THE COUNCIL OF TRENT ABOLISHED THE OFFICE OF PARDONER, AND IN 1567, POPE PIUS V CANCELLED ALL INDULGENCES THAT HAD BEEN BOUGHT AND SOLD.

DECEPTION

Religious deceit

Military subterfuge

Financial fraud

Fake or counterfeit

**Imposture or cross-dressing**

Confidence trick

Scientific deception

# THREE'S A CROWD: THE FALSE DIMITRYS

**Main Culprits:** The false Dimitrys; Russian *boyars*; Sigismund III; Charles IX

**Motivation:** Power

**Damage Done:** Death and destruction caused by civil and foreign wars; violent death of the impostors

*The mob threw themselves on him with horrible cries of triumph, and beating him, dragged him into a room of the palace.... He was stripped and dressed in a baker's robe.... Later, a disfigured corpse with the stomach slit open and the arms slashed was thrown onto the steps of the palace.*

**Prosper Mérimée (1803–70) on the death of the first false Dimitry**

Every young nation experiences growing pains, often accompanied by periods of internal bloodletting, during which rival groups jostle for power. In the medieval period, this meant great feudal lords, who fought one another for the crown. Such was the savagery of these conflicts that many claimants vanished without a trace, often murdered by their own relatives or allies. To the enterprising, this presented a prime opportunity to claim royal titles for themselves. In the stories of Perkin Warbeck and Lambert Simnel, we met two such royal impostors who appeared during England's Wars of the Roses (see pp. 35–40). The equivalent period in the history of Russia is called the 'Time of Troubles', when in less than a decade no less than three men claimed to be Prince Dimitry Ivanovitch (1582–91), third son of Ivan IV of Russia, better known as Ivan 'the Terrible' (1530–84).

**TROUBLESOME TIMES**
Russia suffered decades of political turmoil after the death of Ivan 'the Terrible'.

Russia had first emerged in the mid-ninth century as a pagan kingdom, an amalgam of Viking raiders and Slavic tribes. In the tenth century, the people, by then called the Rus, converted to Byzantine Orthodox Christianity. The Mongol invasions almost wiped out the fledgling Russian principalities in the thirteenth century, and the Rus also faced a threat from the West in the shape of the Catholic Poles and Lithuanians. The Grand Duchy of Moscow, however, survived and thrived, eventually expelling the Mongols from Russia and defeating the invading Catholic Teutonic knights from the West. Ivan III (1440–1505) and his grandson Ivan the Terrible, Russia's first tsar (also *czar*; from the Latin title Caesar), converted the Grand Duchy into a formidable empire with vast territories stretching from Central Asia to the borders of Europe.

Ivan, however, more than amply lived up to his sobriquet, 'the Terrible'. He was prone to fits of fury, though several historians now believe that he may have suffered from periodic bouts of mental illness. In 1581, he murdered both his unborn grandson, and his heir, the Tsarevitch Ivan (1554–81), in bouts of rage. This left the succession to his second son, Feodor I (1557–98), whose only interests were religion and bellringing. It is now thought that he suffered from a mental disability. Feodor succeeded in 1584 but was tsar in name only; the real ruler of the country was his scheming brother-in-law, the *boyar* (nobleman) Boris Godunov (c. 1551–1605).

Feodor did not seem to be able to father an heir, and until he did, the likelihood was that the throne would go to Ivan the Terrible's third son, Dimitry. The boy stood in the path of Boris' imperial ambitions. Not content with exiling him from Moscow to the city of Uglich, he had the boy murdered when he was nine years old. The murder, however, did not serve Boris well in the long run. When the childless Feodor died in 1598, Boris had himself elected as his successor. His reign was ill-fated and was marked by one of the worst famines in Russian history.

**DIMITRY THE UNDEAD**

Around 1600, rumours began to circulate that Dimitry Ivanovitch had miraculously survived Boris' assassination attempt, or had risen, Christ-like, from the grave, and would liberate the people from the tyrannical rule of the hated Boris. On cue, in 1603, a young man presented himself to Prince Adam Wisnowiecki (1566–1622), a powerful Polish-Lithuanian nobleman, claiming to be the missing Russian prince. He told a tale of escape from Godunov's assassins, who had murdered another boy in his place, and of travelling from monastery to monastery to evade capture. He had finally fled Russian soil when recognised by a fellow monk, and he had sought refuge in the city of Ostroh (now in Ukraine), then part of the Polish-Lithuanian Commonwealth.

Dissatisfied with the help Wisnowiecki was able or willing to provide, Dimitry found a new noble protector in the Commonwealth, Jerzy Mniszech (c. 1548–1613). In 1604, Mniszech presented Dimitry to Sigismund III Vasa (1566–1632), king of the Commonwealth. Sigismund recognised Dimitry as the rightful heir to the Russian throne, but there was too much opposition in the Polish Senate to a military adventure in Russia, so the king did not offer any military help. He did not, however, attempt to prevent Mniszech from outfitting a private army for the pretender. To seal their alliance, Mniszech married Dimitry to his daughter, the strong-willed Marina (c. 1588–1614). He was determined to be father-in-law and grandfather to Russia's future tsars. In order to garner as much support as he could for his cause, Dimitry converted to Roman Catholicism, the religion of the Commonwealth.

Back in Moscow, Boris Godunov, the one person who was likely to know for sure what had become of the real Dimitry, instantly denounced him as an impostor and identified him as a runaway Orthodox monk by the name of Grigory Otrepyev (c. 1580–1606). All this was to no avail, however, and Dimitry crossed the border into Russia with a small Commonwealth force. He won the support of disaffected Cossacks and boyars opposed to Boris, but his military position was at best precarious. In 1605, he won a minor skirmish against Boris' forces but lost another. He was facing certain defeat and capture when the news reached him that Boris had died suddenly in Moscow, leaving his sixteen-year-old son, Feodor II (1589–1605) to succeed him.

**DIMITRY WON THE SUPPORT OF DISAFFECTED COSSACKS AND BOYARS OPPOSED TO BORIS, BUT HIS MILITARY POSITION WAS AT BEST PRECARIOUS.**

The new tsar was both intelligent and physically strong, but he was no match for the plotting and counter-plotting that surrounded him in the Kremlin. The rule of the Godunovs that had begun in blood ended in blood. The sixteen-year-old Feodor II was murdered after a few months on the throne, leaving the road open for Dimitry to make a triumphal entry into Moscow, where he was crowned Dimitry II. He ruled with the support of his Roman Catholic Polish-Lithuanian backers, which quickly made him unpopular with the Russian boyars, the Russian Orthodox Church, and the people at large.

A plot soon hatched to have Dimitry deposed, led by Prince Vasily Shuisky (1552–1612). Shuisky had once been a close ally of Boris Godunov, and had been sent to Uglich to investigate the circumstances of the real Dimitry's death. In 1591, he had reported that the boy had committed suicide by stabbing himself in the throat. Upon Boris' death, Shuisky retracted this account and recognised the false Dimitry as genuine, precipitating Feodor's murder. Now he changed his story once again, denouncing Dimitry as an impostor. Less than a year after his coronation, Dimitry II was assassinated by conspirators led by Shuisky. His dismembered body was thrown out of the palace (see quote), burned to ashes, and the ashes fired from a canon out of the city gates in the direction of the hereditary enemy, the Polish-Lithuanian Commonwealth. The Russians also massacred Dimitry's Commonwealth bodyguard, giving Sigismund III a motive to interfere in Russia's affairs. Shuisky then ascended the throne as Vasily IV.

Vasily's reign was even less successful than that of the other murderous usurper, Boris Godunov. He had made an enemy of Sigismund and alienated many of the boyars. To ward off the Commonwealth threat Vasily signed a treaty with Charles IX of Sweden (1550–1611). The alliance prompted Sigismund to declare war on Russia. In the meantime another man emerged claiming to be the murdered Dimitry Ivanovitch. The second false Dimitry (c. 1580–1610) first appeared in 1607 in the Russian town of Starodub. He told an even more unlikely story of a second escape at the hands of Shuisky's assassins, claiming that they had murdered a double in his place. Little is known about his true origins. Several sources agree that his family name was Verevkin, and that he might have been the son of a priest or a minor nobleman, or of Jewish extraction. Nevertheless he was 'recognised' by his 'widow' Marina Mniszech, and won the support of her father, the usually disaffected Cossacks, and the boyars opposed to Vasily.

In 1610, Dimitry defeated Vasily's forces near Moscow but did not take the capital. The ineffective Vasily was forced to abdicate, and died in a Commonwealth prison two years later. Russia was in the midst of a tripartite power struggle: between Dimitry's rebel army, an invading Polish-Lithuanian force under King Sigismund, and a Russo-Swedish army under the command of Vasily's cousin. The throne was vacant, and Dimitry, with growing popular support, was poised to make good his claim. How good his chances were, we shall never know, as at this crucial moment in history, Dimitry number two died at the hands of a disgruntled nobleman. Marina was by then pregnant and would be delivered of a son whom she christened Ivan (after his supposed grandfather, Ivan IV) Dimitryevitch (1611–14), claiming for him the title of tsarevitch. She found a new protector in the Cossack adventurer Ivan Zarutsky (d. 1614). This 'alternative' imperial family survived for another three years, until they, too, fell into Russian hands. Zarutsky and the little Ivan were executed in Moscow, and Marina died in prison soon after.

**FATAL OATH**
The first false Dimitry obtained foreign support by promising to convert his subjects to Catholicism. The oath cost him his life.

With the throne still vacant, and the country at war with two foreign powers, a group of boyars elected Sigismund III's fifteen-year-old son Władysław (1595–1648) as the new tsar. This may appear to be a strange move on their part, but had the proposal been accepted it would have forestalled Sigismund's invasion of Russia. One of their conditions was that Władysław convert to the Russian Orthodox rite. Sigismund refused the terms and the election and occupied Moscow, thinking to claim the throne himself and convert the country to Roman Catholicism.

In 1611, the third and most enigmatic Dimitry appeared in the Baltic city of Ivangorod, claiming improbably to have escaped assassination for a third time. The pretender, who may have been a defrocked cleric called Sidorka (d. 1612), temporarily won the support of Charles IX of Sweden. However, when Charles turned against him and planned to put his own son on the Russian throne, Dimitry was handed over to Moscow by his former 'subjects' and hastily executed.

In the space of 14 years, Russia had seen two usurpers on the throne, three impostors pretending to be Dimitry Ivanovitch, a foreign prince elected to tsardom, and another half-dozen minor pretenders, including Marina's son Ivan. Finally, in 1613, the boyars elected one of their own to the throne and united behind him to expel the Commonwealth and Swedish invaders. They chose the seventeen-year-old Mikhail I Romanov (1596–1645). This time, it seemed, the Russians had learned their lesson, and the Romanov dynasty ruled until 1917, when the last tsar, Nicholas II (1868–1918), was overthrown in the Russian Revolution. The story of Russian imperial imposture was not quite over, however. The murder of Nicholas and his family in 1918 by the Bolsheviks provided one final opportunity for an impostor to claim that she was of royal blood before the Russian monarchy disappeared forever (see Anna Anderson, pp. 102–6).

**THIRD TIME NOT SO LUCKY**

## DECEPTION

Religious deceit

Military subterfuge

Financial fraud

Fake or counterfeit

Imposture or cross-dressing

**Confidence trick**

Scientific deception

# THE BOGUS MAGUS: 'COUNT' CAGLIOSTRO

**Main Culprit:** Giuseppe Balsamo

**Motivation:** Financial gain and fame

**Damage Done:** Hoodwinked the credulous

*The quest of treasure had been all the rage a century before. Young Balsamo became a treasure-seeker. He was a clever youth, and got a rich goldsmith of Palermo, one Marano, to believe that there lay in a grotto […] an immense treasure, of which he could make him the owner[…] Balsamo began his incantations. All at once a band of demons, clothed in deep black, appeared, fell on Marano, and gave him a sound thrashing. The good man was cudgelled and robbed.*

**From *Cagliostro and Company* by G. Maidment and F. Funck-Brentano, 2008**

The eighteenth century is often called the 'Age of Reason' and the 'Century of the Enlightenment', because it was the age of the great French *philosophes*, including Voltaire (1694–1778) and Jean-Jacques Rousseau (1712–78). However, as is often the case in periods of intellectual and social ferment when old certainties are overturned, a space is opened for the clever confidence trickster to fill the vacuum of belief. When humans lose faith in their traditional god or gods, as has often been observed, they will believe in almost anything. A parallel can be drawn with our own times: as conventional church-going decreases, interest in all kinds of fringe and non-Christian religions, and 'New Age' beliefs increases. Through the intellectual doors that the Enlightenment had opened came in a strange mix of ancient esotericism and pseudo-scientific charlatanism. For example, ancient Egyptian hieroglyphs, first reproduced in Europe in the late sixteenth century, were believed to be a code containing the secrets of Egyptian hermetic magic.

At the same time, eighteenth-century society was socially extremely conservative. In France, Austria and Russia, the classes were kept separate by laws and customs as strict as those of the Indian caste system. One of the causes of the French Revolution of 1789 was the rigidity of the *Ancien Régime* class system, which prevented the growing and affluent middle class from accessing political power that was reserved to the aristocracy. In this society, a name and a title were the passports to success, and those who claimed them were not always what they seemed. Travelling to a foreign country naturally helped. A few hundred miles and a couple of borders could turn a plain mister into a marquis or a mistress into a countess.

The final element in this story was the belief in alchemy. Although the science of chemistry was fast dispelling ancient beliefs, there were plenty who still believed in the search for the elixir of immortality – the Philosopher's Stone – and for the process through which base metals could be transmuted into gold. Books of magic abounded and were filled with incantations that the credulous believed would lead them to buried treasure.

**ROYAL ROCKS**
Cagliostro was implicated in the Affair of the Diamond Necklace, involving Marie Antoinette (above), that rocked the French court.

## THE TRICKSTER FROM PALERMO

Giuseppe Balsamo (1743–95) was born in the city of Palermo, capital of the Italian island of Sicily. Italy had not been a single united country since the fall of the Western Roman Empire (476 CE), but remained divided into a patchwork of states, large and small, until the end of the nineteenth century. The north of the country was in the Austrian zone of influence, the south in Spain's, and central Italy was ruled by the pope. In Italy, one did not have to travel far to change identities and social class.

Balsamo was a commoner by birth, though from a relatively well-to-do family. He received a good education for the period, and was sent to be a novice at a monastery. Holy orders, however, did not interest the young Giuseppe. While at the monastery he acquired a rudimentary knowledge of alchemy, Catholic ritual and pharmacology, which would serve him well in later life. He also developed an interest in the occult, though more to take advantage of the gullible rather than as a true believer (see quote). Marano, the man he had tricked and robbed, realised that he had been duped and tried to have the seventeen-year-old Balsamo arrested, but the bird had flown to Messina. In Messina, Balsamo had a wealthy and aged aunt whose surname was Cagliostro. He hoped to inherit from her, but on her death, she left her wealth to the Church. Instead of the money he had hoped for, all that Giuseppe obtained was his aunt's name, which he believed was more mysterious than his own.

In the next few years, Giuseppe Balsamo would morph into Alessandro di Cagliostro, a count with a rather mysterious and exotic pedigree. He claimed to be the son of a princely house of the Empire of Trebizond, a Byzantine state that had been created after the fall of Constantinople to the Crusaders in 1204, which survived the capture of the great city by the Ottoman Turks in 1453 by eight years. Later on, Cagliostro was in Malta where another element of his biography was contrived, claiming that he had been raised as a Christian in Muslim Morocco and rescued by the Grand Master of the Knights of St John, the old crusader order that ruled the island of Malta until the end of the eighteenth century. He would later claim to have visited Egypt to learn its ancient occult lore.

In 1768, Cagliostro was back in Italy, in Rome, where he managed to get the job of secretary to a Roman Catholic cardinal. While in the service of the Church, Cagliostro was conducting a lucrative business selling magic charms covered in Egyptian hieroglyphs, consorting with Rome's criminal underworld, and improving his skills as a forger and confidence trickster. He met and married the fourteen-year-old Lorenza Feliciani, and moved into her parents' home. However, Cagliostro soon argued with the Felicianis, and the couple left Rome and embarked on a grand European tour.

Cagliostro and his young wife visited the courts of France, England and Russia, peddling an entertaining mix of spiritualism, magic and medicine to jaded aristocrats, who lapped up his bogus claims and bought his love potions for extortionate amounts. During a visit to England, he was initiated into the Masonic movement. He later went on to found his own esoteric Egyptian style of Freemasonry, which had little to do with the rationalist, secular aims of the wider Masonic movement. Although all forms of magic were punishable by death in the countries where Cagliostro plied his trade, he had the protection of senior nobles and even crowned heads. He came close to losing his liberty and his head, however, when he became embroiled in the Affair of the Diamond Necklace (1785–6), a confidence trick that rocked the very foundations of the French monarchy. He was acquitted, however, and returned to Italy. This last move was to prove fatal.

**MAGIC MAN**
Cagliostro blended the discoveries of the 'Age of Reason' with the superstitions of earlier centuries of unreason.

Freemasonry was illegal in papal Catholic Rome, and Cagliostro was either tricked into revealing his Masonic activities to spies of the Holy Inquisition or denounced by his own wife Lorenza, who wanted out of her marriage. He was arrested and sentenced to death in 1789. The pope, however, commuted his sentence to life imprisonment, and he was interned in the Castel Sant'Angelo, the large fortress opposite Saint Peter's Basilica. After a failed escape attempt, he was transferred to the forbidding medieval fortress of San Leo in central Italy. Despite his many claims to know the secrets of eternal life and many other occult mysteries, he died a broken man at the relatively early age of 52 in 1795.

**DECEPTION**

Religious deceit

Military subterfuge

Financial fraud

**Fake or counterfeit**

Imposture or cross-dressing

Confidence trick

Scientific deception

# TO FAKE OR NOT TO FAKE: WILLIAM IRELAND

**Main Culprit:** William Ireland

**Motivation:** To please his father

**Damage Done:** Ruin of his own and his father's reputation

*Vortigern:*

*And when this solemn mockery is o'er,*

*With icy hand thou tak'st him by the feet,*

*And upward so, till thou dost reach the heart,*

*And wrap him in the cloak of lasting night.*

**From *Vortigern, an Historical Play*, Act V, Scene 2 (1795)**

William Shakespeare (1564–1616) is probably the best-known dramatist in the English-speaking world. Despite his fame, surprisingly little is known about his life. What is known has been pieced together through painstaking research, and much remains uncertain. In the late eighteenth century, though his plays were regularly performed by the leading theatrical companies of the day, Shakespeare's biography was a mix of a few known facts, a great deal of guesswork, and a host of apocryphal stories and traditions. The mystery of Shakespeare's life naturally elicited considerable interest among men of letters and historians, who avidly collected anything remotely connected with the 'Bard of Avon'. One such man was the engraver and author of travelogues (what we would call a travel writer today) Samuel Ireland (1744–1800). Imagine the joy such a man would feel, not only if he discovered letters and documents by Shakespeare's own hand, but also the manuscript of two long-lost plays by England's most eminent playwright.

Shakespeare's birthday is given as St George's Day (23 April) 1564, but this is a traditional rather than actual birth date. He was the son of John Shakespeare (c. 1530–1601), a merchant and civic official in the English town of Stratford-upon-Avon, Warwickshire. It is not known where he was educated, but it was probably at the local 'grammar' school, where he would have studied the Latin and Greek classics and English history. In 1582, aged 18, he married the 26-year-old Anne Hathaway (1556–1623 – she of the famous cottage), possibly because she was pregnant with their first child, Susanna (1583–1649). He then dropped out of sight between 1585, when his twin boy and girl Hamnet (d. 1596) and Judith (d. 1662) were born, and 1592 when he appeared in London as a successful actor and playwright. He spent the remaining years of his life dividing his time between Stratford and London, and died a well-respected and wealthy man in Stratford in 1616. Although his work had appeared piecemeal during his lifetime, the first publication of 36 of his 38 plays dates to the First Folio of 1623. Scholars take this to be the authoritative list, although two plays were later added to the Shakespeare canon.

**THE BARD**
In the eighteenth century, Shakespeare's biography was made up of a few known facts and a great many fanciful anecdotes.

Samuel Ireland was originally a weaver, but he abandoned this trade in favour of his true passion, engraving. In the 1780s he exhibited at the Royal Academy of Arts in London, winning prizes for his work, and he made a living from dealing in antiquarian engravings, books and prints, which he himself also collected. In the 1790s he published several travelogues of Holland, Belgium and France, and of several English counties, including *Picturesque Views on the Warwickshire Avon* (1795). Ireland visited Stratford-upon-Avon with his son – eighteen-year-old William Henry Ireland (1775–1835) – in 1793, to draw the scenes he would later publish in *Picturesque Views*.

While he was in Stratford, Samuel visited all the places traditionally associated with Shakespeare's life and collected as much information as he could about the playwright, a good deal of it invented for his benefit by the locals. He heard of a cache of original documents in the house of a local man, but on arriving there was told that the papers had been destroyed a week earlier. Bitterly disappointed, the gullible engraver returned to London. The loss of these presumed Shakespeare originals was witnessed by Samuel's loving son, William Henry Ireland.

WILLIAM SHARED HIS FATHER'S INTEREST IN LITERARY MEMORABILIA, BUT HE TOOK A MUCH MORE HANDS-ON APPROACH WHEN IT CAME TO ITS 'DISCOVERY'.

William shared his father's interest in literary memorabilia, but he took a much more hands-on approach when it came to its 'discovery'. He was apprenticed to a law firm in London, which gave him access to early legal documents, and a store of ancient paper stock. He probably practised his forger's trade secretly at work, until he was ready to present his great 'finds' to his father in 1794, a year after their disappointing visit to Stratford. William gave his father a mortgage deed signed by Shakespeare, several letters, including one from Queen Elizabeth I (1533–1603) to the playwright, books that the great man had annotated, handwritten manuscripts of *King Lear* and *Hamlet*, and, best of all, two hitherto unknown plays: *Vortigern, An Historical Tragedy* and *Henry II*. He claimed these had been found in a trunk belonging to a mysterious Mr H., whose identity he refused to divulge.

Samuel was delighted, and much to his son's dismay, immediately displayed the documents, inviting many of London's literary luminaries to view them. The biographer and diarist James Boswell (1740–95) was so moved that he knelt before the documents and devoutly kissed them as one would a religious relic. The visitors enthusiastically declared the finds to be genuine. The papers were on display for over a year, and the Irelands took them to Carlton House to show them to the Prince of Wales. Again against William's wishes, Samuel decided to publish engraved copies of the papers, including the unknown plays *Vortigern* and *Henry II*, in 1795. If William had intended the deception to please his disappointed father, it had now seriously got out of hand.

Publication finally made the papers widely available to the academic community, including the leading Shakespeare scholar and editor of the day, Edmund Malone (1741–1812), who had not been invited to view the documents. In early 1796 Malone wrote a 400-page rebuttal of the documents, accusing Samuel of forging them. He cited as evidence the handwriting of Queen Elizabeth that did not match other authentic examples; anachronistic use of language; bizarre spellings that did not match Elizabethan or any known historical English orthography; and several glaring historical errors, including references to the Globe Theatre in London before it was actually built. Despite this devastating attack, the Irelands retained some eminent defenders, and the controversy raged back and forth in the pages of newspapers and magazines.

**ALL THE WORLD'S A STAGE**

The *coup de grâce* for the Ireland forgeries was not Malone's book, however; it was the one and only performance of one of the recently 're-discovered' plays, *Vortigern and Rowena* or *Vortigern, An Historical Tragedy*, which was staged at the Drury Lane Theatre, London, on 2 April, 1796. Unsurprisingly, the performance was sold out, and the packed house was abuzz with excitement. The producer was none other than the playwright Richard Sheridan (1751–1816), and the leading Shakespearean actor of the day, John Kemble (1757–1823), took the leading role of Vortigern.

The historical Vortigern was an obscure figure from early British history. He lived some time after the Romans had abandoned Britain (fourth century CE). The play opens with Vortigern's murder of King Constantius, whose throne he then usurps. The dead king's sons Aurelius and Uther go to Scotland to raise an army to avenge their father's murder. Meanwhile, the usurper invites the Saxons under Hengist and Horsus to England to fight for him. Vortigern falls in love with Hengist's daughter Rowena and deserts his own wife and children. Aurelius and Uther, accompanied by Vortigern's children, invade England and defeat Vortigern and the Saxons. Despite being advertised as a tragedy, the play ends untragically, and Aurelius spares Vortigern and marries his daughter Flavia.

The subject matter of the play was not an unusual one for Shakespeare, who had used themes from Antiquity and early British history in his own work: for example, *Julius Caesar*, *Macbeth* and *Cymbeline*. However, the structure, characterisation and themes of the play fell far short of Shakespeare's own plays. The audience managed to listen to the first acts of *Vortigern* with its Fool lifted from *Hamlet*, and its murderous usurper lifted from *Macbeth*, with a certain amount of restraint. But when Kemble repeated the line 'And when this solemn mockery is o'er' (see quote), the audience, unable to hold back, finally erupted into catcalls and laughter.

Samuel Ireland was outraged, accusing Kemble of being in league with Malone to discredit the play. He wrote *Mr Ireland's Vindication of His Conduct Respecting the Publication of the Supposed Shakespeare MSS* (1796), attacking Malone's work and methods. Worried that his father's reputation was now fatally compromised as the author of the forged documents, William published a full confession, exonerating Samuel. This did not placate the Irelands' critics. They accused father and son of collusion. Amazingly, even after his son's full confession, Samuel continued to believe that the documents were genuine. He died an embittered man in 1800.

**OVERCOME**
The famous diarist James Boswell was so moved by the forgeries that he knelt before them and kissed them.

In 1805, William Ireland published *The Confessions of William Henry Ireland*, once again trying to clear his father's name, but it was only seventy years later that research finally confirmed that Samuel Ireland was his own son's dupe and not his collaborator. William tried his hand as an author of gothic novels and history books, but never achieved much success. In 1832 he published *Vortigern* as his own play but it was not given another performance until 2008. He died in London, impoverished and forgotten, in 1832.

# TRANSGENDER SPY: THE CHEVALIER AND CHEVALIÈRE D'ÉON

**DECEPTION**

Religious deceit

Military subterfuge

Financial fraud

Fake or counterfeit

**Imposture or cross-dressing**

Confidence trick

Scientific deception

**Main Culprit:** Chevalier d'Éon

**Motivation:** To live as a transgendered person

**Damage Done:** Embarrassed the French crown; exiled from his/her native France

*The history of the women who disguised their sex in order to consecrate themselves to God and to adopt the monastic life and who have been recognised as saints by the Greek and Latin Church.*

**Subtitle of *Pious Metamorphoses* by Mlle La Chevalière d'Éon (1728–1810)**

In the past forty years, social scientists have realised that social gender, biological sex and sexual orientation do not define one another. For example, a biological female can play the gender role of a man, and at the same time consider 'himself' to be a lesbian; or a biological male can adopt a female gender role, and yet continue to be a heterosexual in his choice of female partners. The exact definition of these individuals becomes complicated if we stick to the terms 'man' and 'woman', taking for granted that these describe fixed social, sexual and physiological characteristics. In recent year, the term 'transgendered', or 'trans' for short, has come into use, to describe persons who are either biologically male or female, who do not necessarily play the conventional social gender role usually ascribed to their biological sex.

**DRESSED TO DECEIVE**

In the eighteenth century, such fine social distinctions did not exist. Men were taken to be socially, sexually and physiologically male, and women, to be socially, sexually and physiologically female. We have seen in the stories of Pope Joan (pp. 27–31) and Hua Mulan (pp. 32–5) that ambitious women could disguise themselves as men in order to go beyond the limited opportunities open to their sex. But these were conscious deceptions, and their social and biological identities as women were never in doubt. Until modern times, it would have been much less advantageous for a man to disguise himself as a woman, unless it were to evade some danger. There existed in eighteenth-century England a group of gay men called 'the Mollies', who cross-dressed as part of sexual role-playing games, which signals to several scholars the beginnings of both modern gay and transsexual subcultures.

In the life of the Chevalier/Chevalière d'Éon (1728–1810), we also find a very modern formulation of the concept of biological sex, gender and sexual identity. D'Éon was taken to be a biological woman during his lifetime, and he himself claimed that he had been born female, had been raised as a male, and had later reverted to his original sex. In reality, he was, as far as can be ascertained, physiologically male, and consciously decided to play the female gender in later life. He carried out a double deception, pretending to be a female-to-male-to-female, while in reality being a male-to-female. His motives are difficult to ascertain, as his autobiography weaves real facts with deceits and exaggerations. He admired and wanted to emulate women who had played the male gender – especially women like Pope Joan, whom he believed had cross-dressed in the service of God (see quote). In d'Éon's mind, adopting a female identity and serving God and his country were deeply intertwined.

Like that other Enlightenment sexual revolutionary, his contemporary, the Marquis de Sade (1740–1814), d'Éon was born in the final decades of France's monarchical *Ancien Régime*, the son of a well-to-do provincial family. His father was an official in the town of Tonnerre in Burgundy in eastern France. He excelled at school, and aged 15 was sent to France's most prestigious high school, the Collège Mazarin in Paris. While there he was in the care of his uncle, the Inspector General of the Paris Police. Through his family connections, he was able to obtain the job of royal censor, which gave him an income and the leisure to study and lead the life of a young nobleman about town with good prospects. Interested in public service, he wrote a book on fiscal policy (1756) and another on the history of taxation (1758).

In 1756, King Louis XV (1710–74) appointed this promising young man to the post of secretary to the French Ambassador to the court of Empress Elizabeth of Russia (1709–62). His diplomatic work was only part of his service to the king. He was also initiated into the *Secret du Roi* (the King's Secret), a private intelligence-gathering organisation – the French CIA of its day – that answered to the king alone, and that not even the king's own ministers knew about. In 1760, he returned to France to enlist as a captain in a dragoons regiment and fight in the Seven Years' War (1754–63). The conflict involved all the major European countries and pitted France against her hereditary enemy, England. At the end of the war, d'Éon travelled to London with the French delegation to negotiate the peace treaty. For this and other services in the king's employ he was decorated and knighted, taking the title Chevalier ('Sir' in British usage) d'Éon.

**INTELLIGENCE**
King Louis maintained a private secret service that even his ministers were not aware of. D'Éon was one of his most trusted agents.

In 1763, he was sent back to London, as temporary French envoy to the court of George III (1738–1820), and continued his spying activities for King Louis. One of his assignments was to obtain information for possible landing sites for a French invasion of England – a scheme

Louis had not revealed to his own government, but had unwisely, as it turned out, discussed in writing with d'Éon. The Chevalier's future looked bright. He had the confidence of the king, and he expected to be appointed permanent envoy to England. But at this point, the political situation changed at the French court. The king took a new mistress, Madame de Pompadour (1721–64), and d'Éon's patrons at court fell out of favour. He was passed over for the post of ambassador and demoted to secretary, and the Comte de Guerchy (1715–67) was appointed in his place. D'Éon was outraged and refused to serve the count, and went as far as accusing him of attempted murder. The case caused a scandal in England and France, and the king recalled d'Éon, but he refused to return to France – an open act of rebellion against his sovereign.

THE KING TOOK A NEW MISTRESS, MADAME DE POMPADOUR, AND D'ÉON'S PATRONS AT COURT FELL OUT OF FAVOUR.

D'Éon, however, had an 'insurance policy' in the shape of the king's letters to him about a planned invasion of England. He was dismissed from his diplomatic post, but the king secretly continued to pay him a pension, and the Chevalier continued to spy for Louis until his death in 1774. In the early 1770s, rumours began to circulate that d'Éon was really a woman. The story was probably started by d'Éon himself, and he did nothing to deny or confirm it. Louis sent a spy to England to verify the truth of the matter in 1772, and the man returned convinced that d'Éon was really a woman. The English, always the sporting gentlemen, bet the staggering sum of £200,000 (several tens of millions of dollars at today's values) on whether d'Éon was male or female. As d'Éon refused to let himself be examined, the matter had to be settled in court in 1777, when the Lord Chief Justice of England ruled that d'Éon was indeed of the female sex.

## FROM SIR TO LADY D'ÉON

When the mild-mannered Louis XVI (1754–93) came to the throne, he decided to disband the King's Secret and pension off its spies. D'Éon, still in England, remained a tricky problem. Louis sent the flamboyant playwright Pierre Caron de Beaumarchais (1732–99) to negotiate with d'Éon. Beaumarchais offered him a pension and official recognition as a woman, and in 1777, d'Éon returned to France dressed in his dragoons uniform, which he continued to wear in Paris until the king ordered him to wear only female clothing, as befitted his 'true' sex. With the official recognition of his female identity, d'Éon, now la Chevalière, had achieved his aim. However, he remained restless and dissatisfied. In 1778, he offered to lead an all-women regiment to fight in the American War of Independence (1775–83), which France had joined on the American side. The king would have none of it and exiled him to Tonnerre to live out his days with his widowed mother. Forbidden to live to Paris, d'Éon returned to the more congenial surroundings of London, where he continued to live as a woman on his French government pension. To entertain himself, he took part in fencing competitions until seriously injured in 1796, when he had reached the then advanced age of 68.

Unfortunately for 'Madame' d'Éon, the French Revolution intervened in 1789. He lost his pension, and King Louis his head. Now living in straitened circumstances, d'Éon was forced to take lodgings with the widow of a British naval officer. He died in her house in 1810. When doctors examined the body, it was determined to be physiologically male. Thus ended the career of one of the most colourful figures of the late eighteenth-century who has been called the first 'philosopher of gender'. In his autobiography, which was not published until 2001 (see Further Reading, pp. 252–6), it is clear that he had invented four crucial episodes to justify his female identity: that his father had raised him as a boy to get an inheritance; that he had cross-dressed when spying in Russia to become a confidante of the Empress Elizabeth; that his 'true' female sex had been discovered after he had a riding accident in London in the 1770s; and that his mother had repeatedly written to him telling him to abandon his 'false' manhood and embrace his 'womanhood'.

© Getty Images

**HALF AND HALF**
D'Éon perplexed his contemporaries, as shown by this drawing of him as both male and female.

In death, d'Éon received the accolade that he had dearly wanted in life, when a French journalist called him a 'modern Joan of Arc', writing the following epitaph:

*Joan of Arc needed a still-Gothic century*

*To make a name for herself*

*But this philosophical century*

*Pays a double homage to d'Éon.*

## DECEPTION

Religious deceit

Military subterfuge

Financial fraud

Fake or counterfeit

**Imposture or cross-dressing**

Confidence trick

Scientific deception

# THE ALMONDSBURY PRINCESS: CARABOO OF JAVASU

**Main Culprit:** Mary Willcocks

**Motivation:** To escape the poorhouse and get enough money to emigrate to the United States

**Damage Done:** Severe embarrassment for the people she had fooled

*Her dark complexion and shining black hair, large lustrous eyes and black eyebrows, gave her a very Oriental appearance, and her costume was very becoming. It was soon known that there was a Malay Princess staying at Mrs. Worrell's, and her door was besieged with visitors, curious to see this novelty, and all went away satisfied that she was really the Princess Caraboo.*

**From *A Recollection of Seventy Years* by Mrs John Farrar (1866)**

Previous entries (see Lambert Simnel and Perkin Warbeck, pp. 35–40, and the False Dimitrys, pp. 49–54) introduced royal impostors whose aim was to acquire power, status and wealth through their deceptions. But this latest royal impostor had a far more modest motive for her deceit – to remain out of that dreadful British institution so vividly described in the works of Charles Dickens (1812–70), the 'workhouse' or 'poorhouse' – a prison that masqueraded as a charitable hospice, where men and women convicted of vagrancy were locked up in dreadful conditions and forced to work. While earlier impostors had chosen to impersonate real princes, Mary Willcocks (1791–1864) not only invented a princely identity, but also created a whole country, with its own culture, language and alphabet.

Early nineteenth-century England was not the cosmopolitan country that it is today. Britain was in the process of acquiring a vast empire that would stretch from Canada to the Far East, but outside the capital and the main trading ports, non-European foreigners were still a rarity. In 1817, the country was suffering the after-effects of twenty years of hostilities with France during the Revolutionary (1792–1803) and Napoleonic Wars (1803–15), which made the population even more suspicious of strangers. Unemployment and food prices were high, and the thousands of returning soldiers placed a serious burden on the archaic system of poor relief established under the reign of Elizabeth I (1533–1603). The country's unsettled state, however, also presented opportunities for the enterprising to leave their usual occupations and places of residence. In other words, it was a period well suited to the clever impostor and fraudster.

**THE EXOTIC STRANGER**

On 3 April 1817, a young woman was found wandering in a distressed condition in Almondsbury, a small village in Gloucestershire, southwest England, 17 km (10.5 miles) from the port of Bristol. No one could understand the language that she was speaking, and her dark hair and eyes gave her an exotic appearance. Her clothes, however, were of local manufacture. She was taken to the parish's overseer of the poor, who, at a loss at what to do, took her to the local magistrate, Samuel Worrall, who lived at the local manor house with his American-born wife, Elizabeth.

Mrs. Worrall was immediately fascinated by her apparently exotic visitor, whom she described as being in her mid-twenties, clean about her person, and with hands that showed no signs of hard physical labour, which, at the time, was a sign that a person was of a certain social class. She was able to learn that her name was 'Caraboo'; and the girl recognised Chinese imagery shown to her, seeming to say that it belonged to her native country. However, she did not have East Asian features, which puzzled Mrs. Worrall and made Mr. Worrall suspicious.

Mrs. Worrall sent Caraboo to the local inn, where she refused to eat meat or drink beer, the usual drink of the period, or to sleep in a bed. She drank tea after saying a prayer in an unknown language, and insisted on washing her cup each time she drank. Mr. Worrall, who was less easily impressed than his wife, decided to commit her for trial for vagrancy in Bristol. If the girl had been found guilty, she could have been sent to the poorhouse or transported to Australia. However, after Caraboo had spent ten days in detention in Bristol, Elizabeth intervened on her behalf and persuaded her husband to bring her back to Almondsbury.

© Getty Images

**SQUALOR**
Workhouses, like this one in Andover, England, subjected young vagrants to harsh living conditions.

Life in the small Gloucestershire village was very tame and predictable, so the arrival of this eastern 'princess' caused quite a stir. Visitors began to arrive to see Caraboo, some to marvel at her exoticism, and others to test her claims. The local parson interviewed her and paid her the most outrageous compliments, trying to make her blush to show that she only pretended not to understand English but, as Mrs. Worrall recorded with some satisfaction in her journal, the girl did not react in any way. This convinced her that Caraboo was genuine. At this point, a local squire brought a Portuguese sailor, Manuel Eynesso, to meet Caraboo. Eynesso had, or claimed to have, spent time in the East Indies (now Indonesia) and the Far East, and to be able to speak the Malay language. He conversed with Caraboo and apparently understood what she said. The story Eynesso told was later elaborated by a Captain Palmer, who spent time with Caraboo, noting down everything she said and did.

Caraboo, Eynesso and Palmer revealed to an expectant world, was a princess from the Malay island of Javasu, the daughter of a Chinese father and a Malay mother, which explained why she did not have East Asian features. She had been abducted by pirates, and taken to Batavia (now Jakarta, Indonesia), where she had been sold to a Portuguese captain, whose ship was bound for Europe. The ship had called in at the Cape of Good Hope (South Africa) and the island of Saint Helena, where the British held Napoleon Bonaparte (1769–1821) from 1815 to 1821. On sighting the British coast, she had jumped ship and swum ashore not far from Bristol. As her clothing was soaked and in tatters, she had begged for clothing from an unidentified cottage, which explained why she had been found in English clothes. She had then made her way to Almondsbury.

At home with the Worralls, Caraboo played her part with increasing confidence and obvious enjoyment. She had 'learned' enough English to communicate but not converse with Mrs. Worrall and the servants. The good lady provided cloth and accessories for Caraboo to make herself an outfit, which consisted of an embroidered gown to the calf, sandals, a shawl worn 'in Malay style', and a turban ornamented with feathers. She had accomplishments that seemed to set her apart from her English female contemporaries: she swam, fenced and could shoot a bow and arrow. She built an 'altar' to her 'god', Allah Tallah, on an island in a lake, where she would make daily animal sacrifices, pray, and cook her meals. On one occasion, which she said was her father's birthday, she dressed herself as a warrior, complete with bow and arrow, 'armour' made from a dinner gong, and her face covered in war paint. She insisted on going to church in the get-up – much to the chagrin of Mr. Worrall and the delight of Mrs. Worrall.

**'PURE HUMBUG'**

News of Caraboo spread, and soon visitors were coming far and wide to meet her. One of her most eminent visitors was Dr. Charles H. Wilkinson (c. 1763–1850) from the neighbouring spa resort town of Bath. He was an eccentric savant who experimented with the medical uses of 'Galvanism' (electricity). He, too, declared Caraboo to be genuine, and arranged to have samples of her writing sent to Oxford University for examination by specialists. At the same time, Mrs. Worrall paid for a portrait of Caraboo to be painted by the Bristol artist Edward Bird (1772–1819). The game, however, was almost up. The Oxford linguists soon returned the judgement that Caraboo's language was 'pure humbug'. What sealed her fate, however, was being recognised by several people she had met before arriving in Almondsbury – her landlady in Bristol, Mrs. Neale, and a young man whom she had met on the road.

Confronted by Mrs. Worrall with this new evidence, Caraboo finally admitted that she was the daughter of a Devon cobbler and that her name was Mary Willcocks. Although ashamed of having been taken in so completely, the kindly Mrs. Worrall was not angry with Mary. She thought it best, however, if Mary left the country quietly, and she arranged for Mary's passage to the United States, where she found her a place as a servant. Before she left, Mary told her story to a Bristol journalist, revealing an adventurous life that included a son, possibly illegitimate, a score of jobs in domestic service, several impostures, and visits to Europe. Her aim, when she had gone to Almondsbury, was to beg the fare of five guineas that would take her to the United States, where she hoped to start a new life.

Mary returned to England in 1821, and tried to cash in on her fame as Caraboo, but with little success. She later married and lived in Bristol where she set up in business selling leeches to the local hospital. She died in 1864 aged 75. As impostures go, Mary's was harmless. Her 'victims' had really fooled themselves, wanting to believe in her for their own reasons: Mrs Worrall and the ladies of Bath and Bristol to enliven their dull provincial lives, and the 'experts' who had been taken in, to borrow some of her celebrity.

ALTHOUGH ASHAMED OF HAVING BEEN TAKEN IN SO COMPLETELY, THE KINDLY MRS. WORRALL WAS NOT ANGRY WITH MARY.

# JESUS' KID BROTHER: HONG XIUQUAN

**DECEPTION**

Religious deceit

Military subterfuge

Financial fraud

Fake or counterfeit

Imposture or cross-dressing

Confidence trick

Scientific deception

**Main Culprit:** Hong Xiuquan

**Motivation:** Power

**Damage Done:** A decade-long civil war in China and the slaughter of millions of soldiers and civilians

*Hong Xiuquan was the sort of fellow who might well have become a sectarian religious leader or founder at any time in Chinese history. A combination of his own visions and guidance from these limited Christian writings convinced Hong that he was 'God's Chinese son', [...] the direct offspring of a monotheistic, basically Judeo-Christian God and thus literally the younger brother of Jesus.*

**From God and Caesar in China by J. Kindopp and C. Hamrin, 2004**

For millennia, the Chinese believed – with some justification – that China was the only civilised country on earth, surrounded by uncouth, illiterate barbarians. After the collapse of the Western Roman Empire (476 CE), when Europe entered its 'Dark Ages', Chinese civilisation grew ever more brilliant and technologically advanced. The inventions the Chinese exported to the rest of the world included paper, gunpowder and gunpowder weapons, silk, movable type, the magnetic compass and banknotes. The peak of Chinese cultural and scientific achievement occurred during the Song (960–1279), Yuan (1271–1368) and Ming (1368–1644) dynasties. For most of this period, China remained outward-looking (even if this meant looking down its nose at everyone else). Chinese fleets sailed as far as East Africa, and European ships came to trade at China's ports to buy its silks and fine porcelains.

The supremacy of China, it seemed, would last forever. Towards the end of the Ming Dynasty, however, the Chinese colossus proved itself to be hollow and in imminent danger of toppling over. Economic woes led to political instability, which the centralised and rigidly conservative imperial bureaucracy was incapable of addressing. Instead of looking outward for solutions, China looked inward and backward to its glorious past. The country was beset with civil unrest and foreign threats, until in 1644, the unthinkable happened: the semi-civilised nomadic Manchu people invaded the empire and established the Qing Dynasty (r. until 1912). At the same time, the Chinese realised that the European 'barbarians' had made great strides and had now surpassed China in the very technologies that it had given them: navigation and gunpowder.

**BITTEREST WAR**
Hong led his soldiers in the Taiping Rebellion, a conflict that claimed the lives of millions of innnocent Chinese civilians.

After the Qing had been in power for two centuries, not only had they made their mark on China, it had also made its mark on them. They had absorbed China's deep conservatism and superiority complex when dealing with foreigners. They had also gone soft, giving up the warlike customs that had given them the edge over the Chinese. The age-old dream of China's pre-eminence was shattered when the empire was defeated in the First Opium War (1839–1842) against Britain, and the Second Opium War (1856–60) against Britain and France. China was forced to sue for peace on the most humiliating terms, open its ports to foreign trade and cede territory to the victors. It seemed to be the beginning of the biggest land grab in history since Columbus' discovery of America.

Although China's emperor was an absolute monarch, who was called the 'Son of Heaven', he was not immune to political challenges. Chinese political philosophy held that the 'Mandate of Heaven' that gave the emperor his authority could be lost, if a dynasty proved to be an economic, social or military failure. By the mid-nineteenth century, the Qing had failed on all three counts: the country had been defeated in two wars with the Western powers, social unrest was widespread, and the economy had all but collapsed. The time was ripe for a new leader to emerge from the chaos to establish a new mandate and dynasty. That man was the self-styled younger brother of Jesus Christ, Hong Xiuquan (1814–64).

Hong was born in Guangdong province in Southern China and was a Hakka – an important Han Chinese ethnic group that has been called the 'Jews of China'. His parents were farmers, but they ensured that he received a classical Confucian education that would prepare him to take the prestigious imperial civil service examination. In 1836, aged 22, Hong travelled to the provincial capital of Guangzhou to take the entrance examination. In the next few years, he attempted the examination another three times without success. Having failed to enter government service, he became a teacher in his native village.

During his first visit to Guangzhou he had heard a Christian missionary preach, and read Chinese Christian tracts. In 1837, after failing his examination for a second time, Hong had a nervous breakdown. While he was convalescing, he had several mystical experiences and visions in which he saw two figures, whom he later claimed were Jehovah, his Heavenly Father, and his older brother, Jesus Christ. They instructed him to cleanse China of 'demon-worship', meaning the main religions of Buddhism, Confucian ancestor-worship and Daoism. His knowledge of Christianity remained slight, however, until he studied with the American Baptist minister Issachar Roberts (1802–71) in Guangdong ten years later. However, Hong's understanding of Christian teaching was so idiosyncratic that Roberts refused to baptise him.

## CREATING HEAVEN ON EARTH

Hong waited until 1844 to act upon the revelation that had been given him. He started by 'cleansing' his own home of 'demons' by burning all his Confucian and Buddhist books and statues and encouraging his relatives to do the same. When Hong's iconoclastic activities extended to the village temple, the authorities moved against him, and he and his relatives were forced to flee on foot to the neighbouring province of Guangxi, home to a large Hakka community. It was there that his mission began in earnest, and he developed a social and political program that became the blueprint for the later Heavenly Kingdom of Great Peace (Taiping), which combined pseudo-Christian beliefs with communitarian social and economic policies: all property was to be held in common; society was declared classless; and women were given full equality with men, though the sexes were rigidly segregated and even married couples had to live apart. He banned various Qing practices, including polygamy, footbinding and the wearing of the traditional queue hairstyle, and also abolished opium smoking, prostitution and gambling. In practice, however, the rule of 'Heavenly Peace' was authoritarian, militaristic and corrupt, and the Taiping leaders or 'kings' did not abide by the strict moral code they imposed on their followers.

**ONWARD TAIPING SOLDIERS**

The Qing government, beset by other problems, ignored the Taiping movement until it was too late. In 1850, the authorities sent a small force to demand Hong's surrender, but he defeated it easily, killing its general. The Qing next launched a full-scale attack, which was again repulsed after heavy fighting and high casualties on both sides. With nothing left to lose, Hong proclaimed the foundation of the Taiping Heavenly Kingdom in 1851. Hong captured the important city of Nanjing in 1853, slaughtering its 30,000-strong imperial garrison and many thousands of civilians. He renamed the city Tianjing (Heavenly Capital). Once installed in his Heavenly Palace, Hong withdrew from the day-to-day running of the kingdom, preferring the role of ruler and religious prophet, issuing a string of religious decrees and moral codes. He left earthly matters to lesser 'kings' and 'princes', which led to internal feuding and assassinations among the rival Taiping leaders.

Throughout the 1850s, the Western powers, safe in their trading concessions in Shanghai, had remained neutral in the rebellion, as it diverted the attention and manpower of the Qing government and allowed them a free hand in China. However, when the Taiping attempted to take the port of Shanghai in 1860, the Western powers were finally forced to intervene. A joint European-Chinese force repulsed the initial Taiping attack. From this point on the Qing, backed by the European powers, began to regain the upper hand. They fought their way to Tianjing, which they reached in 1864. Hong had abdicated in favour of his son a few months before the Qing army arrived, and died of food poisoning before the capture of the city.

The dream of the egalitarian Kingdom of Heavenly Peace was drowned in an ocean of blood as over the next ten years the surviving Taiping were tracked down and executed. In earlier times, Hong might have succeeded in overthrowing the Qing and establishing a new dynasty. However, at that time, the foreign powers backed the established regime because they preferred a corrupt, weak government to the radical Taiping. The Qing Dynasty limped on in power for another 58 years until it, too, was overthrown in the republican revolution of 1912.

China is no stranger to reformist religious cults. At the close of the nineteenth century, the Qing government of the formidable Empress Dowager Cixi (1835–1908) unwisely backed the anti-Christian and anti-foreign Boxer Rebellion (1898–1900), which attempted to expel all foreigners from China. In modern times, a parallel can be drawn between the Taiping and the Falun Gong movement. Falun Gong, founded in 1992 by Li Hongzhi (b. 1951), became so popular that the Chinese Communist authorities banned it in 1999. Unlike the pseudo-Christian Taiping, Falun Gong is based on traditional Buddhist and Daoist ideas, but it represents the same heady mix of religious beliefs and practices and a social and political reform agenda that terrifies the conservative, anti-democratic Communist establishment.

THE FOREIGN POWERS BACKED THE ESTABLISHED REGIME BECAUSE THEY PREFERRED A CORRUPT, WEAK GOVERNMENT TO THE RADICAL TAIPING.

**DECEPTION**

Religious deceit

Military subterfuge

Financial fraud

**Fake or counterfeit**

Imposture or cross-dressing

Confidence trick

Scientific deception

# BARNUM'S WONDER: THE FEEJEE MERMAID

**Main Culprit:** P. T. Barnum

**Motivation:** Financial gain

**Damage Done:** Hoodwinked the credulous

*We've seen it! What? Why that Mermaid! The mischief you have! Where? What is it? It's twin sister to the deucedest looking thing imaginable – half fish, half flesh; and 'taken by and large,' the most odd of all oddities earth or sea has ever produced.*

**From *The New York Sun*, 5 August 1842**

There is a little bit of a child in all of us that wants to believe that fantastical creatures such as unicorns, centaurs, elves and fairies (see pp. 91–5) really exist somewhere in the world. One of the most enduring myths of this kind is the story of the 'merpeople', who live in an underwater realm – a mirror of the surface world, with its own submerged houses, fields, workshops, temples and palaces. The tradition is ancient and universal, spanning the globe from British Columbia to Southeast Asia, but our own view of mermaids has been shaped by classical mythology. In the story of Odysseus (pp. 15–19) we encountered the Sirens, which were half human, half bird, but there are also legends of sea creatures that were half human, half fish from ancient Greece and the Near East, which have been retold and embellished during later ages. As a rule, ancient mermaids and mermen are not the cuddly, lovable creatures we meet in Disney's *The Little Mermaid* (1989); they are usually evil monsters that embody the destructive potential of the sea. They lure ships to their doom on the reefs, or drown sailors by pulling them under the waves.

Scholars have put forward several theories to explain the origins of the mermaid myth. One likely explanation is that several animal species were taken to be mermaids and mermen. In the frame are the order *Sirenia*, the dugongs and manatees, large aquatic mammals that live in warm tropical rivers, swamps and coastal wetlands; seals in the temperate and northern seas; and finally dolphins, who are known to follow boats. Another possible explanation is the extremely rare genetic condition sirenomelia, in which the legs of a newborn are fused together to resemble a fishtail. The condition affects one in every 100,000 births and is usually fatal within a day or two of birth. Yet a third theory is the deliberate manufacture of mermaids, using the body and head of a primate and the tail of a fish. This was not always created in order to deceive, as these manufactured 'mermaids' were used in religious rituals in Japan and the islands of Southeast Asia.

**SEA COWS**
See mammals such as manatees and seals are thought to be the origin of many of the world's legends of mermaids and mermen.

In the early 1840s, the world, or at least the most credulous part of it, was ready to believe in the existence of mermaids and mermen. However, it took the genius of America's greatest showman, P. T. Barnum (1810–91) to pull off one of the greatest hoaxes of the nineteenth century, the arrival and exhibition in New York of the fabled Feejee (Fiji) Mermaid.

**USE A FISH TO CATCH A HUMAN**

In the summer of 1842, a British naturalist by the name of Dr. J. Griffin arrived in New York bringing with him an extremely rare specimen, the Feejee Mermaid, which he claimed had been caught off the coast of the Pacific island of Fiji. The New York press (see quote) had been tipped off, and they arrived in force at Griffin's hotel. The good doctor was at first very reluctant to admit them, but let himself be persuaded, and finally showed them the specimen. The eager reporters were convinced that the mermaid was genuine, but as photography had not yet been perfected, no pictures accompanied their enthusiastic reviews. P. T. Barnum, however, stepped in to fill the pictorial gap, when he visited all the newspaper offices in the city with engravings of beautiful bare-breasted mermaids, which he said were useless because Dr. Griffin had refused to let him exhibit the mermaid at his American Museum (on the corner of Broadway and Ann Street). The editor of each paper, thinking he had the exclusive, published the engraving, giving Barnum free, citywide publicity.

At this point Dr. Griffin conveniently changed his mind and agreed to display the mermaid at the Concert Hall on Broadway. The exhibit was the centrepiece of his lectures on his experiences as an explorer and naturalist in the South Seas and his bizarre theories on marine natural history. After a week of packed lectures at the Concert Hall, the doctor allowed the mermaid to be moved to Barnum's American Museum, where it drew immense crowds, tripling the museum's average monthly takings. After a month at the museum the mermaid went on tour to the Southern states, but controversy over its authenticity forced Barnum to bring it back to New York. For the next twenty years the mermaid was exhibited in New York at Barnum's American Museum and in the Boston Museum owned by Boston's very own 'Barnum', Moses Kimball (1809–95).

Barnum had pulled off a brilliant triple deception on the New York public. First, he knew that the mermaid was a fake. He had purchased it himself from Moses Kimball and had had it examined by a naturalist.

The mermaid was probably a Southeast Asian religious artifact (see above), made of the mummified head and torso of a small ape sewn to the tail of a fish. Kimball had bought it from an American sea captain called Eades, who himself had acquired it in the Far East in 1822. Eades had sold his ship and borrowed heavily in order to purchase the specimen for the then astronomical sum of $6,000, and hoped to recoup on his investment by exhibiting the mermaid in London. Eades was no Barnum, however. The scheme failed, and he was left penniless and in hock to creditors. Desperate for cash, he sold the mermaid to Kimball for a fraction of the price he had paid for it.

Barnum's second masterstroke was creating the hype around the arrival of the mermaid in New York by planting letters about its 'discovery' and forthcoming 'arrival' in New York to the press and later distributing the engravings to the newspapers, which gave him free citywide advertising. The engravings, showing the classical image of a nubile bare-breasted mermaid, would certainly have caught the imagination of members of the New York public. In reality, the mermaid was a small, wizened creature, with its arms outstretched and no obvious breasts, and looked as if it had died in some pain. The third and final deceit was the invention of the British naturalist, 'Dr. J. Griffin', whose presence would give the mermaid the gloss of scientific respectability. In reality, Griffin was not a naturalist or even a British subject: he was an associate of Barnum's called Levi Lyman, hired to play the part.

The mermaid disappeared in around 1860. It may have been destroyed in a fire at Barnum's American Museum in 1865, or during another blaze at Kimball's Boston Museum twenty or so years later. The Kimball family donated an artifact claimed to be the Feejee Mermaid to the Peabody Museum in Harvard; however, the Harvard specimen does not match the descriptions and engravings of Barnum's mermaid and is so poorly put together that it is unlikely ever to have fooled anyone. To quote the hit TV show, *The X-Files*, which featured the Feejee Mermaid in one of its episodes, the truth is definitely out there, but it is very likely that the truth about the Feejee Mermaid is that it was a very clever fake, sold to the credulous by an even cleverer showman.

THE THIRD AND FINAL DECEIT WAS THE INVENTION OF THE BRITISH NATURALIST, 'DR. J. GRIFFIN', WHOSE PRESENCE WOULD GIVE THE MERMAID THE GLOSS OF SCIENTIFIC RESPECTABILITY.

**DECEPTION**

Religious deceit

Military subterfuge

Financial fraud

**Fake or counterfeit**

Imposture or cross-dressing

Confidence trick

Scientific deception

# FISHY TALES: *OMPAX SPATULOIDES* AND THE FURRY TROUT

**Main Culprits:** Australian pranksters

**Motivation:** A joke

**Damage Done:** Misled the scientific community for sixty years

'In 1879, a naturalist was sent by station hands a creature, part platypus, part lungfish and part eel. The naturalist described it to Castelnau, who reported it to the Linnean Society in Sydney as an archaic fish which he named Ompax spatuloides.'

**From the *Australian Dictionary of Biography*, online edition (2009)**

Since the beginning of history, the mysterious world of the oceans has been the home to a multitude of sea monsters, both real and imagined. Ancient mariners believed in huge sea serpents that could sink ships, and half human, half fish 'merpeople' (see previous chapter), while modern science has discovered monster whale sharks, fish that glow in the dark, and giant squid big enough to eat whales. By contrast, inland waters, with a few exceptions (see Loch Ness Monster Hoaxes, pp. 133–8), are much more placid environments, whose denizens have been well documented for centuries. At the end of the nineteenth century, however, there were still discoveries to be made in the far-flung corners of the British Empire. In 1869, for example, an entirely new species of primitive fish, the lungfish, which retains the ability to breathe air, had been discovered in Australia. It was only ten years since Charles Darwin (1809–82) had published his *On the Origin of Species*, and naturalists were busily looking for animals that might be intermediary forms between fish and amphibians.

**EATING THE 'PLATYFISH'**

In 1872, a strange-looking fish was reported in the Burnett River area of northern Queensland, Australia. Its head was similar to that of the *Neoceratodus* lungfish, with a long tail, and the strangest characteristic of all, a duck-shaped bill like that of a platypus. Workers on the Gayndah Cattle Station claimed that Native Australians had caught the fish in a local waterhole, where it was living with other species of lungfish. The 'platyfish' was cooked and served to Carl Staiger, the former director of the Brisbane Museum, for dinner. His presence at the very same moment of such an important discovery should have aroused suspicions, but instead Staiger drew the fish and then ate it. He had swallowed the hoax (literally),

**CRITTERS**
The hoaxers took advantage of Australia's unusual fauna to fabricate their entirely fictional fish.

hook, line and sinker. He sent his observations and drawings to François Laporte, Count of Castlenau (1810–80), who was one of the most eminent naturalists of the day. Laporte accepted Staiger's description in good faith and reported the discovery to the Linnaean Society in Sydney, giving it the name *Ompax spatuloides*.

Although no other specimens of *Ompax* were ever found, the strange fish remained in the list of Australian wildlife for three decades. When naturalists re-examined Staiger's original drawings, however, they realised that the sample had probably been assembled from parts of other animals: the head of a lungfish, the body of a mullet, the tail of an eel and the bill of a platypus. Staiger had been taken in by the hoax because the fish had been presented to him cooked.

**THE TROUT FUR COAT?**

Another thirty years and half a world away, another piscine oddity was reported in the Colorado state press: the furry trout. Tales of a fish covered in fur living in the chill waters of North America's rivers and lakes emerged as early as the seventeenth century. In this case, the explanation was not a concocted specimen but the result of a natural infection known as cotton-mould (*Saprolegnia*). A fish infected with the mould shows white or grey fur-like tufts on its body. When the fish dies, the mould continues to grow, sometimes covering the whole body. The mould, however, cannot be preserved through taxidermy, so the extant examples of 'furry trout' that are found in museums and private collections are undoubtedly fakes.

# GOING APE: PILTDOWN MAN

**DECEPTION**

Religious deceit

Military subterfuge

Financial fraud

Fake or counterfeit

Imposture or cross-dressing

Confidence trick

**Scientific deception**

**Main Culprits:** Charles Dawson and others

**Motivation:** Fame

**Damage Done:** Put back the study of human evolution by several decades

'On 18 December 1912 Arthur Smith Woodward and Charles Dawson announced to a great and expectant scientific audience the epoch-making discovery of a remote ancestral form of man – The Dawn Man of Piltdown [...] There was great excitement and enthusiasm which is still remembered by those who were there; for, in Piltdown man, here in England, was at last tangible, well-nigh incontrovertible proof of Man's ape-like ancestry; here was evidence, in a form long predicted, of a creature which could be regarded as a veritable confirmation of evolutionary theory.'

**From The Piltdown Forgery (2003) by J.S. Weiner and C. Stringer**

When Charles Darwin (1809–82) published *On the Origin of Species* in 1859, he revolutionised our view of the origin and evolution of animal species. However, he waited until 1871 to publish *The Descent of Man*, which applied his theory to humans. The popular misinterpretation of this idea at the time was that humans were descended from the great apes – gorillas, orangutans and chimps. In fact, the great apes are not our ancestors but our distant cousins. It took another twenty years until Eugène Dubois (1858–1940) made the first discovery of one of humanity's early ancestors, *Homo erectus*, on the island of Java; another, *Homo heidelbergensis*, a common forebear of modern humans and Neanderthals, was discovered by a German workman in 1907. These two species of extinct hominids occur relatively late in humanity's evolution. *H. erectus* lived between 1.4 million and 200,000 years BP (Before Present) and *H. heidelbergensis* between 600,000 and 350,000 years BP.

We now know that the first bipedal human ancestors, the australopithecines (first discovered in South Africa in 1924), date back almost four million years BP, and that there have been dozens of hominid species, now long extinct, between them and us, including several evolutionary dead-ends, such as the Neanderthals. Although the full complexity of human evolutionary history was not fully understood in the early 1910s, a few pieces of the puzzle had been found. The great scientific prize, however, was the discovery of a fossil that would display the ape-like characteristics of early hominids and a telltale feature that would show conclusively that it was a direct human ancestor – the so-called 'missing link'.

**DARWIN'S APE**
The father of evolutionary science, Charles Darwin, mistakenly predicted a hominid ancestor with an ape's jaw and a human's skull.

In 1912, amateur archeologist and geologist Charles Dawson (1864–1916) announced to an expectant world that he had found bone fragments from the missing link in humanity's ancestral line in the Piltdown gravel pit near the East Sussex village of Uckfield. Dawson christened his find 'Piltdown Man', and a grateful scientific community awarded Dawson the ultimate accolade by giving the new hominid the Latin name *Eoanthropus dawsoni*, 'Dawson's dawn man'.

At a meeting of the Geological Society in 1912, Charles Dawson and Sir Arthur Smith Woodward (1864–1944), the Keeper of Geology at the British Museum and president of the society, made a joint presentation about Dawson's discovery of the fossilised remains of the skull and jaw of an early hominid. The bone fragments had been found in a geological stratum containing the bones of animals long extinct in England, including hippos, rhinos and mammoths, as well as ancient species of deer, beaver and horse, and primitive flint and bone tools, all of which led Dawson to estimate the find to be half a million years old. The cranial fragments, apart from being unusually thick, showed marked similarities with modern human skulls; the jaw, which had two molars still in place, was very different. Smith Woodward concluded: 'While the skull is essentially human […] the mandible appears to be that of an ape, with nothing human except the molar teeth.' Of particular importance was the human-like wear pattern on the teeth. It seemed that the missing link in humanity's ancestry had been found. He would have been ape-like in appearance, with a large jaw and teeth, but an enlarged braincase.

Although the hominid and animal fragments showed the dark-brown staining of ancient fossilised remains, and the stratigraphic evidence seemed compelling, the meeting of the Geological Society divided into two camps. There was no question yet of a suspected fraud, but several scholars present did not believe that the ape-like jaw and human-like cranium could be from the same individual. They put forward the alternate (and, with hindsight, fairly accurate) theory that they came from two distinct animals: the heavy jaw from a chimp-like ape of the Pliocene period (5.3 million to 2.6 million years BP) and the cranium from a hominid of the Pleistocene period (2.6 million to 12,000 BP), which had been washed up together in the Piltdown gravel beds, along with remains of animals from both periods and the stone implements Dawson had found. However, the meeting was carried by Smith Woodward's strongly argued case. He reconstructed the skull, which, though human in shape, was about two-thirds of the size of that of a modern human. Attached to this diminutive human braincase was a distinctly ape-like jaw.

**A FORTUITOUS FIND**

It is not entirely surprising that so many in the scientific community believed the discovery to be genuine. The hoaxer had prepared his ground carefully. First he had planned the circumstances of the find, which had taken place over a period of a year, and had involved several individuals in the locality, as well as respected scientists, such as Smith Woodward. Dawson claimed to have come upon the site quite by accident when he had seen workmen mending a road with gravel, which contained flints that reminded him of similar deposits from another English locality where significant animal fossil finds had been made. On being told that the gravel came from the Piltdown gravel pit on a neighbouring farm, he went to investigate. He claimed that workmen had found the first bone fragment, and that he had found other fragments on subsequent visits. Dawson and Smith Woodward discovered the most important piece, the jawbone and teeth, together. Dawson's involvement of Smith Woodward in the find was his second masterstroke. Although it would mean sharing some of the glory, the man's reputation and position made him above suspicion.

The final piece in the hoaxer's scheme was to create a specimen of a hominid that conformed exactly to the preconceived notions of the scientific community of the day. Darwin had put forward a very

© Getty Images

**FAKING IT**
Anatomists quickly realised that the Piltdown skull was a composite of human and ape fragments.

similar human ancestor in his *Descent of Man*: a hominid who would have large ape-like fighting teeth and also an enlarged braincase. The belief then prevalent was that human evolution had begun with an increase in brain size. Later discoveries placed the evolutionary milestone not as an enlarged cranium but bipedalism, which entailed a number of other morphological, behavioural and dietary changes that led to bigger and bigger brains. Another factor not to be underestimated during the late days of Britain's imperial greatness was the discovery of humanity's ancestor not in distant Java, China, Africa or even Europe, but in southeast England. It confirmed that the nation that had given the world the 'Mother of Parliaments' had also quite possibly given humankind one of its earliest ancestors.

The sceptics still needed to be convinced, however, and, as if on cue, further evidence was found in the vicinity of Uckfield. The French geologist and paleontologist Pierre Teilhard de Chardin (1881–1955) found the canine (or eyetooth) of Piltdown Man in 1913, which was large by human standards but showed the same human-like wear patterns as the molars. In 1914, an unusual bone tool was found at Piltdown, and in 1915, Dawson found remains of a second individual at another site two miles away, again in proximity to ancient animal fossil fragments. Surprisingly, the second site was never properly scientifically documented, and Smith Woodward never bothered to visit it. With this array of fresh evidence, even the most diehard sceptic must be convinced, and indeed many were. Dawson died suddenly in 1916. Subsequent investigations of the Piltdown site, which continued sporadically until 1950, never produced any new discoveries of hominid or animal fossils.

As early as 1923, the German anatomist Franz Weidenreich (1873–1948) had already correctly identified the fragments as coming from a human skull, albeit one that was unusually thick – probably because of disease – and the jaw of an orangutan. These had been chemically stained to give them the appearance of fossilised material. Of the other associated finds, several were fakes, such as the bone tool, and others genuine, such as the animal fossils, but Dawson, alone or with accomplices, had planted them on site and then claimed that he had found them there. When the remains were submitted to rigorous scientific examination in 1953, it was found that the skull was probably no more than 500 years old; the jaw came from a species of orangutan native to the island of Borneo; and the fossilised teeth came from a chimpanzee. The hoaxer had carefully filed down the teeth to give them human-like wear patterns.

**THE IDENTIKIT HOMINID**

The identity of the forger, however, has never been confirmed beyond doubt, though it seems likely that Charles Dawson was either the sole or principal instigator of the hoax. His death at the age of 52, a mere five years after the initial 'find', meant that he could not be quizzed about its exact circumstances. However, modern investigations of Dawson's other archeological and fossil discoveries reveal that he had been creating fakes for at least two decades before the 'discovery' of Piltdown Man. Having fooled local museums and geological societies with his earlier fraudulent finds, which included the filed-down teeth of a non-existent reptile–mammal hybrid and a fake Roman statuette made of cast iron, he decided to pull off the scientific hoax of the century by discovering the missing link.

Dawson's aim was not financial gain but fame. He coveted the prestigious title of Fellow of the Royal Society, then the world's most eminent scientific body. Several others have been implicated as Dawson's accomplices, including Teilhard de Chardin, who had so fortuitously found Piltdown Man's eyetooth. Why an ordained Jesuit priest, who would later become a respected paleontologist and do much valuable (and genuine) work on *H. erectus* in China, would get involved in the hoax has never been satisfactorily explained. Smith Woodward is unlikely to have been in on the fraud, as after retiring from the British Museum, he moved to a house near the site and funded several fruitless private excavations of the gravel pit.

The main impact of the Piltdown Man hoax was to put back the study of human evolution for several decades. When Raymond Dart (1893–1988) discovered the first australopithecine specimen, *Australopithecus africanus*, in 1924, its place in evolution was at first disregarded because instead of having an enlarged braincase and large simian teeth like Piltdown Man, it had a small braincase and small human-like teeth. Evolution had declined to stick to the blueprint set out by Darwin and accepted by Smith Woodward and his contemporaries. Another unintended consequence of the hoax was to give succour and ammunition to the Creationists, who argued that paleontologists had developed their theory of human evolution on the basis of a few, and in the case of Piltdown Man, faked, specimens.

# ELEMENTAL, MY DEAR CONAN DOYLE: THE COTTINGLEY FAIRIES

**DECEPTION**

Religious deceit

Military subterfuge

Financial fraud

**Fake or counterfeit**

Imposture or cross-dressing

Confidence trick

Scientific deception

**Main Culprits:** Elsie Wright, Frances Griffiths and Sir Arthur Conan Doyle

**Motivation:** Hoax by the girls to get back at Elsie's sceptical father; Conan Doyle's genuine belief in Spiritualism

**Damage Done:** Hoodwinked the credulous

*There are fairies at the bottom of our garden!*
*It's not so very, very far away;*
*You pass the gardener's shed and you just keep straight ahead –*
*I do so hope they've really come to stay.*
*There's a little wood, with moss in it and beetles,*
*And a little stream that quietly runs through;*
*You wouldn't think they'd dare to come merrymaking there –*
*Well, they do.*

**From 'The Fairies' by Rose Fyleman (1877–1957)**

As we have seen in the tale of the Feejee Mermaid (pp. 78–81), the success or failure of a hoax depends more on the hoaxer's ability to persuade than the plausibility of the hoax itself. P. T. Barnum was the ultimate showman and huckster, and he prepared his hoax with enormous care, taking full advantage of the mass media of his day to reach the largest possible audience. Unlike Piltdown Man (see previous entry), the mermaid hoax would not have survived the scrutiny of science – even mid-nineteenth century science. But the hype Barnum managed to create persuaded the entrance-fee-paying public for several weeks. It was never a question of fooling 'all of the people, all of the time,' to quote Abraham Lincoln (1809–65), but to fool just enough people for just long enough to recoup on his investment.

**FAIRYTALE**
Frances posing in front of the dancing 'fairies', which were probably painted paper or cloth cutouts made by Elsie.

In contrast, the photographs of the 'Cottingley Fairies', taken between 1917 and 1920, were not produced by masters of deception but by two young girls: Elsie Wright (1901–88) and her younger cousin Frances Griffiths (1907–86). Had it been left to the girls, the hoax would have been quickly forgotten; however, the photographs came to the attention of none other than Sir Arthur Conan Doyle (1859–1930), the creator of the great fictional detective, Sherlock Holmes. In addition to his literary work, Conan Doyle was a self-proclaimed expert on all things paranormal. It was his belief that the photographs were genuine that turned them into an international sensation.

A famous poem written about the same time, 'The Fairies' (see quote), expresses the wonder that people still felt for all things supernatural at the beginning of the twentieth century. Fairies occur in many European traditions, and there are several explanations about their origins. Our tradition of fairy-folk is thought to be the result of the Christianisation of supernatural beings from pagan religions: elemental spirits such as nymphs and satyrs, who inhabited the forests and streams of the classical and Celtic worlds.

The late teens and early twenties of the twentieth century were a difficult time in Western Europe. The 'war to end all wars', the First World War (1914–18), was taking place, with the slaughter of an entire generation of young men. It was just the right time for a little magic to brighten up the drab wartime gloom. Elsie and her younger cousin Frances were spending the summer of 1917 together at Elsie's home in the village of Cottingley on the outskirts of the northern British town of Bradford. Elsie's father was an electrical engineer, and was the proud owner of a quarter-plate camera. One July day, the girls came back from a walk by a small stream that ran behind the family home, claiming to have seen fairies. Elsie's sceptical father teased them for telling stories.

Determined to prove her father wrong, Elsie asked to borrow his camera. As Mr. Wright believed that his daughter had never used a camera before, he loaded the plate, set the aperture for her, and gave her basic operating instructions. The girls came back an hour later, claiming to have successfully snapped the fairies. Elsie's father developed the plate himself. The photograph shows Frances, looking straight into camera, with a group of four diminutive winged creatures dancing in front of her in the greenery. There is a waterfall and rocks in the background. Although the setting is undoubtedly genuine, what is immediately striking about the photograph is that Frances, instead of staring entranced at the fairies, is looking straight past them as if they weren't there. Additionally, although the fairies are blurred as if moving, they also have a flat, two-dimensional appearance. In September, there followed more photographs, which showed Elsie with a grotesque-looking winged gnome, complete with pointy hat, tights and beard. When he developed the first photograph, Elsie's father was sure that the girls had stood paper cutouts in front of Frances; Elsie's mother, who was interested in the occult, however, believed they were genuine.

A year later, Frances sent a letter to a friend in Cape Town, South Africa, casually mentioning the fairies, and including copies of the two photographs. Frances, who had grown up in South Africa, added on the back of one of the photographs: 'It is funny I never used to see [fairies] in Africa. It must be too hot for them there.' In 1919, Elsie's mother went to a meeting of the Theosophical Society to listen to a lecture on

**'THERE ARE FAIRIES AT THE BOTTOM OF OUR GARDEN'**

fairies. She mentioned her daughter and niece's fairy photographs, and in 1920 they came to the attention of the Theosophist Edward Gardner. As soon as he saw the photographs, Gardner was convinced that they were genuine. He showed them to his friend and fellow spiritualist Sir Arthur Conan Doyle, who had coincidentally been commissioned to write an article about fairies for the *Strand Magazine*. Conan Doyle showed them to other paranormal experts, who were divided as to whether the photographs were genuine or fake.

To resolve the matter, Conan Doyle asked Gardner to go to Cottingley to meet the Wrights, and give the girls cameras and photographic plates to take more photographs. The plates had been secretly marked to ensure that they were not switched or tampered with by the girls or by Elsie's father, who was suspected of being in on a possible deception. The trip produced a further three pictures: one of each girl, each pictured with a single fairy, and the most mysterious and evocative, entitled 'A Fairy Sunbath', which showed translucent fairies around a cocoon-like structure – the 'sunbath' in the title. Gardner and Conan Doyle were exultant, believing that the photographs provided proof of their belief in the world of spirits. In 1922, Conan Doyle published the photographs among other accounts of fairy sightings in *The Coming of the Fairies*. The press and public opinion, however, remained divided.

**MISGUIDED**
Sir Arthur Conan Doyle was a committed spiritualist and wrote a book about the Cottingley fairies.

Gardner and Conan Doyle showed the plates to photographic experts, including the Kodak Company. Kodak confirmed that the negatives were single exposures – meaning that the plates had not been exposed twice so that two distinct images could be superimposed – and that there was no evidence that the plates had been tampered with in any other obvious way. However, they refused to certify that the pictures were genuine, as they could have been faked, for example, by taking photographs of already doctored photographs. The appearance of the fairies in the snapshots also raised some doubts. Not only were the creatures the traditional 'fairytale' fairies – pretty young women with gossamer or butterfly wings and dressed in Grecian draperies – but they also had suspiciously contemporary, modish hairstyles.

If we accept that the photographs were fakes, who conceived and carried out the hoax? Mr. Wright, the electrical engineer, probably had the technical know-how, but he remained sceptical throughout his life. Mrs. Wright was a believer but had no obvious technical expertise. That left the girls, Elsie and Frances. Frances was ten in 1917, and too young to be responsible in anything but being an accomplice. However, Elsie, who was sixteen that year, was a talented artist and had worked creating composites in a photographic laboratory during the war. She had the skill and the technical know-how to create the fakes.

**A HATPIN HOAX**

The most likely explanation, however, was not complicated technical wizardry in a lab, but was most likely the simplest and easiest to realise, and the one suggested by Elsie's father when he had seen the first photograph: he had asked the girls what the bits of paper were doing in the snapshot. The simplest way to create the fairies was to cut them out of paper, card or cloth, colour them, and hold them up with pins or wire. Air movement during the lengthy exposure required by early cameras would have given the figures the blurring of apparent movement. Elsie and Frances were interviewed several times about the photographs. In two interviews in the 1970s, they steadfastly denied that the photographs had been faked, but in 1981 and again in 1986, when most of the people involved had died, Elsie finally admitted that the fairies had been cutouts held up by hatpins. Frances, however, while she confirmed that the pictures were not genuine, continued to maintain that she had seen fairies as a little girl 'at the bottom of our garden.' Maybe, seventy years on, for Frances, believing had really become seeing.

## DECEPTION

Religious deceit

Military subterfuge

**Financial fraud**

Fake or counterfeit

Imposture or cross-dressing

Confidence trick

Scientific deception

# GET-POOR-QUICK SCAMMER: CHARLES PONZI

**Main Culprit:** Charles Ponzi

**Motivation:** Financial gain

**Damage Done:** Defrauded and ruined thousands of investors; went to prison several times; died penniless and alone

*Charles Ponzi was a deft practitioner of that special type of deliberate, premeditated fraud best described as, well, a 'Ponzi scheme'. And it didn't end with the collapse of his first big-time scam in Boston; when he got out on parole there, he went to Florida under an assumed name and was jailed again, this time for real estate fraud, returned to do more time in a Massachusetts prison, and was finally deported.*

**From *Wall Street People* (2003) by C. Ellis and J. Vertin**

There has been no shortage of thieves, embezzlers and fraudsters throughout history, but for a financial criminal to merit inclusion in these pages, he or she must have had a certain vision and ambition. Take the Emperor Nero, for example, the man who defrauded an entire empire by debasing its currency (see pp. 20–2); but we have to wait until the modern period until a single man can match his feat. The type of fraud that we shall examine in this article, the 'Ponzi scheme', has similarities to other financial phenomena: economic 'bubbles' and 'pyramid' schemes.

This book's companion volume *History's Worst Inventions* examined the bursting of two economic bubbles (see 'Tulip Mania' and 'Subprime Mortgages'). Despite what many who have suffered in the Credit Crunch might think, there is no intention to defraud in a bubble. Public and experts alike display a certain lemming-like behaviour, fooling themselves into believing that the price of an asset, stock or investment vehicle is going to increase in value forever – until it doesn't, of course, and the bubble 'bursts'. The asset or stock plummets in value, and everyone loses their money; the investors and, with some justice, the bankers and brokers.

Similar to a bubble in the hype that it needs to succeed is the fraudulent investment scam known as the pyramid scheme. The organiser, or 'pharaoh', sits atop a pyramid of investors, who pay him a commission or joining fee for being part of the scheme, and buy the goods or services the scheme is notionally set up to sell. They in turn recruit further investors who also make single payments. As the number of investors grows, so the profile of the scheme begins to resemble a pyramid. In theory, each investor is supposed to get a cut of the payments and profits, though in practice only the people at the very top actually net any money. When the scheme inevitably collapses because of lack of new investment, the victims are left holding unsaleable goods or services and have lost all their money. The 'Ponzi scheme' is a type of pyramid scheme, although in this case, most of the profits are funnelled into the pockets of the fraudster.

**TRUST ME**
Ponzi made 'robbing Peter to pay Paul' into the economic principle with which he built his fortune.

**THE MAN WITHOUT A PLAN**

Charles Ponzi (1882–1949) was born in the small northern Italian town of Lugo. The exact details of his life before he emigrated to the United States are confused by the many lies that he later fabricated about his own past. His later career, however, does not demonstrate any particular financial acumen or specialist knowledge of investment or banking. Quite to the contrary, one investigator thought that he was a fiscal incompetent and barely numerate. He disembarked in the New World in Boston in 1903 with $2.50 in his pocket, having gambled away his savings during the crossing. During the next few years, he drifted from city to city, and from dead-end job to dead-end job, often getting himself fired for petty pilfering and theft. He did not seem to be a man destined to go down in the annals of crime as the nation's biggest fraudster before Bernard Madoff (see pp. 246–51).

Ponzi did not invent the financial scam that was named after him, the 'Ponzi scheme'. In 1899, a New York businessman, William Miller, started the Franklin Syndicate, which promised investors the suspiciously high return of ten per cent on their investment. Instead of using the profits from legitimate investments to pay out on his promises, Miller merely persuaded his investors to re-invest their gains, and persuaded others to join the scheme, and used their money to pay off any investors wise enough to cash in their gains. The scam managed to net Miller $1 million before it was shut down. It's unlikely that Ponzi had heard of Miller's Franklin Syndicate, as he was not even in the country at the time; however, the early part of the twentieth century, when there was lax or non-existent financial regulation, offered plenty of examples of similar financial double-dealing by seemingly honest bankers and businessmen.

In 1907, Ponzi got his first proper lesson in fraud when he went to work for the Zarossi Bank in Montreal, Canada. The bank had been set up by Luigi Zarossi to cater for the growing number of Italian immigrants arriving in Canada. He offered the unusually high rate of six per cent on cash deposits. Ponzi was promoted from junior bank teller to manager, and then realised that the bank was funding its high interest payments on accounts not from investments in property but by using funds deposited in new accounts. In essence the bank was operating as a Ponzi scheme, and it must have given the young man a great deal to think about. Unfortunately for Ponzi and his employer, the bank failed because of bad real-estate loans, and Zarossi fled the country, taking as much of the bank's money as he could carry.

Ponzi was again left jobless and penniless. He decided to return to the United States, and in order to pay his travelling expenses and set himself up, he hatched a scheme to forge a cheque drawn on the account of a firm that had once had been a Zarossi Bank customer. Ponzi's talents as a forger were no better than his abilities as a petty thief: he was immediately arrested by the Canadian police, convicted, and sent to prison for three years. It was to be the first of many periods of incarceration. He finally made it back to the United States in 1911, where he got mixed up in a scam to smuggle illegal immigrants into the country and was sent to prison for another two years. While in prison in Atlanta, he made two interesting acquaintances: the Sicilian mobster Ignazio 'Lupo' (Wolf) Saietta (1877–1947) and the Wall Street financier Charles Wyman Morse (1856–1933). It is interesting to speculate on the lessons Ponzi learned from a racketeer and a crooked financier, and one can be pretty sure that reform and rehabilitation were not high on the curriculum.

'The cheque's in the post' is one of the three things that you should never believe. In any dealings with Charles Ponzi, this was probably sound advice, and when he finally returned to Boston, he tried his hand at several businesses, all of which failed. One of these was a business-listings directory. Although the listings idea never got off the drawing board, he received a letter of interest from a European firm, accompanied by an international reply coupon (IRC). The U.S. addressee could redeem the coupon to defray the cost of return postage in U.S. postage stamps. In the aftermath of World War One (1914–18), the relative rates of postage between Italy and the U.S. had got seriously out of kilter. Ponzi realised that you could buy IRCs in Italy and redeem them for a higher value in American stamps. Although the profit from a single IRC was small, bulk transactions could theoretically have made the business very lucrative.

On the surface, Ponzi had finally hit upon a viable and, above all, honest idea to make his fortune. Another name for this type of (perfectly legal) financial operation is 'arbitrage', in which dealers take advantage of

**'THE CHEQUE'S IN THE POST'**

price differentials in two markets. Arbitrage is routinely applied to securities, bonds, derivatives, currencies and commodities. Where Ponzi came unstuck was in the total number of IRCs in circulation, and the time and expense needed to redeem each coupon, as they had to be cashed in one at a time. In other words, there was no way to make a profit from redeeming IRCs.

Undaunted, Ponzi went ahead with the scheme regardless. He started small, getting friends to invest by promising to double their investment in three months. He was as good as his word, and soon succeeded in attracting new investors. In 1919, he started the Securities Exchange Company to promote the business, hired agents paid on a commission basis, and was soon taking money from all over New England. By the summer of 1920, Ponzi was worth several million dollars – enough to take a controlling stake in the Hanover Trust Bank of Boston. He bought himself a mansion and began to live the life of a successful businessman that he had craved for so many years.

What was really happening combined an economic bubble with a Ponzi scheme. The hype around the scheme made people careless and over-optimistic about the value and soundness of the investment. They borrowed heavily and mortgaged their homes to get the funds to invest in the scheme that promised astounding returns of 50 per cent in 45 days. It was a Ponzi scheme they were investing in, however, because the company was not making any legitimate profits on IRC arbitrage, but merely paying existing investors with monies obtained from new ones. The survival of the scam depended on the willingness of people to re-invest their profits, which they did with alacrity. However, it was only a matter of time before the authorities realised what was really going on.

**MENTORS**
Ponzi met crooked financier C.W. Morse and Mafia boss Lupo Saietta while he was in prison.

Articles appeared in the press questioning the whole basis of the scheme, and there were several runs on the company that Ponzi struggled to pay off. Finally, in August 1920, an audit revealed that the scheme was $7 million in hock, and the authorities moved in to close down the Securities Exchange Company and Hanover Trust Bank. Ponzi pleaded guilty to mail fraud and was sentenced to five years in jail.

Charles Ponzi was down but by no means out. He was convicted on further charges in Massachusetts, but he appealed and managed to remain at liberty long enough to start a real-estate scam in Florida selling parcels of swampland to investors. In 1925, he was convicted of violating the state's trust and securities laws and sentenced to a year in prison. After his release, he tried to leave the country but was arrested and sent back to serve out a seven-year prison term in Massachusetts. Released in 1934, he was immediately deported to Italy as an illegal alien, having failed during his many years in the U.S. to apply for citizenship. He spent a few years in Italy, where he worked in the finance ministry of that other crook, the dictator Benito Mussolini (1883–1945). Incompetence and dishonesty obliged him to flee to South America. He ended his days penniless and alone in a charity hospice in Rio de Janeiro, Brazil, where he died blind and partially paralysed at the age of 67.

**DECEPTION**

Religious deceit

Military subterfuge

Financial fraud

Fake or counterfeit

**Imposture or cross-dressing**

Confidence trick

Scientific deception

# MY FAIR LADY: ANNA ANDERSON

**Main Culprits:** Anna Anderson and her supporters

**Motivation:** Fame and financial gain

**Damage Done:** Prevented Anna from getting proper medical treatment

*The Grand Duchess Anastasia, I believe, was seventeen. She was over-developed for her age; she was stout and short, too stout for her height; her characteristic feature was to see the weak point of other people and to make fun of them. She was a comedian by nature and always made everybody laugh. She preferred her father to her mother and loved Maria Nicholaevna more than the other sisters.*

**From *The Last Days of the Romanovs* (1993) by G. Telberg**

In times when an accident of birth rather than ability determines all the status, wealth and power you'll have for the rest of your life, it's not surprising that imposture is so attractive. During Russia's 'Time of Troubles' (1598–1613), three men claimed to be Prince Dimitry Ivanovich (see the False Dimitrys, pp. 48–53), and one succeeded in becoming tsar, albeit very briefly. This last case of royal Russian imposture, however, was very different. The Romanov Dynasty that had put an end to the Time of Troubles had been in power for three centuries, when the doctrine of the divine right of the tsar came into conflict with the modern ideologies of capitalism, liberal democracy and socialism. To everyone but Tsar Nicholas II (1868–1918) and his wife the Tsarina Alexandra (1872–1918), the outcome was a foregone conclusion. All that remained to be decided was the exact manner in which Russia's *Ancien Régime* would be replaced by the new order.

Russia's first revolution in February 1917 ushered in a provisional government led by the moderate Alexander Kerensky (1881–1970). Nicholas abdicated but held on to the hope that his son the Tsarevitch Alexei (1904–18) or his younger brother Grand Duke Michael (1878–1918) would become Russia's first constitutional monarch. All these plans were swept away when Lenin (1870–1924) overthrew Kerensky in the Bolshevik Revolution of October 1917. Kerensky had sent Nicholas and his wife, son and four daughters, the Grand Duchesses Olga (1895–1918), Tatiana (1897–1918), Maria (1899–1918) and Anastasia (1901–18), to Tobolsk in Siberia, to keep them safe from the Bolsheviks and away from supporters who might stage a rescue attempt. In Tobolsk the family and their servants lived in the relative comfort of the governor's mansion.

**REAL MCCOY**
Grand Duchess Anastasia died in a hail of bullets with the rest of the Romanov family in Yekaterinburg.

In April 1918, Lenin's government moved the family into much more cramped and uncomfortable quarters in the city of Yekaterinburg in central Russia. Nicholas still prayed for rescue, and Lenin might have had some thought of sparing the tsar to put him on trial, but then suddenly in July, the Russian imperial family vanished from history. Not long after, rumours began to spread that the Romanovs had been murdered, but that Tsarevitch Alexei and one of his sisters had escaped the massacre and were now living in hiding. Of such stories are impostures made.

Almost two years after the disappearance of the Romanovs in Russia, in February 1920, a young woman was admitted to a mental hospital in Berlin after a failed suicide attempt. Having no papers and refusing to reveal her identity, she was admitted under the name *Fräulein Unbekannt*, the German equivalent of Jane Doe. In 1922, a fellow patient at the asylum claimed that the young woman was Grand Duchess Tatiana, the tsar's second daughter. She confided her suspicions to a Russian émigré, who contacted former members of the imperial household and friends of the German-born Tsarina Alexandra. While several believed her to be the missing Romanov princess, a former lady-in-waiting of the tsarina said flatly that she was too short to be Tatiana. However, the still unidentified girl reportedly said that she had never claimed to be Tatiana, and her supporters now identified her as the younger sister, Anastasia.

When she was released from hospital, the young woman, who took the name Anna Tchaikovsky, was taken in by a former tsarist official now living in Germany. She was introduced to Princess Irene of Hesse (1866–1953), Tsarina Alexandra's sister, and therefore her presumed aunt, but the princess failed to recognise her as her niece. She commented: 'I saw immediately that she could not be one of my nieces. Even though I had not seen them for nine years, the fundamental facial characteristics could not have altered to that degree.' Under normal circumstances, that would probably have been enough to discredit Anna once and for all, but Russian émigré circles immediately after the Revolution were far from normal. Russia was in the midst of a second Time of Troubles: the country was embroiled in a civil war and fending off foreign invasions from both east and west. Many still hoped for the restoration of the old order, and a surviving member of the ruling family – even one as suspect as Anna – was worth holding on to.

In 1925, Anna was hospitalised with a serious infection and came close to death. Several members of the tsar's family and household, including Nicholas' sister and Anastasia's former tutor and nursemaid, visited her in hospital, but none of them recognised her as the grand duchess.

Nevertheless, doubt remained and investigations continued. The Danish royal family, relations of the murdered Alexandra, funded her convalescence. She then passed into the care of Alexandra's brother, the Grand Duke of Hesse, who initiated the first serious inquiries as to his guest's identity. He concluded that Anna was Franziska Schanzkowska, a Polish citizen who had worked in a German munitions factory during the First World War (1914–18). She had been declared insane in 1916 after an industrial accident had injured her and killed a fellow worker. She had gone missing in 1920 just around the time Anna had surfaced in Berlin. The grand duke arranged a meeting between Anna-Franziska and her brother, but he refused to confirm that she was his missing sister. In later life, he admitted that he had left her in Hesse's care because her life as Anastasia would be much better than as the poor mad Franziska.

In 1927, Anna found a new champion in Gleb Botkin (1900–1969), the son of the tsar's personal physician, who had been murdered with the family in 1918. Botkin had known Anastasia as a child in Tobolsk. He had managed to escape to Japan and had subsequently emigrated to the United States. With the help of wealthy Russian émigrés living in the U.S., he paid for Anna's passage. In order to avoid the attentions of the press, she took the name under which she would be known for the rest of her life, Anna Anderson (1896–1984).

© Getty Images

**DNA PROOF**
Anderson's true identity as a Polish factory worker was only revealed by DNA tests in the twenty-first century.

The year 1928 marked an important anniversary for the supporters and relatives of the former tsar. It was ten years since Nicholas and his family had disappeared, presumed murdered by the Bolsheviks, and his relations were entitled to claim any of his property outside the Soviet Union. There were rumours of Romanov millions held in banks in London and Berlin. Anna, if proved to be Anastasia, would be entitled to a share of the loot as the tsar's only surviving daughter. Botkin and his American attorney Edward Fallows set up a corporation to obtain the Romanov fortune in Anna's name. The surviving Romanovs immediately denounced her as an impostor. Anna returned to Germany to pursue her claim through the courts, starting one of the longest civil actions in German legal history. In the end, the Romanov millions proved to be as illusory as Anna's claims. There was some money in Germany, but by no means a fortune, and it was divided between the tsar's surviving relations.

ANNA SURVIVED AN INVESTIGATION BY THE NAZIS AND WORLD WAR TWO, AND ESCAPED INTO FRENCH-OCCUPIED WEST GERMANY.

Anna survived an investigation by the Nazis and World War Two (1939–45), and escaped into French-occupied West Germany when the Soviet Army occupied what was to become East Germany. She remained in West Germany until 1968, cared for by German aristocratic supporters. They found her a home in the small village of Unterlengenhardt near the Black Forest. In the years after the war, she continued to receive visitors, relatives of the tsar and tsarina, and former acquaintances of Anastasia. Several confirmed her identity while others denounced her as an impostor. Anna became increasingly reclusive and eccentric, acquiring a dog and dozens of cats. In 1968, she was admitted to hospital gravely ill, and the authorities had her animals put down. Released from hospital, the now distraught Anna was about to embark on her final adventure. Botkin and John Manahan, a history professor from Charlottesville, VA, paid for a second trip to the United States. Manahan later married Anna so that she could remain in the country. The couple lived increasingly reclusive and eccentric lives until Anna's death from pneumonia in 1984 at the presumed age of 88.

It may seem improbable to the modern-day reader that the true identity of Anna Anderson was not confirmed beyond reasonable doubt until the twenty-first century. However, DNA tests were not developed until 1985, one year after Anna's death. Adding to the confusion was the fact that after the murder of Nicholas and his family in 1918, two of the bodies – that of his son and of one of his daughters – had been buried separately in Yekaterinburg in order to conceal the murders from tsarist loyalists. This was the source of the rumours that Alexei and either Tatiana or Anastasia had survived the massacre. However, the remains of the prince and princess were discovered in 2007. DNA tests on tissue taken from Anna Anderson during surgery in the United States confirmed that she was not related to the Romanov family and was in fact the missing Polish factory worker, Franziska Schanzkowska.

# TRUE FAKES:
# ARTUR ALVES REIS

**DECEPTION**

Religious deceit

Military subterfuge

**Financial fraud**

Fake or counterfeit

Imposture or cross-dressing

Confidence trick

Scientific deception

**Main Culprit:** Artur Alves Reis

**Motivation:** Financial gain

**Damage Done:** Disrupted the Portuguese economy, led to the collapse of the First Republic and the establishment of a fascist dictatorship

*The profound impact of [Reis'] success gave Portugal its worst shock since the great earthquake of 1755, brought on the most enduring dictatorship of our time, wracked the Lord Mayor of London, almost ruined one of the world's great printing firms, and culminated in one of the longest and costliest cases in British legal history.*

**From *The Man Who Stole Portugal* (1966) by M. Teigh Bloom**

© iStockphoto

When a government prints money it hasn't earned, it's euphemistically called 'quantitative easing', and while many may consider it a crime against economic reason, it is not a crime against the law. The authorities, however, take a very dim view when an individual indulges in a bit of 'quantitative easing' – counterfeiting, in other words. One of the major problems for criminals is the physical manufacture of the counterfeit currency. The printing of banknotes and the minting of coins are major industrial processes. As modern coinage contains no precious metals, there is no profit in debasing quarters, pound coins and euros, and modern forgers concentrate on banknotes. The production of banknotes, however, is also a complex process, involving large quantities of special papers, inks and a printing press. However, no matter how good a counterfeit is, it will never be quite as good as the real thing – lacking the correct serial numbers and seals, and the other built-in security measures official government printers include on their banknotes.

As printing counterfeits is difficult and costly, in its own right, and stealing money from banks attracts the unwelcome attention of the police, the ideal for the criminal would be to have access the government's own supply of banknotes. In the United States, the Department of the Treasury's Bureau of Engraving and Printing in Washington, DC, and Fort Worth, TX, are the only two facilities producing dollar bills, and the bureau does not take private orders. However, smaller countries, which lack such secure printing facilities of their own, often have recourse to reputable firms of overseas printers to produce their banknotes. In the early part of the twentieth century, the government of Portugal obtained its printed currency from the highly respected British firm of Waterlow and Sons, who also printed certain denominations for the Bank of England.

**DEVALUED**
The Reis fraud almost spelled the end for Portugal's national bank.

The geographic gap between the producer of the banknotes in the United Kingdom, and the client, the Bank of Portugal in Lisbon, was the weakness exploited by Artur Alves Reis (1898–1955), the mastermind behind what was to go down in history as the 'Portuguese Banknote Crisis'.

The young Artur did not have a good start in life. His father was an insolvent funeral director, and he himself dropped out of college where he had been studying for an engineering degree. However, Artur wasn't going to let a lack of qualifications stand in his way of a bright future as long as he had access to pen and paper. He forged himself an engineering degree from Oxford University and set sail for the Portuguese colony of Angola on the west coast of Africa. On the strength of his bogus credentials, he got a job in the colony's Sanitation Department, and made a fortune by buying stock in a local railway company with an unsecured cheque.

Having succeeded in making one fortune through forgery and embezzlement, he returned to Portugal in 1922 determined to make an even bigger one. He forged a cheque to the value of $100,000, with which he bought one firm and then attempted to take control of another. He was arrested in 1924 and indicted for embezzlement but escaped conviction on a technicality. He later claimed that he had been the victim of a criminal conspiracy. His short stay in prison, however, rather than acting as a warning that a life of crime did not pay, gave him the leisure to hatch one of the most daring counterfeiting schemes in banking history: the illegitimate production of legitimate banknotes in the name of the Bank of Portugal.

Three factors made Artur Alves Reis' ambitious forgery plan possible. The first was the parlous state of Portuguese politics in the first quarter of the twentieth century. Portugal had won its independence from its larger and more powerful neighbour Spain in the seventeenth century. After a brief French interregnum during the Napoleonic Wars (1799–1815), when Portugal was nominally ruled from its former colony of Brazil, the ultra-conservative Catholic Portuguese monarchy held power until 1910, when it was replaced by the aggressively secular First Republic. The republic, however, was no more of a success than the monarchy. Between 1910 and 1926, when it too was finally overthrown, there were 45 governments – an average of 2.8 a year.

The second factor that allowed his scheme to succeed was that Portugal had gone off the gold standard in 1891. This meant that its currency, the escudo, did not have to be backed by gold reserves (as was the case in the U.S. and UK at the time). This removed a further form of oversight

**NATURAL-BORN FORGER**

on the production of banknotes. During the republic, the partially private Bank of Portugal was responsible for issuing banknotes in the name of the Portuguese government. While in prison, Reis studied how the bank went about issuing notes, and he realised that in addition to the usual official government channels, the bank could issue notes without telling the government. Furthermore, there was no department in the bank that checked for duplicate serial numbers. According to Henry Wigan of the London School of Economics, 'Reis estimated that a personal issue of 300 million escudos (the equivalent to £3,023,889 at the 1925 rate of exchange) would neither alert suspicion nor disrupt the central banking mechanism of the state.' The third and final factor that Reis was counting on was that the contract for printing the large-denomination 500-escudo bill was held by the highly respected firm of 'secure' printers, Waterlows in Watford, England.

**MAKING MONEY**

With the help of Dutch businessman Karel Marang, the German spy Adolf Hennies and José Bandeira, whose brother was Portuguese ambassador in The Netherlands, Reis put his scheme into motion. He claimed to be acting on secret instructions from the Bank of Portugal, which needed the funds as a loan to the colonial administration of Angola. In 1924 Marang opened the negotiations with Waterlows using documents Reis had forged with Bandeira's help. Waterlows asked for written confirmation from the Bank of Portugal and its governor, but unwisely made their request not directly but through Marang. Reis duly presented him with forged letters of authorisation. As the notes were destined for Angolan use, Marang explained, Waterlows could use serial numbers already in use in Portugal. Satisfied, Waterlows printed 100 million escudos in 500-escudo bills bearing the distinctive likeness of the first circumnavigator, Vasco da Gama. Marang and Bandeira delivered the first consignment to Reis in Portugal by means of the Portuguese diplomatic bag.

Reis smuggled in around 100 million escudos, which represented 0.9 per cent of Portugal's GDP. He employed agents to convert it into genuine currency and invested heavily in the Portuguese stock market. At the same time, he was spending lavishly on the lifestyle of a successful business tycoon, buying a mansion, expensive clothes and jewellery for his wife. In June 1925, Reis opened his own bank, the

Bank of Angola and Metropole, to ease the importation and disposal of the 'real' counterfeit millions. But his most audacious ploy, which had it succeeded would have been the greatest scam of the century, was his attempt to buy a controlling interest in the Bank of Portugal. As the bank was the only institution that could detect the fraud, he reasoned that if he succeeded in buying a controlling stake, he could stop any inquiry. Reis needed 45,000 shares to achieve his ends, and by November 1925, he had managed to acquire 10,000.

But the game was almost up for Reis and his accomplices. In early December, a Portuguese newspaper published a series of articles attacking the probity of the Bank of Angola and Metropole and its links with German interests. It suggested, incorrectly, that the bank was being funded by the German government, as part of a plot to acquire Portugal's African colonies. Although the story turned out to be completely wrong, it prompted an investigation into the bank. The investigators discovered that the bank possessed 500-escudo bills that matched existing serial numbers, but that they were otherwise indistinguishable from the real ones. Moves to remove all 500-escudo bills from circulation caused panic all over Portugal. The Bank of Portugal contacted Waterlows, and Reis' scheme was discovered. He and his accomplices were arrested, the Angola and Metropole Bank closed, and Reis was sentenced to twenty years in prison.

© Getty Images

The repercussions of Reis' crime, however, were to be far greater than his and his accomplices' incarceration. The incident ruined Waterlow and Sons, which lost its UK government contracts. Much worse was the effect on the already rocky Portuguese government and economy. In 1926 the First Republic succumbed to a military coup. The succeeding *Estado Novo* (New State) was one of the world's longest-lasting fascist dictatorships, surviving until the bloodless revolution of 1974.

**DICTATOR**
The true beneficiary of the Alves Reis fraud was Antonio Salazar, whose dictatorship lasted until 1974.

## DECEPTION

Religious deceit

Military subterfuge

Financial fraud

**Fake or counterfeit**

Imposture or cross-dressing

Confidence trick

Scientific deception

# REDS UNDER THE BEDS: THE ZINOVIEV LETTER

**Main Culprits:** Desmond Morton and Joseph Ball; British Intelligence; the Conservative Party; the *Daily Mail* newspaper

**Motivation:** To discredit the Labour government

**Damage Done:** Led to the downfall of the Labour government

*A settlement of relations between the two countries will assist in the revolutionising of the international and British proletariat not less than a successful rising in any of the working districts of England, as the establishment of close contact between the British and Russian proletariat, the exchange of delegations and workers, etc., will make it possible for us to extend and develop the propaganda of ideas of Leninism in England and the Colonies. Armed warfare must be preceded by a struggle against the inclinations to compromise which are embedded among the majority of British workmen, against the ideas of evolution and peaceful extermination of capitalism. Only then will it be possible to count upon complete success of an armed insurrection.*

**Excerpt from the text of the *Zinoviev Letter* (1924)**

For many in Europe and North America, the Russian Revolution of 1917 was a dreadful warning of things to come. During and after the First World War (1914–18), the thrones of Russia, Austria-Hungary and Germany had fallen, and the surviving European royals looked on with some alarm at the growth of anti-monarchist sentiment fanned by the growing socialist and communist movement known as the 'Comintern', or the Third International (1919–43). The Third International, founded in Moscow at the height of the Russian Civil War (1917–23), was the final incarnation of a communist organisation whose aims were stated as working: 'by all available means, including armed force, for the overthrow of the international bourgeoisie and for the creation of an international Soviet republic as a transition stage to the complete abolition of the State.' It gathered together left-wing parties and trade unions from all over the world. The man appointed to be its head was the charismatic Bolshevik leader Grigory Zinoviev (1883–1936).

**REVOLUTIONARY**
Zinoviev issued an immediate denial, saying that he was on leave when the letter was written.

However, instead of being a highly organised and well-funded organisation with a clear revolutionary agenda and a secret network of agents ready to do Moscow's bidding, in the early 1920s the Third International was a chaotic talking shop made up of small political parties and workers' groups with conflicting aims and beliefs. It had been set up when the newly born Soviet Union was fighting for its very survival and needed all the support it could muster overseas. Zinoviev was an interesting choice as its leader and showed that Lenin (1870–1924) had a rather ambiguous attitude to the organisation. The two men had fallen out during the early days of the October Revolution, when Lenin accused Zinoviev of being a 'deserter'. Lenin, however, fell ill in 1922, and died two years later. Zinoviev allied himself with Joseph Stalin (1878–1953), and for a time he became one of the most influential Soviet leaders.

**THE QUIET REFORMER**

In postwar Britain, society was changing, too, but at a much more sedate pace. The socialist Labour Party of Prime Minister Ramsay MacDonald (1866–1937) had come to power in 1924, but the king was still on his throne, and the streets of London, Manchester and Liverpool were not awash with the blood of the bourgeoisie. The British Labour Party was a socialist party with a small 's', and it did not endorse armed revolution as its preferred means to achieve reform.

MacDonald's main aims in government were twofold. He pursued a relatively modest program of domestic reform, including the extension of benefits to the unemployed and an increase in the supply of public housing. In foreign policy, he wanted to repair the damage done by the 1919 Treaty of Versailles, which had imposed heavy reparations on Germany and the occupation of part of her territory by France. He believed rightly that too harsh treatment of Germany would lead to a nationalist backlash and a renewed threat of war. He also wanted to regularise Britain's relations with the Soviet Union (SU) to bring her back into the international community. His plans included two commercial treaties and a loan to the Bolshevik government. His administration, however, did not have an outright majority in Parliament and governed with the support of the Liberal Party.

MacDonald's extension of the hand of friendship to the SU, however, had made him extremely unpopular with the Conservative Party and the right-wing press, and their allies in the British establishment. His enemies were on the lookout for anything that would discredit the Labour government, especially something that would suggest that the party had been infiltrated by communist sympathisers. In 1924, two separate incidents gave them the ammunition they needed to attack the Labour government: the Campbell Case and the Zinoviev letter.

**HIS ENEMIES WERE ON THE LOOKOUT FOR ANYTHING THAT WOULD DISCREDIT THE LABOUR GOVERNMENT, ESPECIALLY SOMETHING THAT WOULD SUGGEST THAT THE PARTY HAD BEEN INFILTRATED BY COMMUNIST SYMPATHISERS.**

John Ross Campbell (1894–1969) was a gift to any right-wing newspaper editor wishing to make trouble for a left-leaning government. He was a member of the Communist Party of Great Britain (CPGB), and in 1924 became the acting editor of the party's official paper, the *Workers' Weekly*. In an article entitled 'An Open Letter to the Fighting Forces', on 24 July, Campbell wrote:

> *Soldiers, sailors, airmen, flesh of our flesh and bone of our bone, the Communist Party calls upon you to begin the task of not only organising passive resistance when war is declared, or when an industrial dispute involves you, but to definitely and categorically let it be known that, neither in the class war nor a military war, will you turn your guns on your fellow workers, but instead will line up with your*

*fellow workers in an attack upon the exploiters and capitalists, and will use your arms on the side of your own class.*

It was a rousing call to arms, and in the eyes of the law, an incitement to the armed forces to mutiny against their officers and government. Members of the Conservative and Liberal parties called for Campbell's arrest, but MacDonald's government refused to prosecute him. The opposition countered by accusing sections of the Labour Party of being infiltrated by communists, and forced a vote of no confidence in the government, which MacDonald lost. A general election was called for 29 October 1924. The short campaign focused on the proposed treaties between the United Kingdom and the Soviet Union.

Four days before the election was due to be held, on 25 October, the right-wing newspaper, the *Daily Mail*, published a letter supposedly written on 15 September 1924, by Grigory Zinoviev, president of the Third International, and addressed to the members of the Central Committee of the CPGB. The page-one headlines read: 'Civil War Plot by Socialists' Masters: Moscow Orders To Our Reds; Great Plot Disclosed.' The Zinoviev letter, as the document became known, suggested links between the CPGB and the Parliamentary Labour Party: 'It is imperative that the group in the Labour Party sympathising with the Treaty should bring increased pressure to bear upon the Government and Parliamentary circles in favour of the ratification of the Treaty.' The rest of the letter dealt with Comintern plans to foment a workers' revolution in Britain and the subversion of the armed forces (see quote).

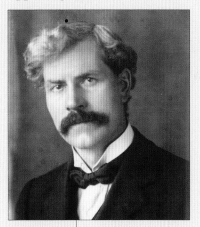

**REFORMER**
The publication of the Zinoviev letter cost Labour Party Prime Minister Ramsay MacDonald the election.

Zinoviev immediately issued a rebuttal of the letter, pointing out several factual errors, and explaining that he had been away on leave on the day he was supposed to have written the letter. However, the damage had been done. The Conservative Party won the election, and prevented an inquiry into the origins of the letter or how it had been leaked from the Foreign Office to the press. In 1967, journalists working for the *Sunday Times* of London claimed that the letter had been forged by Russian émigrés living in Germany. Their aim was to sabotage relations between Britain and Russia. This prompted a first internal investigation by the

Foreign Office, but the report was never published because it was considered to be too sensitive from an intelligence point of view.

Thirty years later, in 1998, the New Labour government of Tony Blair commissioned Gill Bennett, chief historian at the Foreign Office, to conduct the definitive study of the Zinoviev letter affair. According to Bennett, the letter was probably written by White Russians in Riga, Estonia, where it was passed on to British intelligence agents. She did not discount the possibility that the British secret service had commissioned the letter, but in all likelihood it merely took advantage of a useful anti-Soviet forgery. The letter was sent back to London, where it was examined by officers of SIS (Secret Intelligence Service), now known as MI6. Bennett implicated two intelligence officers, Desmond Morton and Major Joseph Ball, both of whom had close links with the Conservative Party. They passed the letter on to the Foreign Office suggesting that it was a genuine document. At the same time they organised the letter to be leaked to the *Daily Mail* a few days before the general election. Bennett concluded her report by saying that she had not found any evidence for an institutional conspiracy by SIS to bring down the Labour government, but that many of its officers were men who through their class affiliations, education and inclinations closely identified with the aims of the Conservative Party.

# TOWER FOR SALE, ONE CAREFUL OWNER: VICTOR LUSTIG

**DECEPTION**

Religious deceit

Military subterfuge

Financial fraud

Fake or counterfeit

Imposture or cross-dressing

**Confidence trick**

Scientific deception

**Main Culprit:** Victor Lustig

**Motivation:** Financial gain

**Damage Done:** Defrauded the gullible; ended his days in Alcatraz

At the meeting, Lustig presented himself as a representative of the Ministry of Posts and Telegraphs explaining that he had been charged with arranging for the scrapping of the [Eiffel] tower, such was the expense of its upkeep, and was inviting bids from the merchants. However, due to the fact that this would provoke a public outcry as by now the tower had become such a landmark, the meeting had to be kept confidential.

**From *Book of Lies* (2005) by Andrews McMeel Publishing**

It would be interesting to speculate whether Robert McCulloch, who bought London Bridge in 1967 for $2,460,000, to re-erect it at Lake Havasu City, Arizona, had a moment's doubt as to whether his deal with the City of London was completely genuine. He might have paused to remember a *cause célèbre* from his childhood, when a confidence trickster had sold Paris' iconic Tour Eiffel (Eiffel Tower) to a gullible businessman.

The Eiffel Tower was built as the entrance arch of the Paris Exposition Universelle (World's Fair) of 1889. Gustave Eiffel (1832–1923) had originally intended the design for the previous year's Barcelona World's Fair, but the city fathers turned down the design as too unusual. The more adventurous Parisians accepted the scheme for their own exhibition, and the distinctive latticework tower took two years to assemble (1887–9). The tower stands 324 m (1,063 ft) high and was the tallest man-made structure in the world until it was dethroned by New York's Chrysler Building in 1930. It is constructed of 18,038 pieces of puddled iron riveted together and weighs around 10,000 metric tons.

© Dreamstime

**FOR SALE**
After the First World War the iconic Eiffel Tower was in a state of disrepair, which gave Lustig the idea of selling it for scrap.

The original building permits gave permission for the tower to stand on the Champ de Mars on the left bank of the Seine for 20 years, until 1909, when it was supposed to be moved to another location or dismantled. Although much criticised as an eyesore when it was first built, the tower gradually won the hearts of Parisians, who grew to love its unique design. Soon the tower had become a symbol of the French capital, a status that was confirmed when it played a role in the French war effort during World War One (1914–18). In the postwar period, however, the city lacked the funds to maintain the tower, and it began to look shabby and run-down. Articles appeared in the press about the state of the tower and what should be done about it. Several even suggested that the tower might have to be dismantled. This gave 'Count' Victor Lustig (1890–1947) the idea for his most audacious scam to date: selling off the Eiffel Tower for scrap.

Although he called himself a count, Lustig was born a commoner in the small Bohemian town of Hostinné (now in the Czech Republic). Like others before him, he found that by crossing a few borders, he could claim an impressive aristocratic pedigree. After the dissolution of the German, Russian and Austro-Hungarian empires after World War One, Europe was awash with displaced aristocrats, both real and bogus. Lustig began his career as an international confidence trickster on the ocean liners that steamed between Paris and New York. One of his scams was the '$100-bill printing machine'. Lustig would demonstrate the device to his astounded mark, while explaining that, regrettably, it took the machine six hours to copy one $100 bill. The machine would change hands for in excess of $30,000, and would 'print' a further two banknotes that Lustig had placed inside. After that the machine only produced blank paper. By then, of course, the 'count' was nowhere to be found.

Although $30,000 was a considerable sum in the early 1920s, Lustig was a man of expensive tastes and even more expensive ambitions. He was looking for a scheme that would not only net him a fortune, but also confirm him in his own eyes as the king of confidence tricksters. In 1925, Lustig read about the run-down condition of the Eiffel Tower, and it gave him the idea of posing as a government official charged with secretly disposing of the monument (see quote). He invited six leading French scrap-metal merchants to the five-star Crillon Hotel in Paris to discuss the deal. Lustig, accompanied by his 'secretary', Dan Collins, took the men on an inspection tour of the tower and asked them to send him sealed bids for the contract. His real aim was to discover which of the six men would make the best mark for the scam. He selected the gullible André Poisson, who saw the deal as a means to ingratiate himself with the French government.

His wife, however, was not so easily convinced. She wondered if Lustig was really all that he claimed to be and asked why the deal had to be done so quickly and with such secrecy. Poisson arranged another meeting with Lustig, who managed to suggest that what he was really after was the bribe to award the contract to Poisson's firm. Curiously, the revelation that Lustig was a corrupt French official after a backhander reassured the Poissons. As is often the case in confidence

**BOHEMIAN RHAPSODISER**

tricks, the mark is made to believe that it is he or she who is in the know and has the upper hand over the confidence trickster. Poisson paid Lustig 250,000 francs (in the region of $1 million) plus a bribe and received a bill of sale for the tower.

Lustig and Collins quickly left Paris for Austria with their ill-gotten gains. They were expecting news of the affair to be splashed all over the French papers at any moment, but the Poissons were so embarrassed by having been taken in that they had not reported the matter to the police. Thinking that he had got away with the scam, Lustig returned to Paris six months later to try the trick again. This time, however, one of his intended victims reported the matter to the police, and Lustig and Collins had to make a quick exit. By this time, Lustig had been arrested 45 times under 22 aliases in different European countries. He decided to quit Old World once and for all and made his way to the Land of the Free.

In the United States, Prohibition (1919–33) was in full swing. The country was fertile ground for shysters and confidence tricksters of every kind. Lustig immediately resumed his criminal activities. One daring sting operation involved the notorious Chicago mobster, Al Capone (1899–1947). He obtained $50,000 from Capone, on the pretext of investing it for him in the stock market. Instead, Lustig kept the money in a safety deposit box for two years, and then returned it to Capone, explaining that the deal had fallen through. Capone was so impressed by Lustig's 'honesty' that he gave him a $5,000 reward.

**JUST REWARD**
Lustig finished his days in prison in Alcatraz alongside his one-time mark, gangster Al Capone.

Despite such successes, Lustig's luck was finally running out. In 1934, he was arrested on a charge of counterfeiting in New York. He escaped prison the day before his trial and went on the run only to be captured in Pittsburgh a month later. He pleaded guilty and was sentenced to 20 years in Federal prison, which he served out at Alcatraz alongside his one-time mark, Al Capone. Lustig died of pneumonia in prison in 1947.

# SEXING SPORT: STANISŁAWA WALASIEWICZ

**DECEPTION**

Religious deceit

Military subterfuge

Financial fraud

Fake or counterfeit

**Imposture or cross-dressing**

Confidence trick

Scientific deception

**Main Culprit:** Stanisława Walasiewicz

**Motivation:** Sporting accomplishment

**Damage Done:** Embarrassment to the Olympic movement

*Stella Walsh lived in the United States but competed for Poland. In her 20-year career she set nearly 100 world records at distances up to 200 metres. Competing under her given name, Stanisława Walasiewicz, she won the women's 100 metres in the 1932 summer Olympics with a time of 11.9 seconds. She also held the women's 200-metre record from 1926 to 1942.*

**From *Running through the Ages* (2001) by E. Seldon Sears**

The recent case of middle-distance runner and 2009 800-metre gold medallist Mokgadi Caster Semenya (b. 1991) highlights the difficult issue of biological sex in sport. While in certain areas of life, the biological sex of an individual may pose legal, social or moral questions, in sport it raises the additional issue of the physical advantage males have over females – especially with regard to height and muscular strength. The current 100-metre world record holder Usain Bolt (b. 1986) owes a good deal of his success to his 1.96 m (6'5") frame, which gives him an extremely long and efficient stride. In the 1920s and '30s, the biological sex of one of Poland's greatest athletes, Stanisława Walasiewicz (1911–80), was questioned, but it wasn't until her death in 1980 that her biological sex was finally determined.

## THE FLYING POLE

Stanisława Walasiewicz was born in Poland. Her birth certificate states that she was born female. She emigrated to the United States with her family when she was three months old. The Wałasiewicz family settled in Cleveland, Ohio, where her father took a job in a steel mill. Although a U.S. resident, Stanisława – or Stella, as she was known to her American fans – did not become a citizen until 1947. She showed her sporting ability at school, again as a girl, and at the age of 16 she was offered a place on the American Olympic team sponsored by the *Cleveland Press* newspaper. However, she was not allowed to take part in the Amsterdam Olympic Games of 1928 because she was not a U.S. citizen. Instead she competed in the Pan-Slavic games in Poznan, Poland, where she won gold in several running events and the long jump.

In 1930, the American Athletic Union (AAU) persuaded the government to offer Walasiewicz U.S. citizenship so that she could compete for the United States at the Los Angeles Olympic Games of 1932. However, days before she was due to take the oath of allegiance, she changed her mind and decided to remain a Polish citizen. She ran for Poland at Los Angeles, and won gold in the 100 metres, equalling the world record of 11.9 seconds. She received a hero's welcome in Poland, was decorated by the Polish government, and was voted Polish sporting personality of the year four years running. After a break because of an injury, Walasiewicz returned to competition in 1933. She was undoubtedly an athlete of unusual ability. During her career, she set over 100 Polish,

European and world records, and won over 40 U.S. national titles. Her European record for the 100 yards has remained unbeaten. During her career, journalists commented on her masculine appearance, and one described her as having 'long man-like strides' and a 'deep-bass voice'.

At her second Olympic Games, held in Berlin under the auspices of the Nazis in 1936, Walasiewicz had to defend her title against Missouri-born Helen Stephens (1918–94), nicknamed the 'Fulton Flash'. Stephens won the race in 11.5 seconds, beating Walasiewicz into second place. Walasiewicz was outraged and accused Stephens of being a man. In an irony that will not be lost on readers, she insisted that Stephens be examined to prove her biological sex. In the days before genetic testing, these tests confined themselves to physical examinations by a doctor. In the event, the exam proved Stephens to be female.

© Getty Images

**SORE LOSER**
Beaten into second place
at the 1936 Olympics,
Walasiewicz (right) accused
the winner of being a man.

Walasiewicz continued her sporting career in the United States during the war, and finally became a citizen in 1947 after the communist takeover of her native Poland. That same year, she married the boxer Neil Olson, though the marriage was short-lived. She kept the name Stella Walsh Olson until her death. She won her final U.S. title in 1951 at the age of 40. After her retirement she continued to be an active figure in the expatriate Polish sporting community, organising meets and sponsoring young athletes.

In 1980, aged 69, Walasiewicz was caught in the crossfire during an armed robbery in Cleveland and was killed. An autopsy revealed that she showed both male and female sexual characteristics, and further investigation revealed that she had chromosomal abnormalities, possessing both the XY and XX chromosomes. She was what is now called an 'intersex' individual – that is, neither entirely male nor female but a combination of the two. Socially, Walasiewicz, had been raised as a girl, and it is likely that she herself considered herself to be completely female. However, under today's Olympic rules, she would not have been admitted as a female competitor.

**DECEPTION**

Religious deceit

Military subterfuge

Financial fraud

Fake or counterfeit

Imposture or cross-dressing

Confidence trick

**Scientific deception**

# PSEUDO-GENETICS: LYSENKOISM

**Main Culprit:** Trofim Lysenko

**Motivation:** Power and fame

**Damage Done:** The imprisonment and execution of genuine scientists; held back the study of agronomy and genetic science in the Soviet Union for decades

*Trofim Lysenko single-handedly obliterated the study of genetics within the Soviet Union for the best part of twenty-five years, replacing it with his own phony scientific theories on the inheritance of acquired characteristics in the plant world. Much of Lysenko's bogus research was only exposed after his scientific dictatorship had done a great deal of long-term damage to Soviet agriculture.*

**From *Joseph Stalin: A Biographical Companion* (1999) by H. Rappaport**

In the modern-day creationist vs. evolutionist debate, we are used to the idea that the 'believers' in the debate put faith, in this case, in God's creation, over the scientific evidence of evolution presented by paleontologists, geneticists and biologists. We take it for granted that atheism must stand for scientific objectivity, if nothing else. However, wind back the clock seventy years, and you will find that an extreme atheist position sometimes entails its own form of blind faith in ideological dogma. During the rule of Joseph Stalin (1878–1953), the Soviet Union developed its own brand of scientific dogmatism, based not on empirical evidence but on Marxist-Leninist ideology. The pseudo-scientific theory known as Lysenkoism after its creator, Trofim Lysenko (1898–1976), was applied to genetics and agriculture with disastrous consequences.

Tsarist Russia was a land of farmers, and over 80 per cent of the population lived directly from the land. Until the mid-nineteenth century, peasants were still tied to the land as serfs on the estates of large aristocratic landowners and of the crown, much as they had been in medieval Europe. However, between 1861 and 1866, during the reign of Alexander II (1818–81), the serfs were emancipated, and in theory, if not always in practice, were encouraged to buy and own their own land. The problem was that the former serfs did not have the money to buy or effectively develop the land.

**PROPAGANDA**
While Russia starved, the Soviet media reported bumper harvests from Stalin's collectivised farms.

The process of agrarian reform continued and accelerated during the administration of Pyotr Stolypin (1862–1911), who served as prime minister to Nicholas II (1868–1918) from 1906 to 1911. It was thanks to Stolypin rather than the Bolsheviks that Russian agriculture modernised in the early part of the twentieth century. He intended to create a class of capitalist farmers, who owned their land and would be able to produce the agricultural surpluses needed to feed Russia's growing urban population. The First World War (1914–18) and the Russian Revolution and subsequent civil war (1917–23) interrupted the process of reform, and then sent it in an entirely new direction.

**STALIN'S SCIENTIST**

Lysenko was not born into imperial Russia's academia. He was the son of Ukrainian peasants and he completed his education, not at a prestigious metropolitan high school and university, but at the Uman School for Horticulture (1917–21) and the Kiev Agricultural Institute (1921–25). After graduating, he took a job at the Kirovabad Experimental Station in the southern republic of Azerbaijan. In the late 1920s, he published accounts of his experiments with vernalisation. *Vernus* is the Latin word for spring, and vernalisation is a process during which plant seeds require a period of cold before they can germinate and flower. Certain fruit-bearing trees and shrubs, including the blackcurrant, will not flower and fruit if the preceding winter has not been cold enough.

In Azerbaijan Lysenko experimented with artificial vernalisation, claiming that the process would not only permit crops to be grown in areas where they had not been grown before, but would also triple or quadruple the yields of subsistence crops such as wheat, rye and barley. Although the Soviet media credited Lysenko with the invention of vernalisation, in which seeds were first soaked in water and then stored in the snow before sowing, this was a traditional practice in Russian agriculture known since the mid-nineteenth century.

Lysenko went on to make other much more contentious claims, including that he had managed to grow a winter crop of peas without the use of mineral fertilisers, and that the effects of vernalisation could be inherited. That is, that the offspring of vernalised plants would not need to undergo the process in order to flower and fruit. In human terms, this would mean that a child would be able to inherit his or her parent's ability to play tennis, for example, as long as the parent had learned to play before the child's conception. This ran contrary to the principles of heredity established by Gregor Mendel (1822–84), which stated that any acquired characteristic developed by a parent organism during its lifetime cannot be passed on to its offspring. This was confirmed by the work of British geneticist Thomas Hunt Morgan (1866–1945), who studied mutations in fruit flies and identified chromosomes and genes as the mechanisms of heredity in 1910.

What made Lysenko's work so attractive to the Soviet leadership under Stalin was that it offered a simple, cheap and Russian solution to the country's agricultural crisis. In 1921, Lenin had launched the New Economic Policy (NEP), which allowed private ownership in agriculture and industry in order to stimulate economic growth. The NEP saved the Russian economy from collapse, but it also had an unforeseen impact on agricultural production. Although yields increased and returned to pre-revolutionary levels, farmers were less likely to sell their produce to buy consumer goods and preferred to consume it themselves. A massive shortfall in the supply of grain in 1928 led the government to requisition grain from farmers, who responded with violent resistance and hoarding. Instead of increasing the grain supplies, they became even scarcer.

In response, Stalin abandoned the NEP and ordered the collectivisation of Russian agriculture. Henceforth, private landholdings would be abolished and all land would be held by the state and farmed collectively. This proved to be even more unpopular than the requisition policy. Many farmers refused to work their land, and others burned their crops and slaughtered their animals. The result was famine on a national scale. It is estimated that at the height of the famine during 1932–3 between five and a half and eight and a half million people starved to death. Instead of appealing for international food aid, Stalin hushed up the disaster. As Russians and Ukrainians starved, the Soviet media carried reports of high crop yields and showed images of happy, well-fed farmers.

While conventional biologists and agronomists could provide little help to solve what was essentially a man-made crisis, Lysenko offered inexpensive, fast and ideologically sound 'communist' solutions. These solutions, however, were based on his faked experiments and did not deliver; they merely led to lower crop yields and yet more shortages and famines. Despite Lysenko's failures, Stalin appointed him head of the Lenin All-Union Academy of Agricultural Sciences in 1936, a member of the Presidium of the Soviet Academy of Sciences in 1938, and director of the Academy's Institute of Genetics in 1940. He used his position to silence his critics, and to denounce Mendelian genetics as an 'alien foreign bourgeois biology'. After World War Two (1939–45), the link was also made between the murderous eugenic theories of the

**ICEMAN**
Lysenko claimed that he could make crops grow in poor soils and cold climates without fertilisers.

Nazis and Mendelian genetics, because Mendel was an ethnic German living in Austria.

Instead of conventional genetics, Lysenko proposed the homegrown pseudo-science of agrobiology – a bizarre amalgam of biology, genetics and agronomy based on his own faked research findings and his crank theories of the inheritance of acquired characteristics. His predecessor as head of the Lenin All-Union Academy of Agricultural Sciences, the eminent botanist and geneticist Nikolai Vavilov (1887–1943) was arrested and sent to prison, where he died of malnutrition. By 1948 Lysenko had obtained supreme power over the Soviet agricultural and genetic establishment. He forbade the study of Mendelian genetics and decreed that criticism of Lysenkoism was henceforth illegal.

**FALL FROM GRACE**

When Stalin died in 1953, the more liberal Nikita Khrushchev (1894–1971) became supreme leader. Although Lysenko and his pseudo-scientific theories came under increasing scrutiny during his rule, Khrushchev nevertheless continued to protect him. It was only after Khrushchev's fall from power in 1964 that Lysenko himself was finally discredited. He was removed from his post as director of the Institute of Genetics in 1965, and his nefarious impact on scientific research in the Soviet Union finally came to an end. By the mid-1960s the science of genetics had made enormous strides in the West, especially after the discovery in the structure of DNA by Watson and Crick in 1953. Because of Lysenko, Soviet geneticists were decades behind their American and Western European counterparts.

It would not be an exaggeration to say that Lysenkoism played a role in the collapse of the Soviet Union in 1990. It was part of an ideological apparatus that stifled advances in science and technology that meant that communist Russia fell further and further behind her capitalist competitors.

We are used to considering fundamentalist dogma as the greatest obstacle to the pursuit of scientific truth; however, the two worst examples of the perversion of science come from atheistic regimes during the twentieth century: Nazi eugenics and Soviet Lysenkoism.

# A LITTLE FAKE MUSIC: MARIUS CASADESUS

**DECEPTION**

Religious deceit

Military subterfuge

Financial fraud

**Fake or counterfeit**

Imposture or cross-dressing

Confidence trick

Scientific deception

**Main Culprit:** Marius Casadesus

**Motivation:** To prove he was as good as Mozart

**Damage Done:** Embarrassed music critics, musicians and musical cognoscenti

*A Concerto in D major for violin and orchestra attributed to Mozart, K. Anhang 294a. The work exists in a simple two-stave sketch, supposedly written in 1766, and dedicated to the French Princess Adélaïde. Although a letter exists in which Mozart dedicates such a work to the Princess, it is almost certainly not his concerto.*

**Excerpt from 'Adélaïde Concerto' in *The Harvard Concise Dictionary of Music and Musicians* (1999) by D. M. Randel**

We have already seen one case of literary forgery (see William Ireland, pp. 58–62), and we shall also learn about a famous forger of Picassos and Impressionist masters (see Elmyr de Hory, pp. 151–5). Although not always the case, money is often the principle motivation for the forgery of the work of a famous artist. The case of music, however, is slightly different. While a handwritten manuscript by a famous author or a painting can be a valuable object in its own right, a musical score, if not in the hand of the original composer, is worthless. The value of a musical piece is the music itself; hence the musical forger cannot hope to benefit materially from his fakery. His or her aim might be quite different, however, such as proving that the forger is as good a composer as his or her illustrious predecessor.

Among the names Mozart (1756–91), Handel (1685–1769), C.P.E. Bach (1714–88) and Marius Casadesus (1892–1981), who does not

belong in the list – that is, who is not a household name in the pantheon of classical music? It must be galling for a musician to know that, no matter what his achievements as an instrumentalist or composer, he or she will never attain the fame of a Mozart, a Bach or a Handel. How tempting would it be to borrow a little of their glory by passing off one of your own compositions as one of theirs? And if the musical world, including expert musicologists, critics, recording labels and artists, and fellow composers are taken in: what delicious irony – a moment of pleasure to savour. Although we cannot be sure of Marius Casadesus' motivation, he was responsible for one of the great musical hoaxes of the twentieth century when he published an undiscovered violin concerto by Wolfgang Amadeus Mozart.

**PRODIGY**
Mozart was so prolific that experts were not surprised when Casadesus produced the unknown concerto.

Mozart died famously young, at the age of 35, in 1791, but by then he had written over 600 works, including sonatas, concerti, symphonies, sacred choral pieces, masses and operas. The task of cataloguing Mozart's prolific output, which began at the tender age of five years old, defeated every musicologist until Ludwig von Köchel (1800–77). In 1862 he published his 551-page catalogue, entitled *Chronological-Thematic Catalogue of the Complete Musical Works of Wolfgang Amadé Mozart*, better known as the Köchel catalogue. The Köchel has been re-edited three times, to include new discoveries and remove works of doubtful authenticity.

Many works have been misattributed to Mozart because he himself transcribed the work of other composers, and also included the work of younger, upcoming composers along with his own. Other manuscripts were lost and have been rediscovered in Vienna and Salzburg. The discovery of a new work, such as the 'Adélaïde Concerto', written when Mozart was ten years old, would not have come as a huge surprise to the musical community, and it was duly included in the third revision of the Köchel and given the number K. Anhang 294a – 'Anhang' signifying that it was in the appendix (see quote). The man who had 'rediscovered' the Adélaïde was the French violinist and composer Marius Casadesus.

The Casadesus family is an extraordinary musical dynasty, which according to the family's website (www.casadesus.com, 2009) is now in its fifth generation. The patriarch, Luis Casadesus (1850–1919), was born in the Catalan town of Figueres. He emigrated to France where he married and fathered nine children. Luis was an amateur musician who played the violin, guitar and mandolin and also wrote a popular teaching method for the guitar. He taught all his children to play musical instruments, and eight of them took up music professionally, four of them – Francis (1870–1954), Robert-Guillaume (1878–1940), Henri (1879–1947) and Marius – as instrumentalists and composers.

**SCION OF A MUSICAL DYNASTY**

Even for a Casadesus, Marius was a particularly gifted musician. He studied at the Paris Conservatoire, where he won first prize for the violin in his graduation class of 1914. After graduating, he embarked on a successful international touring career as a violinist, founding the Marius Casadesus String Quartet. He later joined his brother Henri's Société des Instruments Anciens, and was a founder member of its successor, the Société Nouvelle des Instruments Anciens; both ensembles were dedicated to the use of period instruments in order to recreate the authentic sound of early music. In addition to the violin, he played the guitar, lute, mandolin and viola da gamba. Marius was also a composer in his own right, and published several symphonic works and chamber pieces.

In 1931, Marius announced the discovery of the Adélaïde Concerto, edited and orchestrated by himself from an original sketch by Mozart. The piece was dedicated to one of Louis XV's (1710–1774) daughters, Madame Adélaïde de France (1732–1800), and dated 1766, which fitted into the period when the young Mozart had toured Europe dazzling his audiences with displays of virtuosity on the keyboard. Mozart himself had mentioned the dedication of a work to the princess in one of his letters home, but the work had never been found. The concerto was premiered in Paris at one of the prestigious weekly Lamoureux Concerts.

The Adélaïde Concerto for Violin in D Major, published in 1933, is in three movements: Allegro, Adagio and Allegro. Casadesus described his find as 'an autograph manuscript in two staves, of which the upper stave carries the solo part […] and the lower carries the bass.' The title page was inscribed with Mozart's dedication. The leading Mozart scholar of the day accepted the concerto as genuine and included it in his revision of the Köchel catalogue. Not all were taken in, however, and when Marius failed to provide the original documents, doubts were raised about the concerto's authenticity. However, the deception lasted more than 40 years. The concerto was played and recorded by leading soloists, including the violin virtuoso Yehudi Menuhin (1916–99). The truth finally came out in 1977, during a court case concerning the copyright for the concerto's orchestration. Rather than lose the copyright, Marius admitted that he had composed the work in its entirety.

**FAMILY MAN**
Luis Casadesus fathered a musical dynasty of successful composers and instrumentalists.

The Casadesus family, for all their eminence on the French musical scene, were not strangers to the art of forgery. At one time, Henri Casadesus and not Marius was thought to be the author of the Adélaïde hoax. Henri is also credited with several works attributed to other composers, including the Concerto in D Major for Viola attributed to C.P.E. Bach (son of the great J.S.), and concertos attributed for a time to Handel and J.C. Bach (1735–82). Marius died four years after his admission, but his page on the Casadesus family website still lists the 'Violin concerto dedicated to Princess Adélaïde by Mozart' as one of his 'orchestrations'.

# PLUMBING THE DEPTHS OF CREDULITY: LOCH NESS MONSTER HOAXES

**DECEPTION**

Religious deceit

Military subterfuge

Financial fraud

**Fake or counterfeit**

Imposture or cross-dressing

Confidence trick

Scientific deception

**Main Culprits:** Ian Spurling, Marmaduke Wetherell and Robert Wilson

**Motivation:** Revenge

**Damage Done:** Fooled the credulous; wasted millions of dollars in pointless research

*During 1933 and 1934, when there was an enormous amount of publicity worldwide about Loch Ness, many other silly hoaxes were attempted, and the tomfoolery has continued up to the present. Within a week of the purported sonar contact in 1954 a faked sonar chart was shown to reporters [...] In 1969 the* Daily Mail *was again on the receiving end of a hoax, being presented with a mysterious giant bone found at Loch Ness. The bone, it turned out, came originally from a whale and more recently from a museum in Yorkshire.*

**From *The Enigma of Loch Ness* (1986) by H. Bauer**

© Getty Images

There are some places in the world that speak to visitors of the mysterious, the magical, and sometimes the monstrous. Loch (lake) Ness, 37 km (23 miles) southwest of Inverness in the Scottish Highlands, is just such a place. Dark, brooding fir-tree-populated slopes dominate the peat-rich waters of the loch, guarded by isolated castles and ruined watchtowers. Mist covers the murky waters, whipped up into strange shapes by the wind and currents. The second-largest loch in Scotland, Loch Ness is nevertheless tiny when compared to such titans as Lakes Michigan or Superior. The loch occupies 40 km (25 miles) of a geological fault that splits the Highlands into two from Inverness to Fort William, and has an average depth of 132 m (430 ft), increasing to a maximum of 230 m (754 ft). It is connected to other lochs by rivers and the Caledonian Canal but has no direct outlet to the sea.

**BLEAK SHORE**
The dark waters of the loch provide the ideal home for the mysterious and elusive aquatic monster.

The loch remained isolated and difficult to reach until a road was opened along the lakeshore in 1933. The new highway gave visitors unobstructed views across the loch. As soon as the road opened, sightings of a large unknown creature – christened 'Nessie', or the 'Loch Ness Monster' – began to surface in the local and then the national and international media. Since the first sighting, several theories have been put forward as to the type of creature Nessie might be: an evergreen favourite is that it is a large reptile – a survivor of the mass extinction of the dinosaurs that has somehow managed to hang on in the bleak, cold, sparsely inhabited Scottish Highlands; another that it could be a giant, and as yet undocumented species of newt; or an equally unrecorded giant worm. To these you have to add the more fantastical giant sea serpent (although the loch is miles away from the sea and is filled with fresh and not salt water), and a species of aquatic dragon.

The many sightings, and since November 1933, the occasional still photograph and cine and video film, have sparked international interest in the loch and its mysterious inhabitant(s). At first the investigations were small and funded by British newspapers, but during the twentieth century, major scientific institutions took an interest, funding in-depth investigations of the waters of the loch with the latest in sonar technology, hydrophones and submersibles. The dark waters of the loch do not lend themselves to underwater photography, but over the years investigators have reported many sonar contacts with large unidentified objects in its depths.

While some hoaxes need an individual of exceptional talent to pull them off – for example, Barnum's Feejee Mermaid (pp. 78–81) – the Loch Ness Monster has never been promoted by an impresario of genius. Nessie, however, has its unrivalled natural setting. In 1933, when the lakeshore road opened, the area was not the busy tourist destination that it is today. On 22 July, a London couple on holiday in the Highlands, Mr. and Mrs. Spicer, were driving along the road when they saw 'a most extraordinary form of animal' cross the road ahead of them. The creature was about 1.2 m (4 ft) high and 8 m (25 ft) long, with a long slender neck as wide as the road (between 3–3.5 m, 10–12 ft). It was carrying a dead animal in its jaws, and it slithered or crawled – the Spicers could not see the lower portion of the body clearly – some 20 m (20 yards) into the loch. Mr. Spicer went on to say that the creature was 'the nearest approach to a dragon or prehistoric animal that I have ever seen in my life.'

The sighting, reported in the *Inverness Courier* on 4 August, led to further reports of sightings. That same month Arthur Grant claimed that he had almost hit a creature when motorcycling on the lakeshore road in the early hours of the morning. He described a similar creature to the Spicers', with a small head attached to a long neck. The creature quickly retreated and vanished into the waters of the moonlit loch. Margaret Munro, a servant at a local house, said that she had seen the creature before the Spicers, on 5 June at around 6.30 am, when she was on her way to work. She described an animal with a grey elephant-like hide, a small head and long neck, and two short flippers or forelegs. Finally, in November 1933, the first photographic evidence appeared in the press. A local villager called Hugh Gray was walking home from church along the lakeshore when he saw an 'object of considerable dimension making a big splash with spray on the surface.' Luckily he was carrying his camera (though why he had it when going to church was never explained), and he began photographing the creature. Only one picture showed a distorted image of something in the water, but not clearly

## THE BIG-GAME HUNTER AND THE HIPPOPOTAMUS-FOOT UMBRELLA STAND

enough to be identified. Critics have suggested that the photograph actually shows his dog running through the water.

Nessie was fast becoming the national sensation of 1933, and the British newspaper the *Daily Mail* hired a big-game hunter, the improbably named Marmaduke Wetherell, to investigate the sightings. We can imagine Marmaduke kitted out in his African pith helmet and carrying an elephant gun trekking through the frozen Scottish Highlands. Wetherell did not see the monster, but in December he found giant footprints on the rocky loch shore, made by a large, heavy animal, apparently returning to the water.

The *Daily Mail* claimed to have discovered the first physical evidence of the monster. However, when casts of the prints were sent to the British Museum of Natural History in London, its expert zoologists reported that they had been manufactured with the help of a hippopotamus-foot umbrella stand – a bizarre item of domestic furniture favoured by the British Victorian and Edwardian middle classes in search of an exotic touch for their entrance halls. The *Mail* and Wetherell had been comprehensively hoaxed by an unknown prankster. The *Mail*'s rivals heaped ridicule on the paper and Wetherell, who, like an old injured lion, retired from public view to lick his wounds.

EXPERT ZOOLOGISTS REPORTED THAT THEY HAD BEEN MANUFACTURED WITH THE HELP OF A HIPPOPOTAMUS-FOOT UMBRELLA STAND.

On 21 April 1934, the *Mail*, which clearly had not learned its lesson, published the 'surgeon's photograph', which purported to show the head and neck of a serpent-like creature emerging from the Loch. The supposed author of the photograph was the respected London doctor, Robert Wilson. He claimed to have taken the snap while driving along the north shore road on the morning of 19 April. He refused to be associated with the photograph, he claimed, for professional reasons, which is why it is still known as the surgeon's photograph. The photo was held to be genuine for decades, and was held up by Nessie believers as evidence of the monster's undoubted existence. Strangely, the photo was not subjected to rigorous investigation until Stewart Campbell published a detailed study in an article in the *British Journal of Photography* in 1984. He concluded that the object was only two to three feet long (1 m or less) and was probably an otter or a bird.

A Discovery Channel documentary from the early 1990s subjected the photograph to its own analysis and concluded: 'It seems to be the source of ripples in the water, almost as if the object was towed by something.' They agreed with Campbell's conclusions that the object could not be more than three feet long, and that the picture had been cropped in such a way as to make the object look larger than it actually was. The suggestion was that Wilson had taken the picture knowing full well that it was not Nessie, but had let others jump to their own conclusions. One bright spark suggested that the neck and small head shown on the photograph was, in fact, the trunk of an elephant from a passing circus that had gone swimming in the chilly waters of the loch.

The truth, as it turned out, was much less fantastic but probably more entertaining. In 1994, Marmaduke Wetherell's stepson, Christian Spurling, revealed that he had been part of a plot devised by Wetherell to avenge himself on his former employer, the *Daily Mail*, and the rest of the British media. According to his son Ian, Wetherell, still smarting from the ridicule heaped on him, had vowed: 'We'll give them their monster!' The others involved were his son, Ian, and Robert Wilson. Spurling admitted that he had sculpted the monster's head, which was then mounted on a toy submarine. The plotters had taken the photograph, and Wilson had passed it to the *Daily Mail* to give it credibility. Even today, not everyone accepts the hoax explanation, and even those true believers who do admit that the picture is a fake or merely shows a bird or an otter, say that any number of hoaxes does not disprove the existence of an unknown creature living in the loch. Sightings and investigations continued long after the surgeon's photograph.

**JURASSIC LOCH**

If there are large aquatic creatures living in the loch – and it must be more than one, because one of anything isn't much good – you'd imagine that there would be reports of sightings in the historical record before 1933. However, there is only one well-attested source for the existence of a 'beast' or monster in the vicinity of Loch Ness before the twentieth century. According to the *Life of Saint Columba* written in the seventh century CE, while visiting the Land of the Picts (Scotland) the saint came upon an aquatic beast in the neighbouring River Ness. The creature had killed one of the local pagan tribesmen, and the saint, to prove the power of the Christian God, ordered one of his monks to swim across the river. When the monster appeared and tried to devour the man, Columba admonished it, and it fled in terror. This in itself, however, is not particularly reliable evidence. The monster did not live in the loch but in the nearby River Ness, and stories of saints confronting and vanquishing demons and monsters are the stock-in-trade of Christian hagiography.

Returning from the realm of faith to that of science, we need to examine the most popular candidate put forward by Nessie believers: the plesiosaur. Plesiosaurs are a long-extinct aquatic reptile that lived in the warm seas of the Jurassic period (200–145.5 million years BP).

They had a broad body, a short tail, a long neck and small head, and two pairs of flippers, which did not give them great speed in the water but did give manoeuvrability. Many species are known, with the smallest being some 3 m (9 ft) long, and the largest up to 20 m (60 ft). So far, so good: the plesiosaur corresponds to the most common descriptions of Nessie. However, contrary to many of the sightings, paleontologists now believe that plesiosaurs could not lift their heads out of the water as shown in the surgeon's photograph – the neck was too inflexible and heavy. In addition the loch is much colder than the waters the plesiosaurs would have lived in, and it does not contain enough fish to feed a group of large carnivorous reptiles.

**LIVING FOSSIL**
A surviving plesiosaur is a popular contender to be Nessie – but the reptile became extinct 65 million years ago.

Much more damning, however, is the fact that the plesiosaurs, along with all their other giant reptile cousins, became extinct in the Cretaceous–Tertiary Extinction Event, when an asteroid collided with the earth, obliterating most life on the planet, 65.5 million years BP. During the last Ice Age, Scotland was frozen solid under a sheet of ice, which only unfroze around 10,000 years BP. For plesiosaurs to live in Loch Ness would mean that they had survived somewhere else for 65.5 million years, and then found their way into a freshwater loch over 20 miles from the sea sometime during the past 10,000 years. A sustainable colony would require dozens if not hundreds of individuals, which, being air-breathing, would need to surface regularly. If plesiosaurs had survived in Loch Ness, the British Isles would have its very own Jurassic Park.

# FOOLING HITLER: OPERATION FORTITUDE

**DECEPTION**

Religious deceit

**Military subterfuge**

Financial fraud

Fake or counterfeit

Imposture or cross-dressing

Confidence trick

Scientific deception

**Main Culprit:** General Dwight D. Eisenhower

**Motivation:** Facilitating the D-Day Landings

**Damage Done:** Aided in the defeat of Hitler and Nazi Germany

*That the German high command believed Calais to be the most likely invasion site is testament to Operation Fortitude – the remarkably effective deception and disinformation campaign that the Allies had been conducting for more than a year. To convince Hitler that the invasion would indeed come across the Channel narrows, a fictitious First U.S. Army Group – FUSAG – ostensibly commanded by General George Patton – 'formed up' in Kent and Sussex. Empty tent camps, plywood trucks, rubber tanks, inflatable artillery pieces, dummy landing craft, and phony radio transmissions were employed – along with some less benign measures.*

**From *War Stories 3* (2006) by J. Musser**

'Into the valley of Death rode the six hundred,' reads the refrain from Alfred Lord Tennyson's (1809–92) poem, 'The Charge of the Light Brigade' (1864). To the nineteenth-century British military mind, the Battle of Balaclava during the Crimean War (1853–6) represented the epitome of martial bravery. Never mind that the suicidal cavalry charge directly at the Russian artillery cost the lives of most of the brave six hundred. Defeating your enemy through trickery and subterfuge, on the other hand, as exemplified by the story of the Trojan Horse (see Odysseus, pp. 15–19), had little bravery, glory or honour, even though it may have shortened the war and saved thousands of lives.

The First World War (1914–18) saw an end to heroic charges of any description. There was no glory in dashing across a muddy barbed-wire-strewn wasteland through poisoned gas into the path of artillery and machine-gun fire. By the time of World War Two (1939–45), warfare had become completely mechanised. Tanks and planes replaced men and horses, and concrete bunkers the mud of the trenches. War was no longer fought with toy soldiers in red and gold uniforms on distant battlefields, but it rained down death on cities and murdered by the million in extermination camps. Under such circumstances, any tactic, no matter how hateful, seemed to be justifiable, such as unleashing the horror of the atomic bomb on Hiroshima and Nagasaki in 1945. Luckily for the Germans, however, when the Allies were ready to strike back in the summer of 1944, the A-bomb was not ready. Continental Europe would have to be liberated the old-fashioned way by a mass invasion. As one army fought its bloody way through North Africa and up the Italian peninsula, another was massing on the south coast of England in preparation for the largest amphibious landing in history, planned for 6 June 1944, the day now remembered as 'D-Day'.

**BLOOD AND GUTS**
The hot-tempered General G. S. Patton was the ideal candidate as the leader of the bogus FUSAG.

For Dwight D. Eisenhower (1890–1969), appointed Supreme Allied Commander in Europe at the end of 1943, the invasion of northern France, known as 'Operation Overlord', presented considerable logistical and tactical challenges. In any military campaign, the element of surprise is always crucial and can make the difference between victory and defeat. But how do you hide history's largest invasion force, numbering over 370,000 men backed up by thousands of ships, landing craft, tanks, artillery and aircraft? The short answer is that you can't. Hitler and the German high command would have had reports of the build-up of men and armaments and knew that it could mean only one thing: the invasion of France. However, northern France has a coastline several hundred miles long from the Dover Strait, where the Channel is only 34 km (21 miles) wide, to the tip of Brittany, where it is at its widest at 240 km (150 miles).

By 1944, the Germans and their allies, the Italians and the Japanese, were on the retreat. The Soviet Red Army, backed by the fierce Russian winter, had defeated Hitler's armoured columns and was pushing them back through Poland towards Germany's eastern borders. The British and Americans had defeated Rommel's Afrika Korps and had landed in Sicily and Italy. But Hitler was by no means defeated. In preparation for an invasion of Europe, the Germans had fortified the coastline of Europe from northern Norway to the Spanish border with a network of bunkers, gun emplacements, barbed wire and minefields known as the Atlantic Wall. Fifty-nine divisions protected the most vulnerable part of the wall: France, Belgium and the Netherlands. If the Germans knew for sure where the Allies were going to land, they could concentrate their forces at those points, and counterattack with enough force to repulse the landings.

Eisenhower had to find a way of keeping the landing sites of the expeditionary force secret for long enough to catch the Germans by surprise. Instead of choosing the narrowest point of the Channel in the region of the French port of Calais, Eisenhower decided to land his joint French, American, Canadian and British forces in Normandy, about 190 km (120 miles) from the British mainland, along an 80-km (50 mile) stretch of the coast on five beaches, code-named Utah, Omaha, Gold, Juno and Sword.

In order to keep their objective secret the Allies prepared a complex web of deceptions known as 'Operation Bodyguard'. The story goes that the operation took its name from a comment by Prime Minister Winston Churchill (1874–1965) to Soviet leader Joseph Stalin at the 1943 Teheran Conference. 'In wartime,' Churchill said, 'truth is so precious that she should always be attended by a bodyguard of lies.'

## A 'BODYGUARD OF LIES'

Operation Bodyguard involved three separate subsidiary operations: 'Operation Fortitude North', a British invasion of Norway from Scotland; 'Operation Fortitude South', an Allied invasion of France via the Pas-de-Calais; and 'Operation Zeppelin', a Soviet invasion of the Balkans. These fictional invasions were designed to keep the Germans guessing as to where the Allies would really strike, and prevent them from massing their forces and mounting a successful counter offensive.

The most important of these three was Operation Fortitude South, whose key element was 'Operation Quicksilver', which Eisenhower hoped would keep Hitler's best troops and armoured divisions pinned down in the Pas-de-Calais, while the Allies made their landings and established their beachheads against much weaker opposition in Normandy. In order to make the scheme believable, the first thing he needed was a big name the Germans feared and respected as the commander-in-chief of the imaginary expeditionary force. The man he chose was the hero of the North African and Sicilian campaigns, General George S. Patton (1885–1945), whom he appointed head of the fictitious First United States Army Group (FUSAG), headquartered at the British port of Dover.

**IN ORDER TO MAKE THE SCHEME BELIEVABLE, THE FIRST THING HE NEEDED WAS A BIG NAME THE GERMANS FEARED AND RESPECTED**

'Blood and guts' Patton was an old warhorse who had seen action in the First World War in France. Unfortunately he was also a man of strong opinions and a very short fuse. In August 1943, when he was visiting wounded servicemen in a military hospital in Sicily, he struck a soldier who he thought was malingering. The man was actually suffering from shell-shock and malaria. This was not the first time that the general had assaulted a soldier. Eisenhower reprimanded him and considered shipping him back to the U.S. However, he decided that Patton was too valuable an asset to waste. Instead of sending Patton home, he gave him extended leave in Sicily, fooling the Germans into believing that the general was planning an Allied landing in the South of France.

When Eisenhower sent Patton to Cairo, the Germans interpreted the move as a preparation for an invasion of the Balkans. His finest role, however, was during Operation Quicksilver when he played the part of the C-in-C of FUSAG, touring the country and giving speeches and press conferences that were reported and carefully analysed in Berlin. Patton played his part with some gusto. Three days before D-Day, during a reception at the Ritz Hotel in London, he shouted across the room to Eisenhower, 'I'll see you in Calais!' The remark must have worked as British intelligence intercepts of German radio transmissions the following day reported troop movements from Normandy towards the Pas-de-Calais.

The man who planned Operations Fortitude and Quicksilver was David Strangeways (1912–98), a colonel in the British military intelligence service, SIS. The aptly named Strangeways was no stranger to deception. During his first posting in Cairo in 1942, he had planted false letters and created fake radio traffic to mislead the enemy. His most audacious and successful ploy until Operation Fortitude was the creation of 'the man who never was'. The body of an alleged British officer was washed ashore in Spain carrying the plans of an Allied invasion of Sardinia and Greece. The German high command moved units to both areas, while the real target was Sicily and the Italian mainland.

## 'THE MAN WHO NEVER WAS'

Strangeways divided Quicksilver into six phases: Q1 was the creation of FUSAG in the southeast of England as the HQ for the fictional landing in the Pas-de-Calais; Q2 was the broadcast of fake radio traffic to give the impression that Allied troops were massing in the southeast, while they were really much farther west; Q3 was the building of dummy landing craft, with their associated wireless traffic; Q4 was the bombing of the Pas-de-Calais beaches and railways just before D-Day; Q5 was increased activity around Dover to suggest that the troops were embarking; and Q6 was night lighting in the areas where the dummy landing craft were located.

In addition to the dummy landing craft, Strangeways had also prepared inflatable Sherman tanks and dummy artillery and trucks made of plywood. However, because the Germans had almost no airborne reconnaissance over the south of England, the replica weapons and landing craft were secondary to the principal means that Strangeways used to fool the Germans. He devised three channels to pass false information to the enemy. There were controlled leaks through diplomatic channels to neutral countries that would then be passed on to the Germans – for example, British diplomats approached the neutral Swedish government

**PAPER TIGER**
Operation Fortitude used dummy tanks, but the main ploys were faked intelligence and radio traffic.

about Operation Fortitude North, hoping that the information would be passed on to Berlin by Nazi sympathisers in the Swedish government; false wireless traffic confused the enemy about the location of the real landing sites; and finally, he used a network of German double agents who had gone over to the Allied side to feed false information to German military intelligence.

The success of the D-Day landings is testament to the effectiveness of Operation Fortitude. Even with the best of Hitler's forces diverted to the Pas-de-Calais, during the first few days, it was touch and go whether the Allies would manage to hold on to their beachheads. However, Hitler was so sure that Normandy was a diversion and that Patton would lead the main invasion of France through the Pas-de-Calais that he kept troops in reserve in the area until the end of July. By then the Allies had become so well established in Northern France that the Germans had no hope of dislodging them.

## OPERATION FORTITUDE: AIR OFFENSIVE

A campaign of bombing raids in an area to the east of the D-Day landing sites helped to successfully divert Nazi forces towards Calais.

Preparatory bombing raids

**D-Day landing sites**

Utah

Omaha

Gold

Juno

Sword

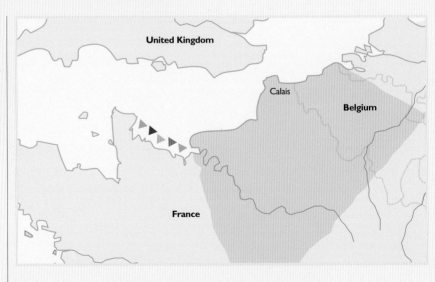

# CLOSE ENCOUNTERS OF THE UNREAL KIND: GEORGE ADAMSKI

**DECEPTION**

Religious deceit

Military subterfuge

Financial fraud

Fake or counterfeit

Imposture or cross-dressing

**Confidence trick**

Scientific deception

**Main Culprit:** George Adamski

**Motivation:** Fame

**Damage Done:** Deluded others into believing in UFOs and alien visitors

*George Adamski supported his experiences with exceptional UFO photographs and colour motion picture footage of these crafts in action throughout the world. His documented, witnessed encounters with Humans from other planets made him one of the most fascinating people of the twentieth century and led to a lifetime of dedication to this subject.*

**Excerpt from the 'George Adamski' page from www.adamskifoundation.com (2009)**

© Nasa

To a generation that has witnessed men walking on the moon and routinely sees images of Earth's neighbouring planets and their moons on the Discovery Channel, it seems unbelievable that someone could claim to have met a 'Venusian human' and travelled to civilisations on the moon, Mars and Saturn. We now know that Mars is a frozen, lifeless desert, and that the gaseous Saturn has no solid ground to stand on. Venusians, were they to exist, would have to be very different from humans. Unlike Earth's benign nitrogen-oxygen-carbon-dioxide atmosphere, Venus' atmosphere consists of a lethal mixture of carbon dioxide and nitrogen, topped by a thick layer of sulphur dioxide clouds filled with liquid sulphuric acid. Although the cloud layer reflects most of the sun's light and keeps the surface in perpetual gloom, the greenhouse effect has superheated the planet so that the average temperature is a broiling 460°C (860°F). Finally, the atmospheric pressure on Venus is a crushing 92 times what it is on Earth.

We only acquired our knowledge of the conditions on Venus in 1962, when the *Mariner 2* probe passed within 35,000 km (22,000 miles) of the planet's surface. In 1952, however, space exploration was barely six years old. German V-2 rockets modified by the USAF carried the first instruments out of Earth's atmosphere in 1946, and our first photograph of Earth from space came from a suborbital V-2 flight in 1947. The Soviet Union successfully launched the first artificial satellite in 1957 and sent the first man into orbit in 1961. Although we knew little about what the planets in the Solar System were like in 1950, there was no shortage of fictional imaginings of extraterrestrials, alien civilisations and space travel. The 1940s and 50s were the heyday of the science fiction B-movie, with titles such as *The Day the Earth Stood Still* (1951), *It Came from Outer Space* (1953) and *Invasion of the Body Snatchers* (1956). A common theme of B-movies was the humanoid alien who travels to Earth in a flying saucer either to destroy humanity or to warn it about the perils of nuclear war.

**VENUS CALLING**
If Venusians did exist, they would not be the blue-eyed, blond Californians of Adamski's fantasies.

© Mary Evans Picture Library / Alamy

The first flying saucer sighting to be widely reported in the American media occurred near Mount Rainier, Washington State, in 1947. It was followed by hundreds of copycat sightings all over the United States, and by the famous Roswell incident, when the USAF initially reported that it had recovered a crashed flying saucer in New Mexico, only to retract the story and say that what they had found were the remains of a high-altitude weather balloon. Add to the flying saucer hysteria a dose of Cold War paranoia, and the secret testing of new aircraft and missiles by the military, and you have a country primed to believe in the existence of aliens, flying saucers and their regular visits to Earth. In George Adamski (1891–1965), the United States found the ufology prophet that it had been waiting for.

George Adamski's family emigrated to the United States from Poland in 1893. He was raised in Dunkirk, NY, but was forced to drop out of school in the fourth grade because his parents couldn't afford to keep him in full-time education. He served in the U.S. Cavalry between 1913 and 1916, seeing action on the Mexican border. He married in 1917, and did low-paid jobs in Wyoming and Oregon before moving to Los Angeles around 1920. In California he joined several esoteric religious cults, including the Theosophical Society, which believed in extraterrestrial intelligences, Atlantis and alien visits to Earth. In the 1920s and 30s Adamski tried his own hand at becoming a cult leader, founding the grandiosely named 'Royal Order of Tibet'. He outlined his philosophy in *Wisdom of the Masters of the Far East* published in 1936. However, his plans to establish a monastic centre for the order in Laguna Beach came to nothing.

In around 1940, he and his handful of followers moved to the Palomar Mountains in San Diego County, where they lived in a primitive commune. Later the group opened a hamburger concession called the Palomar Gardens on the road leading up to the famous Palomar Observatory, where the world's largest optical telescope was commissioned in 1948. Adamski, who began to style himself 'Professor', purchased two telescopes and suggested that he was somehow involved in the Palomar project. The proximity of the observatory and the spate of UFO sightings starting in 1947 gave Adamski the inspiration he needed for the startling revelations he himself would make three years later.

The exact chronology of Adamski's first UFO sighting is a little difficult to establish. Adamski claimed that it took place in 1946, predating the

**'I PHOTOGRAPHED SPACE SHIPS'**

IT SEEMS MORE LIKELY
THAT THE MOUNT
RAINIER UFO WAS
THE INSPIRATION FOR
ADAMSKI'S SIGHTINGS
AND THAT HIS
PHOTOGRAPHS WERE
TAKEN IN 1949.

Mount Rainier sighting by a year, and that his photographs dated from 1948. However, it seems more likely that the Mount Rainier UFO was the inspiration for Adamski's sightings and that his photographs were taken in 1949. That same year, Adamski self-published a sci-fi novel entitled *Pioneers of Space: A Trip to the Moon, Mars and Venus*. The book describes the first fictional expedition from Earth to the moon and the planets of the Solar System, where the explorers encounter races of wise human aliens, whose philosophy is identical to Adamski's own doctrines as laid out in the *Wisdom of the Masters*.

Adamski went public with his own UFO sightings in 1950, and published an account and photographs in an article in the September issue of *Fate* magazine, which specialised in stories about the unexplained, the supernatural and the extraterrestrial. The article, entitled 'I Photographed Space Ships', described his sightings both of flying saucers and of a giant Zeppelin-shaped mother ship, illustrated with photographs of the spacecraft taken with cameras mounted on his telescopes. The pictures do not show the detail of his later productions and are merely blurred lights in the sky. The reception was mixed, with many ufologists accusing him of faking the pictures.

In 1953 Adamski published his first non-fiction book on UFOs called *Flying Saucers Have Landed*, which rehashed many of the more outlandish theories about extraterrestrial visitors to Earth, and their influence on the civilisations of Atlantis, Lemuria and ancient India and Egypt. His most spectacular claim, however, came in a section at the very end of the book, in which he described his meeting with a Venusian human in the Mojave Desert in 1952. The meeting had supposedly taken place near the town of Desert Centre on 20 November, and, he claimed, had been witnessed by five of his followers.

The group was out on a UFO-spotting expedition in the desert when they saw a cigar-shaped mother ship in the skies above them. One of the party recalled later that she thought it might actually have been an aircraft. They followed the 'mother ship' by car until Adamski instructed his companions to drop him off and leave him on his own. He walked away from the highway to set up his telescope and was alone when he witnessed the landing of the scout ship, which Adamski described as a flying saucer made of a translucent metal. The ship's pilot was a Venusian called Orthon, who had long fair hair and tanned skin, and wore futuristic clothing. The Earthman and Venusian communicated by telepathy and sign language and discussed the 'Universal Law' and the dangers of nuclear war. Orthon did not allow Adamski to photograph him, but he was later able to take casts of Orthon's footprints, which were covered in mysterious alien symbols.

Adamski also published what became one of the decade's iconic pictures of a UFO in flight: it shows a saucer-shaped craft with three globes underneath, which he interpreted as part of the propulsion system or the landing gear. Sceptics now believe that the photograph shows a mock-up made up from a lamp or the upper section of an egg incubator, with three light bulbs sticking out of holes cut into a base plate. News of Adamski's alien encounter inspired a spate of copycat reports, several claiming to have been invited into flying saucers and even to have been taken on flights.

**ENCOUNTERS**
One of the many faked UFO photos that have surfaced over the years since Adamski's own creations.

In order to maintain his reputation as Earth's main contact man with the all-wise alien brotherhood, Adamski published *Inside the Space Ships* in 1955. He described further encounters with visitors from Mars, Venus and Saturn – this time, in Los Angeles – as well as a visit to a mother ship. Critics have pointed out that the book has striking similarities with his novel *Pioneers of Space*, and that several passages are lifted word for word from the earlier work. Adamski's descriptions of the flying saucers, mother ship and aliens come straight out of the sci-fi movies of the period, including the rather primitive technology.

From 1953 until his death in 1965, Adamski embarked on a worldwide tour. In his lectures, articles and two further books, *Flying Saucers Farewell* and *Cosmic Philosophy* (both written in 1961), he described the teachings of the spiritually enlightened space brotherhood and the alien civilisations on the moon and the planets Mars, Venus, Saturn and Jupiter. As the years wore on his claims became increasingly outrageous, such as his attendance of a conference of 'masters' on the planet Saturn, and increasingly at odds with the scientific discoveries about the moon and the planets of the Solar System. In 1959, a Soviet probe took the first photographs of the dark side of the moon, showing

**FRAUDULENT PROPHET**

a barren, cratered surface instead of the plants, animals and cities Adamski had described.

Although there is little doubt that Adamski made up his alien encounters, he succeeded in developing a worldwide following, including, he boasted, Queen Juliana of the Netherlands (probably true), and Pope John XXIII and Queen Elizabeth II of England (most probably untrue). Just before his death from a heart attack in 1965, Adamski produced an 8mm film of a flying saucer, but when examined, the footage was found to be faked like the rest of his photographic evidence. Adamski's success was not due to his powers of persuasion, his ability as a public speaker or creativity in his accounts of alien civilisations; however, he correctly gauged the strong belief in aliens and flying saucers among sections of the American public and did his best to exploit it.

# DECEIVING THE EYE: ELMYR DE HORY

**Main Culprit:** Elmyr de Hory

**Motivation:** Financial gain

**Damage Done:** Defrauded galleries, museums and private collectors; was exploited and defrauded himself by unscrupulous associates

*Maybe the word quality isn't the right one speaking about art forgeries but some names have created tremendous respect around them, because of their great skills and impressive ability to cheat even the world's most famous experts.*

**Excerpt from 'Elmyr de Hory' by P. J. Madsen, www.artfakes.dk (2009)**

What connects the impostors, forgers and confidence tricksters whom we have encountered so far is how little any of them have benefited from their deceptions. For all their scheming and cleverness, most of them died alone, miserable, forgotten and in penury. The art forger Elmyr de Hory (1906–76), who was made famous by a biography written by Clifford Irving (b. 1930), himself a forger who later wrote a fake autobiography of de Hory's almost exact contemporary, the reclusive billionaire Howard Hughes (1905–76) (see pp. 199–203) – and by a documentary film made by Orson Welles (1915–85), is a case in point.

**MASTERPIECES**
De Hory faked many famous artists. He painted in the style of Renoir (one of whose paintings is shown here) but never copied existing works.

The particular tragedy of de Hory's life is that he did not want to be a forger, and that he tried to go straight several times. However, he had a special talent for forgery, which was exploited by unscrupulous accomplices and crooked art dealers. What made de Hory's forgeries so difficult to spot was that he did not copy existing works by famous artists, but painted original paintings in their styles. In the Irving biography, he claimed never to have signed the names of other artists on his canvases, and that these had been added by art dealers. He, himself, would have liked nothing better than to paint under his own name but during his lifetime, his own canvases never had the appeal or the monetary value of his forgeries. The tragic irony of his death is that his fake Picassos, Modiglianis, Matisses and Renoirs are now collectable in their own right.

**THE GREAT PAINTER WHO NEVER WAS**

De Hory's early life comes in two versions: his own claimed an aristocratic Austro-Hungarian pedigree, with an ambassador father and a wealthy mother; the reality was probably a little more prosaic and middle-class. He was sent to school in Budapest, the capital of an independent post-First World War Hungary, and later to art school in Berlin. De Hory was clearly a gifted artist, and at the age of 21 he was accepted at one of the leading art schools in France, the Académie de la Grande Chaumière in Paris, where he studied under the French painter, sculptor and filmmaker Fernand Léger (1881–1955). Upon his return to Hungary, de Hory got into trouble with the authorities, possibly because of a homosexual relationship with a suspected British spy. He was arrested and imprisoned as a political dissident.

He was released from prison after the outbreak of World War Two (1939–45), during which Hungary sided with the Germans, only to be re-arrested almost immediately. The fascist Hungarian government, like its German Nazi masters, persecuted its Jewish population and homosexuals. De Hory, who was suspected of being both a Jew and a homosexual, was arrested and deported to a German concentration camp. He managed to survive and escape, and returned to Hungary only to find that his parents had been killed and their property confiscated. At the end of the war, he made his way back to Paris where he hoped to set up as a painter. Postwar Paris was still one of the centres of the world art scene, and wealthy collectors flocked to the city to buy masterworks from the impoverished French and refugees from Soviet-occupied Eastern Europe.

Although de Hory's career as a painter was going nowhere, he discovered a talent for drawing and painting in the style of other artists, in particular for mimicking the work of Pablo Picasso (1881–1973). Picasso, then as now, was one of the best-known and most prolific artists in the world, working in a variety of media, including drawing and painting. De Hory's career as a forger began in 1946, when he sold a 'Picasso drawing' to a British acquaintance, Lady Malcolm Campbell, netting $100. His next sale, of three more Picasso drawings to a French gallery, earned him another $400.

The money allowed him to travel to Scandinavia, with four other Picasso drawings in his suitcase. He offered them for sale to a Stockholm art dealer, who agreed to buy them for the then colossal sum of $6,000, once they had been declared genuine by an expert from Sweden's National Art Gallery. In order to establish the provenance of the drawings and explain his reason for selling them, de Hory claimed that he had rescued them from his aristocratic family's art collection before fleeing Hungary. It was a story that was to serve him well in his early career as a forger. He travelled on to Rio de Janeiro and New York, where he exhibited his own works, with some success, and sold two fakes of the French fauvist painter Raoul Dufy (1877–1953) to the Hungarian-American Hollywood actress Zsa Zsa Gabor (b. 1917). He remained in the U.S., moving from city to city, and expanded his repertoire of artists to include Matisse (1869–1954) and Renoir (1841–1919). Befriended

**DE HORY'S CAREER AS A FORGER BEGAN IN 1946, WHEN HE SOLD A 'PICASSO DRAWING' TO A BRITISH ACQUAINTANCE, LADY MALCOLM CAMPBELL, NETTING $100.**

and exploited by crooked art dealers, de Hory began to sell to leading collectors and major American Museums, including Harvard's Fogg Art Museum.

**DEFRAUDING THE FRAUDSTER**

By 1955 de Hory's luck in the U.S. was running out, as the authorities began to identify several of his fakes. He was forced to skip across the Mexican border to escape arrest on charges of fraud. Despite making it back to the U.S., he was penniless, while the dealers who sold his fakes were making huge profits from his work. Driven to despair, de Hory attempted suicide with an overdose of pills. During his convalescence he met Fernand Legros (1931–83), with whom he would have a tempestuous business and personal relationship for the next decade. Legros and his lover Real Lessart began to sell de Hory's paintings in the U.S., keeping most of the profits for themselves. With the FBI closing in, de Hory returned to Europe, settling first in Paris, and then when that was too dangerous, moving to the Spanish island of Ibiza.

The small Mediterranean island, which is now the capital of rave culture, was then a quiet backwater favoured by artists, bohemians and a few wealthy socialites. For criminals like de Hory, Francoist Spain was an ideal destination as the fascist dictatorship had no extradition treaties with France or the U.S. De Hory continued to paint and to sell his paintings through Legros and Lessart, who peddled his fakes from Tokyo to Texas, netting millions of dollars. In return they paid de Hory a measly stipend of $400 a month, and sometimes they forgot even to pay him that. To placate de Hory, they built him a luxurious villa on the island, where he was able to entertain the visiting 'beautiful people' and continued to produce his fakes.

In 1966, one of Legros' major clients, the oil billionaire Algur H. Meadows (1899–1978) discovered that his 'priceless' collection of French paintings consisted of 56 de Horys. Enraged, he had Legros and Lessart hounded out of the U.S. The pair fled to Ibiza where they moved into de Hory's villa. The three men soon fell out, and Legros evicted de Hory from his own home. However, Legros and his lover's criminal careers were about to come to an end. They were arrested for cheque fraud by the Spanish police and sent to prison. De Hory himself was arrested for homosexual acts, then still illegal in Spain, and served two months in jail.

De Hory returned to Ibiza a year later. At the age of 63, he finally achieved the level of personal fame that had eluded him during most of his life. Clifford Irving wrote his biography, *Fake! The Story of Elmyr de Hory, the Greatest Art Forger of Our Time* (1969), and he took part in Orson Welles' film documentary *F for Fake* (1974). His notoriety allowed him to make a modest living selling his own work for the first time. In 1976, he learned that the new democratic Spanish government had agreed to extradite him to France, where he would face charges of fraud. Unwilling to face this final indignity, the 70-year-old de Hory committed suicide by taking an overdose of pills.

© Time & Life Pictures | Getty Images

**FAKER FAKED**
The forger received a posthumous accolade when forgeries of his fakes appeared on the market.

In his biography, de Hory claimed to have produced more than one thousand fake canvases and drawings, some of which are probably still hanging in private collections and museums as the real thing. Recent reappraisals of his artistic output, both original and in the style of other painters, are beginning to give him the recognition that eluded him during his lifetime. In the 1990s he received the ultimate artist's accolade when reports began to appear in the press that de Hory's forgeries had themselves been faked!

**DECEPTION**

Religious deceit

Military subterfuge

Financial fraud

Fake or counterfeit

Imposture or cross-dressing

**Confidence trick**

Scientific deception

# STACKED: THE BRASSIERE BRIGADE

**Main Culprits:** Betty Corrigan, Marie Orr and Billie Ruth McNabb

**Motivation:** Financial gain

**Damage Done:** Punished for their crimes; serious embarrassment to the Southern Bell Telephone Company

*Just as the 'Brassiere Brigade' saw their lives crashing around them, the case took a strange twist. Southern Bell decided not to press charges. The company's problem was that it couldn't determine the amount stolen on any given day nor could it identify the money as its own. The case, the company feared, was a weak one and a loss in court could lead to catastrophic lawsuits. Some suspected their real reason was embarrassment. They may have just wanted to get the story off the front pages. One joker mailed his monthly payment addressed to Southern Bra Company. It was delivered.*

**From *Murder in the Tropics* (1995) by S. B. McIver**

Having dealt with imaginary monsters and aliens in previous entries (see Loch Ness Monster Hoaxes, pp. 133–8, and George Adamski, pp. 145–50), it's now time to come back down to earth with a good old-fashioned financial scam. This crime did not net the perpetrators billions or even millions of dollars, like the swindles of Ponzi (pp. 96–101) and Madoff (pp. 246–51), nor was it particularly daring or clever, such as the scams of Alves Reis (pp. 107–11) or Lustig (pp. 117–20). However, unlike their crimes, it was almost the perfect crime – the perfect crime being the one you get away with. Clearly, many criminals get away with their crimes. However, we are unlikely to hear about them because unlike Betty Corrigan, Marie Orr and Billie Ruth McNabb, they are not caught, arrested and charged by the police, and they do not give full confessions. This is exactly what happened to the three Florida women employed by the Southern Bell Telephone Company and their accomplices; and even then, they almost got away with their ill-gotten gains.

**THE PERFECT CRIME**

Back in the day before mobile phones and credit-card calls, the only way to make a call away from home was to use a public pay phone with hard currency. In 1950, the General Post Office operated pay phones, or telephone boxes, in the UK, while in the U.S., it was private telephone companies that provided the service. Southern Bell operated the pay phones in Miami, FL, where it made a healthy profit on the operation. Unbeknownst to the company, so did several of its young female employees. The fact that the employees in question were young, female and attractive probably goes some way to explaining why they were not caught earlier. In the 1950s women were thought to be less likely to engage in criminal activity and were less likely to be searched. Sometimes sexism can work in a girl's favour!

Teams of male operatives collected the money from pay phones, and to make sure no one skimmed a bit off the top, it was transferred directly from the phones into sealed containers and into an armoured truck for transportation to the phone company's HQ. As this was the likeliest place for money to go missing, it was also at this stage that the company employed its strictest security measures. Once safely in the building, the money was delivered to a counting room, staffed in Miami by young women, including 23-year-old Betty Corrigan and 21-year-old Marie

Orr. The women's job was to empty the sealed containers into automatic counting machines that would give the company the first official record of how much they had earned that day from their pay phones.

Supervision must have been pretty lax in the counting room, and Betty and Marie realised that if they could hide some of the money and remove it from the premises before it was counted, there was no way the company could find out that it had gone missing. Phase one of their plan was to hide several rolls of quarters inside their brassieres. A roll of 60 25¢ coins weighs 361.5 g (12.75 oz) and is worth $15. If they managed to remove ten rolls a day, they were netting $150. The girls later admitted that they could manage four to five rolls at a time. A modern reader might think that a bra could not take that much extra weight, but we are not talking about the rather flimsy creations of today, but the full industrial-strength underwired 'Bullet' or 'Torpedo' bras as worn by actress Jane Russell.

**GOLD CHEST**
The heavy-duty 'torpedo' bras of the 1950s were ideal for transporting stolen rolls of quarters.

It was too risky for the women to leave the building with the cash stashed in their lingerie, with the clear and present danger of a 'wardrobe malfunction', so they hit on a much easier and safer solution, and one that allowed them to make more than one coin drop a day. Once they had stuffed their bras with quarters, they would go to the ladies' room where they unloaded the loot and passed it on to their waiting accomplice Billie Ruth McNabb. She would then smuggle the coins out of the building in a suitcase. It was never made clear how long the scam had been going on or exactly how much money had been stolen. The police estimated that it could have been as much as several hundred thousand dollars, but out of sheer embarrassment Southern Bell would only ever admit to a fraction of the total.

## MAKING A CLEAN BREAST OF IT

The scam seemed to be the perfect crime, so how did the girls get caught? Marie Orr's 18-year-old sister-in-law Rita reported a theft from her home. Betty Corrigan happened to arrive at the property when the police came to investigate. When they searched the trunk of her car, they found suitcases containing over $4,000 in quarters and $1,000 in bills. Not being seasoned criminals, Betty and Marie confessed to stealing thousands of dollars from the telephone company, with which they bought cars and paid off their mortgages. It was a newspaper editor's dream come true, and each paper vied to come up with the best name for the gang. American readers were treated to 'The case of the silver falsies' and 'The bra bandits', but the most popular name for the group came from a line in an article that read: 'Justice as elastic as the items in which they carried their loot, snapped back today on members of Miami's "Brassiere Brigade".'

Although the girls had confessed verbally to the crime, and the police had found evidence in the shape of around $10,000 in the possession of Orr and Corrigan, there was no actual link between the money and the telephone company. Additionally Southern Bell wasn't able to specify how much money had gone missing or when it had been stolen. The girls immediately withdrew their confessions, and said the money belonged to them. Their lawyers threatened to sue Southern Bell for wrongful dismissal and asked for the money to be returned. When the girls showed up for work, however, they were firmly told that they had been fired and were not allowed back into the building.

Although the girls had been released, the authorities and Southern Bell were only biding their time. The prosecutor for Dade County assured the press, 'If everyone will just keep their brassieres – I mean their shirts – on for a few days we will have some cases. It is a question of assembling evidence.' Accountants painstakingly compared the company's long-distance calls from Miami with the company records held in Jacksonville, FL. They identified discrepancies in the recorded calls from Miami pay phones and the money counted. The amounts were small, less than $500 for any given day, but it was enough to have the women re-arrested and arraigned on a charge of grand larceny. Orr, Corrigan and McNabb were found guilty, sentenced to a year in prison, and ordered to pay back $24,118.

**ALTHOUGH THE GIRLS HAD CONFESSED, THERE WAS NO ACTUAL LINK BETWEEN THE MONEY AND THE TELEPHONE COMPANY.**

# A STUDY IN BLACK AND WHITE: THE 'BLACK ADMIRAL' PORTRAIT

**Main Culprits:** Unknown

**Motivation:** To obtain recognition for the part played by African Americans in the Revolutionary War

**Damage Done:** The discovery of the forgery undermined its aims by raising doubts about the role of African Americans in the war; major financial loss for the owner of the painting

*A few weeks before the painting was due to arrive in New York, Nadezhda Williams, the Fraunces curator, received a call from Dr. McBurney. 'I asked him, "How's our black sailor doing?"' Williams recalled. 'He's just fine, but he's white,' McBurney told her.*

**Excerpt from 'A Painting's Secret', by Erik Baard,**
***The New Yorker* (2006)**

In previous entries we have seen that fakes are not always created for financial gain. The forgery of the *Donation of Constantine* (pp. 23–6) and the Zinoviev letter (pp. 112–16) had clear political motives. The fake Adélaïde Concerto (pp. 129–32) was written to show that the composer could get the better of the musical establishment of his day. In this latest artistic forgery, money does not seem to have been the primary motivation, although in the end the owner of the painting had to accept a major financial loss.

The 'Black Admiral' portrait shows a late eighteenth-century sea captain standing in front of a ship riding at anchor. The man is splendidly attired in red britches, a fine waistcoat with gold buttons, and a naval officer's embroidered blue surcoat, from which emerge the lace cuffs of a white shirt. His left hand rests on the hilt of his sword. Apart from one detail, the picture is not unlike many others from the period of the American Revolutionary War (1775–83). The detail in question, however, is particularly significant, as it is the apparent race of the sitter: he is beyond doubt of African American origin.

**WASHINGTON'S BLACK SAVIOUR?**

The painting, which is of unknown provenance and unsigned, is the property of a retired urologist, Dr. Alexander McBurney, who purchased it from an antique dealer for $1,300 in 1975, in a self-confessed fit of Bicentennial fever. The picture is so unique that it has been featured in books, TV documentaries and exhibitions on African American history and the part African Americans played in the Revolutionary War. In his *The Unknown American Revolution* (2005), historian Gary Nash speculated that the Black Admiral was an American privateer – a state-sponsored pirate made rich from the capture of enemy prizes – because of his demeanour and fine clothes. Another theory was that he was one of the black sailors known to have played a part in the evacuation of George Washington and his troops after the Battle of Brooklyn Heights in August 1776.

In 2006, Nadezhda Williams, the curator of the *Fighting for Freedom: Black Patriots and Loyalists* exhibition, held at New York's Fraunces Tavern Museum, approached McBurney to borrow the painting, which she intended to be the centrepiece of the exhibition. McBurney agreed, but he decided to send the painting to specialist restorer Peter Williams to get it ready for its latest public viewing. Before the restoration,

McBurney had the painting valued and insured it for the sum of $300,000. As soon as the restorer began work, however, he discovered that the portrait had been overpainted, changing the Admiral's skin colour from white to black. The face had been removed altogether, so the true identity of the original sitter remains unknown. The forgery, Williams estimated, dates from sometime in the mid-twentieth century and was done with some care. For example, the forger used a type of varnish that prevents the detection of the additions and overpaintings with ultraviolet light.

The portrait had to be withdrawn from the exhibition, and, once revealed to be a fake, was re-valued at $3,000, losing the good doctor $297,000. However, McBurney remains philosophical about the whole affair. He has had the admiral restored to his fake blackness and continues to give the painting pride of place in his home. The identity and motives of the forger remain unknown, but Peter Williams was probably right when he said, 'We all want black heroes, and that's what's behind this.' In the end, however, the forgery was ultimately counterproductive, as it raised doubts about the authenticity of other evidence of the role played by African Americans in American history.

**RESTORED**
After the Admiral had been exposed as a fake, its owner had him restored to his faux blackness.

# SHANGRI-LALA: CYRIL HOSKIN

**DECEPTION**

Religious deceit

Military subterfuge

Financial fraud

Fake or counterfeit

**Imposture or cross-dressing**

Confidence trick

Scientific deception

**Main Culprit:** Cyril Hoskin

**Motivation:** Fame and financial gain

**Damage Done:** Fooled and exploited the credulous

*Lobsang Rampa was a Buddhist monk and a medical Doctor, who was born in Tibet. After many tribulations and much travelling he eventually settled in Canada near the end of his life and so experienced life in both the East and the West. Dr. Rampa was a revolutionary of his time, one of the first of the Eastern teachers to bring Buddhism and metaphysics to the West in a popular fashion. He wrote many books about spiritual matters, beginning with* The Third Eye.

**Excerpt from www.lobsangrampa.net (2009)**

The story of 'Princess' Caraboo of Javasu (pp. 68–72) is an object lesson in the appeal of the foreign and the exotic. In the early nineteenth century it was possible for an impostor to invent a far-distant land and its culture and claim it as his or her home. By the mid-twentieth, however, the world had shrunk, and only its remotest corners remained unexplored. A modern-day impostor claiming an exotic pedigree would need to pick an area still little known and visited by Westerners. But if the point were to benefit materially from the imposture, he or she would have to choose a country that interested Westerners in some way. In the twentieth century, increasingly wealthy and materialistic Western Europeans and North Americans were turning eastward to search for the spiritual wisdom that they could no longer find in their own Christian culture. George Adamski (pp. 145–50), before he turned his eyes skyward to discover the 'Universal Law' from our alien brothers, had sought it in the wisdom of the East, and in particular, the mysterious land at the top of the world, Tibet.

**TWO'S COMPANY**
Once exposed as a British plumber's son, Hoskin claimed that the spirit of a deceased lama had entered his body.

In the aftermath of the republican Chinese Revolution of 1912, Tibet regained its independence from China, and was ruled by a Buddhist theocracy headed by the Dalai Lama. In 1933, the English novelist James Hilton (1900–54) published *Lost Horizon*, a fictional account of the magical valley of Shangri-La, whose inhabitants were not only permanently blissed out and infuriatingly wise, but also immortal. Hilton built on existing Tibetan legends of a secret valley hidden in the mountains to create his own fictional creation. But such was its appeal that in the late 1930s, the Nazis actually searched for the valley that they thought was the original home of their imaginary Aryan 'master race'.

For all the romance surrounding it, Tibet is a real country, which in the 1940s was populated by an extremely poor, predominantly rural population, which lived in a medieval feudal state. Although the country was notionally independent from China for 36 years, this came to an end when the Communists took over in 1949. While China modernised and reorganised after the upheavals caused by World War Two and the

Revolution, Tibet was left with a degree of autonomy, but this changed in the mid-1950s when the Chinese re-asserted their authority. Finally in 1959, Chinese troops marched into Lhasa. The current Dalai Lama, Tenzin Gyatso (b. 1935, and pictured opposite as a child), fled to India, where he still heads the Tibetan government in exile.

The Chinese instituted a period of brutal cultural persecution in Tibet, closing the monasteries and imprisoning or killing Buddhist monks. Rather than face persecution and death, many monks preferred exile, following their leader to India, and from there, a few travelled to new lives in the West, where they taught their brand of esoteric Buddhism to a Western public hungry for new forms of spiritual insight. There are now many Tibetan Buddhist monasteries in Europe, Australasia and North America. Tibetan Buddhism is an esoteric form of Buddhism, which has elaborate religious rituals and practices designed to help adepts achieve spiritual enlightenment.

**OPENING THE THIRD EYE**

In 1956, the respected British publisher Secker & Warburg published a book entitled *The Third Eye*, which purported to be the autobiography of a Tibetan lama, Tuesday Lobsang Rampa, who had sought refuge in England after many years of exile from his native land. The book described his upbringing in the Chakpori Lamasery in Lhasa. The monastery's curriculum included traditional Tibetan medicine, meditation, yoga, levitation, astrology, telepathy and astral projection. He also claimed to have undergone a painful trepanation of the forehead in order to open his 'third eye', which gave him access to amazing psychic powers, including the ability to see a person's aura – a coloured halo surrounding the body that reveals his or her spiritual attainment and deepest inner thoughts.

A few weeks after the operation, Rampa recalled his first view of an aura:

*Approaching me was a figure smothered in blue smoke, shot through with flecks of angry red. I uttered a squeak of alarm and dashed back into the room. The others looked up at my horrified expression. 'There's a man on fire in the corridor,' I said. The Lama Mingyar Dondup hurried out and came back smiling. 'Lobsang, that is a cleaner in a temper.'*

In a later chapter, Rampa explained the Tibetan theory and practice of 'astral travel':

> *A considerable amount of training was now given to me in the art of astral travelling, where the spirit, or ego, leaves the body and remains connected to life on Earth only by the Silver Cord. Many people find it difficult to believe that we travel in this way. Everyone does, when they sleep. Nearly always in the West it is involuntary; in the East lamas can do it when fully conscious. Thus they have a complete memory of what they have done, what they have seen and where they have been. In the West people have lost the art, and so when they return to wakefulness they think they have had a 'dream'.*

The book had considerable success in Europe and America, and I myself remember reading it decades later one summer holiday, when, as a rather bored and impressionable teenager, I faithfully followed his instructions and willed myself to see auras and float away from my body to travel 'astrally' to faraway (and more interesting) places. Unfortunately, I remained firmly earthbound, and incapable of seeing auras, even when I squinted really hard – some of us clearly don't have what it takes spiritually.

© Creative Commons | Jeff McNeill

**EXOTICISM**
Tibetan Buddhism's esoteric beliefs and rituals lend themselves to misrepresentation by charlatans like Hoskin.

Tibetan scholars were not so quickly taken in as the general public, however. In learned reviews, they countered that Rampa's fantastic revelations were exactly that: completely fantastic and fictitious. Many pointed out that Rampa did not look Asian and that strangely, he also spoke English with the facility and accent of a native speaker. The Tibetan scholar Heinrich Harrer (1912–2006), the author of *Seven Years in Tibet* (1952), who had been a tutor to the Dalai Lama, was determined to prove that Rampa was a fake and a fraud. He hired an English private eye to investigate the mysterious Rampa's origins.

**THE PLYMPTON PLUMBER'S SON**

The private eye published his findings in the British newspaper the *Daily Mail*. He revealed that Tuesday Lobsang Rampa was not an aristocratic Tibetan raised in a Lhasa monastery, who had made a daredevil escape from Tibet, but was in reality Cyril Hoskin (1910–81), the son of a plumber born in the Devon town of Plympton. Hoskin had never been to Tibet, and had acquired his knowledge from books and made up the rest by using his very fertile imagination. In 1948, he had changed his name to the Asian-sounding Carl Kuon Suo, in which guise he had offered the manuscript of *The Third Eye* to Secker & Warburg, only to change it to the more Tibetan Lobsang Rampa when the book had been accepted for publication.

Rampa-Hoskin, however, was to answer his critics in the most ingenious way. He was both Cyril Hoskin and Lobsang Rampa, he explained in a subsequent book, *The Rampa Story* (1960). The spirit of the lama had entered his body and taken it over upon Rampa's death through a process of transmigration of souls. Tibetan Buddhists do indeed believe in reincarnation, and the Dalai Lama and other senior lamas are held to be the reincarnation of their predecessors. However, the process requires the soul of the deceased to enter a newborn baby rather than a full-grown adult.

**THE SPIRIT OF THE LAMA HAD ENTERED HIS BODY AND TAKEN IT OVER UPON RAMPA'S DEATH THROUGH A PROCESS OF TRANSMIGRATION OF SOULS.**

The explanation, while it may have satisfied the most credulous of Rampa's readers, did not prevent constant attacks and lampoons in the British press. To escape the media's unwelcome attentions, Hoskin and his wife moved to Canada in the 1960s, and settled there permanently in 1973. Hoskin changed his name by deed poll to Lobsang Rampa and continued to write, publishing another 18 books, one of which, he claimed, had been dictated to him by his pet Siamese cat. Lobsang Rampa, *né* Cyril Hoskin, passed away in Canada in 1981. He is clearly enjoying an extended holiday somewhere on the astral plane, as he has not yet returned to the earth to impart to us more pearls of wisdom from the mystic East. I must admit that I experienced a certain pang of disappointment when I learned that Rampa was a fraud. He had brought a little bit of magic and wonder into my adolescence.

**DECEPTION**

Religious deceit

Military subterfuge

Financial fraud

**Fake or counterfeit**

Imposture or cross-dressing

Confidence trick

Scientific deception

# AT GREENLAND, TURN LEFT: VINLAND MAP

**Main Culprits:** Unknown

**Motivation:** Financial gain

**Damage Done:** Serious embarrassment for the academic community

*During the seven years it had taken to prepare* The Vinland Map and the Tartar Relation, *the book project was kept just as secret as the existence of the actual map. This secrecy prevented the three authors from freely consulting other scholars when addressing such different subjects as codicological problems, the map's place in the cartographical record, and the map's value to the history of the Norse in America. Once the book had been published, however, a number of scholars willingly expressed their opinions about its authors' statements.*

**From *Maps, Myths and Men* (2004) by K.A. Seaver**

There is now no doubt that the Vikings, or Norse, visited North America some five centuries before Christopher Columbus (1451–1506) 'sailed the ocean blue' in 1492. While Columbus made landfall in the New World in the Caribbean, the Norse travelled via Iceland and Greenland to the far north of the American continent in what is now eastern Canada. Evidence from several Norse epic poems, known as sagas, oral traditions written down between the twelfth and fourteenth centuries, indicate that several expeditions made landfall in lands west of Greenland. These were called Helluland ('land of the flat stones'), thought to be Baffin Island, Markland ('land of forests'), thought to be Labrador, and Vinland ('land of wine' or 'land of meadows'), thought to be Newfoundland.

In 1960, archeologists discovered the remains of a Viking settlement at L'Anse aux Meadows in the north of Newfoundland, proving once and for all that Columbus was a relative latecomer to the New World.

The Norse, however, did not establish permanent settlements in Canada. The saga of Erik the Red (950–1003) refers to the hostility of the native Vinlanders to Viking settlement, and this, and the huge distance from Scandinavia, might explain why North America never underwent major Norse colonisation like Iceland and Greenland.

Prior to the discovery of L'Anse aux Meadows, there was no incontrovertible proof of Norse visits to America. Several stones with runic inscriptions had been produced but most of these are now thought to have been hoaxes. The evidence of the sagas, however, was compelling enough to convince many scholars that the Norse had walked on North American soil. All that was needed was evidence. The discoverer of authentic proof of Norse colonisation would not only earn considerable academic kudos; he or she would also make a great deal of money.

**VINLAND FOUND**
In 1960 archeologists discovered a Viking settlement in Canada dating from 500 years before Columbus.

Three years before archeology confirmed what many historians had long believed, a rare medieval *mappa mundi* (map of the world), thought to date from the early part of the fifteenth century, and predating Columbus by several decades, was discovered bound into a medieval manuscript. The map, which amazed the few academics and museum curators who were shown it, showed the Old World of Europe, Africa and Asia, and to the west of the island of Greenland, a much larger island called Vinland, identified by those who saw it as North America. The map had no certain provenance, and there were many questions regarding its authenticity. However, these were only revealed much later, because for seven years the map and its existence were kept a closely guarded secret, until its proud owner, Yale University, revealed its existence in a blaze of publicity on Columbus Day, 1965.

**THE SECRET REVEALED**

The Vinland map first appeared in 1957, when an Italian antiquary and book dealer resident in Spain, Enzo Ferrajoli de Ry (d. 1967), offered it to the British Museum bound with a handwritten copy of Giovanni da Pian del Carpine's (1180–1252) *Hystoria Tartarum*, the *Tartar Relation*, which told of Carpine's journey to the court of the Mongol Khan in the 1240s. The Relation has no connection with either the Norse or the Americas. The British Museum declined to buy the book because the map and the manuscript did not seem to fit together – wormholes in the book and map did not line up. Later that year, Ferrajoli showed the manuscript to the American book dealer Larry Witten (1926–95), who later claimed to have met the map's putative (and anonymous) Spanish owner with Ferrajoli.

Convinced that the map was genuine, he showed it to experts at his *alma mater*, Yale University. At first, they, too, were sceptical and declined to buy it. Six months later, Ferrajoli produced a second medieval manuscript, this time a copy of Vincent of Beauvais' (c. 1190–1264) *Speculum Historiale* (*Mirror of History*). Beauvais' history of the world was written in the thirteenth century and makes no mention of the Americas or Vinland. However, the wormholes in the *Speculum* matched up with those in the map, suggesting that the map, the *Relation* and the *Speculum* had once been bound together in one volume. The separate sections had somehow become separated, and had been now miraculously reunited. Witten sold the manuscript to billionaire philanthropist Paul Mellon (1907–99), who in turn donated it to Yale.

Yale was now convinced that it had a priceless treasure, and the first proof that the Vikings had visited America and settled there for a time. To keep the find secret it employed the few experts who had seen the map to study it and write a scholarly tome on the discovery and its significance. The task took the men seven years to complete, and during that time, they did not consult experts from other fields who could have helped them to ascertain its authenticity. With much fanfare, Yale presented the map and the book on 21 October 1965.

The ink was barely dry on the copies of *The Vinland Map and the Tartar Relation* before experts from a variety of fields were crying 'fake'. In the past forty years the manuscripts, map, paper and ink have been subjected to the full battery of chemical tests and scholarly analysis by medievalists, linguists and cartographers. Although Yale still maintains that it is genuine, many now believe that it is an extremely good forgery. The evidence against comes from several different fields: linguistics – anachronistic use of language and terminology; cartography – inconsistencies in the depiction of landmasses; and chemistry – the composition of the ink.

To begin with the cartographic evidence, the depiction of the Old World seems to be based on mappae mundi of the 1430s. Asia is a shapeless blob, and Africa is truncated at the Equator; the British Isles, France, Spain, Italy and Greece are recognisable, but Scandinavia is oriented east to west, rather than north to south. The outline of Greenland in contrast, matches a nineteenth-century representation of it as an island, while in the fifteenth century it was believed to be a peninsula attached to Northern Russia. Similarly, the larger island of Vinland is oriented in the correct direction if it is Newfoundland. Linguistically, several of the Latin spellings and usages on the map did not come into common use until the seventeenth century. Finally, most damning of all is the analysis of the ink, which contains the chemical titanium dioxide, an artificial pigment first made in the 1920s. The map's believers continue to argue that the samples were contaminated, or that the titanium dioxide had been produced by some natural chemical process. However, taken together, the evidence strongly suggests a forgery.

**ANACHRONISM**
The Vinland map is a strange mixture of old and new: while Greenland is shown correctly, Africa is a misshapen stump.

**FOLLOW THE MONEY**

If the map is a fake, who could have done it? In the movie *All the President's Men* (1976), Deepthroat tells Bob Woodward (Robert Redford) to 'Follow the money' – sniff out who benefits from the crime and you'll find your criminal. Enzo Ferrajoli is definitely in the frame, as he sold the original manuscripts to Witten. In 1966, Ferrajoli was jailed for taking part in the theft and re-sale of 583 priceless medieval books and manuscripts stolen from the library of Zaragoza's La Seo Cathedral. Ferrajoli would certainly have had access to medieval copies of the *Speculum* and the *Relation*, as well as sheets of original medieval parchment on which to draw the map. However, there is no evidence that he had ever been involved in forgery. Unfortunately for all concerned, he died a year after his arrest, taking the secret of the map with him to his grave. One French investigator, Jacques Victor, has suggested that the unknown forger not only created the map but also the accompanying version of the *Relation* as it shows discrepancies with other extant versions. He could have used blank sheets from a genuine medieval copy of the *Speculum* to manufacture a map and *Relation* that would fit perfectly together.

What about Witten, the respected American book dealer and Yale alumnus? He was one of the main beneficiaries of the sale of the manuscript to Mellon. In 1974, when Yale asked him about the provenance of the map, Witten admitted that he had never met its mysterious Spanish owner, but had obtained the map and the two accompanying manuscripts through Ferrajoli and his associate, an English book dealer. He also revealed that he had paid the Italian a commission on the $300,000 he had received from Mellon. Despite these rather unsavoury revelations, Witten was never accused of improper conduct. He died in 1995, his reputation intact and his antiquarian book business prospering.

By the 1970s, Yale had invested so much of its academic reputation in the authenticity of the Vinland Map that it was unlikely to admit it had bought a forgery made from recycled medieval paper and drawn with twentieth-century ink. At present, the state of play is a draw with a slight advantage to the doubters. The truth, however, will come out one day – either when the perpetrator confesses to the forgery or when a more conclusive set of scientific tests finally settles the matter.

# SPRING FEVER: SPAGHETTI HARVEST

**DECEPTION**

Religious deceit

Military subterfuge

Financial fraud

**Fake or counterfeit**

Imposture or cross-dressing

Confidence trick

Scientific deception

**Main Culprit:** Charles de Jaeger

**Motivation:** April Fools' Day hoax

**Damage Done:** Made a few people believe that spaghetti grew on trees

*'Spaghetti cultivation here in Switzerland is not, of course, carried out on anything like the tremendous scale of the Italian industry. Many of you, I am sure, will have seen pictures of the vast spaghetti plantations in the Po valley. For the Swiss, however, it tends to be more of a family affair.'*

**Excerpt from 'The Swiss Spaghetti Harvest', BBC Television, 1 April 1957**

According to the *Dictionary of Phrase and Fable*, the commonest explanation of the uncertain spring weather on the day on which Jesus Christ was tried as the origins of April Fools' Day cannot be correct, because the tradition exists outside Europe and predates Christianity. More poignant is that it is a survival of the festival of the Roman goddess of agriculture Ceres, the *Cerealea*, which was celebrated at the beginning of April. Ceres, known as Demeter to the Greeks, had a daughter Prosperina (Persephone), who was abducted by Pluto (Hades) and taken to the Underworld. Ceres heard her daughter's cries for help but when she went to find her, she was on a fool's errand, as she found only their echo. Similar traditions of playing practical jokes exist in Israel and Iran, though at different times of year.

Another popular theory put forward is that 1 April was once the last day of the New Year's celebrations when the New Year was feted on 25 March. When the calendar was reformed in the sixteenth century, and the New Year began on 1 January, those people who had not heard of the change or refused to accept it and continued to celebrate the New Year on the old date earned the title of 'April Fools'.

In its modern incarnation, 1 April is the day people play pranks on their friends and family, and on which the media tries to get one over on us all. Many a disbelieving, amazed or outraged newspaper reader, radio listener, TV viewer, and now Internet surfer splutters over an item of breakfast news, realising a split second too late what the date is. In Anglo-Saxon countries, the tradition is that the hoaxes must be carried out before noon; however, as we shall see, this unwritten rule is not always followed. The best April Fools have come from some of the most respected newspapers and TV and radio broadcasters – and who could be more respected than the British Broadcasting Corporation?

© Popperfoto | Getty Images

**DIMBLEBY**
The *Panorama* anchor who was said to have 'enough gravitas to float an aircraft carrier.'

**FOOLS' HARVEST**

Imagine an idyllic rural scene: trees in full blossom by an Alpine lakeside. The background music features the trill of the mandolin, over which the measured, self-assured tones of the British narrator are heard: 'It is not only in Britain that spring, this year, has taken everyone by surprise. Here in the Ticino, on the borders of Switzerland and Italy, the slopes overlooking Lake Lugano have already burst into flower at least a fortnight earlier than usual.'

So far there is nothing very unusual about the report. It is filmed in black and white (as colour had not yet reached British TV screens in 1957), and is in the style of a Movietone newsreel. For all the world it looks like one of those quaint (and if truth be told, fairly patronising) documentary pieces about England's near neighbours on the Continent and their sometimes strange foreign practices. 'But what, you may ask, has the early and welcome arrival of bees and blossom to do with food?' the narrator goes on over shots of trees in full flower. 'Most important of all, it's resulted in an exceptionally heavy spaghetti crop,' he informs his viewers matter-of-factly.

The film cuts to a scene of trees heavily laden with a crop of spaghetti hanging vertically from the branches. Young women in traditional peasant costume pick the ripe pasta from the trees, laying it carefully in flat tray-like baskets. In Switzerland, the narrator explains, spaghetti cultivation is a 'family affair', unlike the industrial scale of Italy's 'vast spaghetti plantations in the Po valley.' All said in the measured tones of authority – not so much teaching the viewer something new, but gently reminding him or her of facts he or she may have forgotten.

The narrator's voice darkens for a moment: 'The last two weeks of March are an anxious time for the spaghetti farmer. There is always the chance of a late frost which, while not entirely ruining the crop, generally impairs the flavour and makes it difficult for him to obtain top prices in world markets.' And then it brightens again: 'But now these dangers are over and the spaghetti harvest goes forward.' Gone also, he tells his no doubt relieved viewers, is the threat of the 'spaghetti weevil'. There follows a description of how the spaghetti is picked and laid out to dry, and an explanation of the crop's amazingly uniform length: 'the result,' the narrator confides, 'of many years of patient endeavour by plant breeders who succeeded in producing the perfect spaghetti.'

The piece closes with images of the traditional meal eaten in honour of the spaghetti harvest, and toasted with special drinking receptacles known as 'boccalinos'. The main course is, of course, a 'ceremonial dish' of 'spaghetti – picked early in the day, dried in the sun, and so brought fresh from garden to table at the very peak of condition.'

## A BOY STUPID ENOUGH TO BELIEVE THAT SPAGHETTI GREW ON TREES

What had made the two-and-a-half minute segment on the Swiss spaghetti harvest so believable was first the medium, second the program that had featured it, and third and most important of all, the man who had provided the voice-over. The spaghetti harvest hoax is thought to be the first April Fool to be broadcast on television. The show in question is still one of the BBC's flagship news and current affairs programs, *Panorama*, which was first aired in 1955. The narrator was the show's anchor, Richard Dimbleby (1913–65), a man described as having 'enough gravitas to float an aircraft carrier.' *Panorama* was broadcast on Monday evenings at 8 pm, and featured in-depth analysis of the main events in the week's news, but often included at the end a segment in a more lighthearted tone. As there were only two TV channels in the UK at the time, the BBC and the independent ITV, the show regularly garnered an audience of ten million viewers.

As soon as the broadcast was over, callers besieged the BBC switchboard with complaints and questions. Some were angry that the BBC had broken the rule that April Fools' Day hoaxes are meant to end at noon. The BBC felt obliged to issue a statement before the end of broadcasts that day, explaining:

> *The BBC has received a mixed reaction to a spoof documentary broadcast this evening about spaghetti crops in Switzerland. The hoax* Panorama *programme, narrated by distinguished broadcaster Richard Dimbleby, featured a family from Ticino in Switzerland carrying out their annual spaghetti harvest. It showed women carefully plucking strands of spaghetti from a tree and laying them in the sun to dry. But some viewers failed to see the funny side of the broadcast and criticised the BBC for airing the item on what is supposed to be a serious factual programme. Others, however, were so intrigued they wanted to find out where they could purchase their very own spaghetti bush.*

Despite the explanation, callers continued to ask the BBC for advice on how to grow their own spaghetti tree. In the end, the exasperated switchboard operators instructed the would-be pasta growers to 'place a sprig of spaghetti in a tin of tomato sauce and hope for the best.'

The spaghetti harvest was not the brainchild of a senior BBC executive or a well-known comedian of the day. The hoax was hatched by Charles de Jaeger (1911–2000), who was then working as a cameraman for *Panorama*. Realising that 1 April 1957 would fall on a Monday, he persuaded the show's editor and producer to let him shoot an extra segment and asked Dimbleby to narrate the voice-over. The group kept the hoax secret from their bosses until the very last minute, thinking rightly that the organisation would have prevented the broadcast.

Charles de Jaeger was Austrian by birth, but fled to Britain in the 1930s when the Nazis invaded his homeland. He worked for the film unit of the Free French government in exile, and joined the BBC in 1943. He became a cameraman five years later, and because he was a talented linguist, he was the first BBC cameraman sent to film outside the UK. De Jaeger later revealed that he'd had the idea for the spaghetti harvest many years before when he was a schoolboy in Vienna. One of his teachers had once taunted his class, saying, 'Boys, you are so stupid, you'd believe me if I told you that spaghetti grew on trees!' De Jaeger was going on assignment in Switzerland, so the expense involved would be minimal. *Panorama*'s editor agreed and provided him with the princely sum of £100 to finance the project.

Now all de Jaeger had to do was film the segment. Contrary to the upbeat voice-over, the spring had not come early in Switzerland that year. The weather that March was cold and misty, and the trees, instead of being early, were late coming into blossom. In the end he had to use stock footage of flowers and trees in bloom that he spliced into the final edit. The location for the hoax harvest was a hotel in the lakeside village of Castiglione, which was surrounded with evergreen trees.

The kind of spaghetti we buy in supermarkets is dry, hard and perfectly straight, so would not be suitable for de Jaeger's purposes, but freshly made pasta is soft and pliable. He got the hotel to make 20 pounds (about 10 kg) of fresh spaghetti and hung it from the branches. However, the pasta dried out too quickly before they could hang it all. De Jaeger next tried cooked pasta, but it was too slippery and heavy, and fell off the branches. One of de Jaeger's Swiss collaborators, however, came up with the solution: they kept the fresh pasta damp until it was ready for use. As soon as the laurel trees had been decked out in the

REALISING THAT 1 APRIL 1957 WOULD FALL ON A MONDAY, HE PERSUADED THE SHOW'S EDITOR AND PRODUCER TO LET HIM SHOOT AN EXTRA SEGMENT AND ASKED DIMBLEBY TO NARRATE THE VOICE-OVER.

fake crop, the extras dressed in peasant costumes began the harvest, carefully lifting the strands off the branches and depositing them in the baskets and then laying them out in the sun to dry. The final touch was the ceremonial meal of spaghetti, prepared in the hotel kitchen, for his Swiss crew.

The spaghetti harvest is thought to have been the first TV April Fool, and it is recognised as one of the best ever made. It is listed as #1 in themuseumofhoaxes.com's 100 best April Fools' Day hoaxes, and has spawned many imitations and tributes in the past fifty years. In 1957, spaghetti was still a relatively rare dish on British tables, but would we fall for it again today? In a world in which people know so little about where their food comes from, on balance, I think we would.

# MAKING CRIME PAY: FRANK W. ABAGNALE, JR.

**DECEPTION**

Religious deceit

Military subterfuge

Financial fraud

Fake or counterfeit

Imposture or cross-dressing

**Confidence trick**

Scientific deception

**Main Culprit:** Frank W. Abagnale, Jr.

**Motivation:** Financial gain

**Damage Done:** Defrauded individuals and institutions

*In a five-year spree of forgery, fraud and impersonation an American called Frank Abagnale earned himself a reputation as America's most gifted con man. Arrested and sentenced to 12 years' jail at the end of the '60s, the 26-year-old was given a second chance by the American government – early release in return for his skill and expertise.*

**From an interview of Frank W. Abagnale with Robert Swan of the Australian Broadcasting Corporation, broadcast on 17 March 2000**

When they were children many of my readers probably dreamed of becoming airline pilots, doctors or lawyers; and there are probably some, who, thanks to hard work, have achieved their ambitions. Most, I imagine, limited themselves to one of these professions, as to succeed in any one of them takes many years of study and then many more years of dedicated practice, and to attempt two, let alone three, would take more time than is allotted to the average human. For the unscrupulous, however, there are much quicker ways than study and dedication to pass as a pilot, doctor or lawyer.

Forgers can easily create all the qualifications they need, but those are often not enough. Impostors also need to play their parts so well that all those they meet will not even bother to ask to see or check their credentials. The right appearance, clothing, manner and tone of voice are often all that is needed to make someone into a doctor, pilot or lawyer. Our image of the members of the professions is that they are men and women of a certain 'weight' and also of a certain age. Would you trust a kid of 16 to be a fully qualified Pan Am pilot? Or a young man of 18, a fully qualified doctor? Or a 20-year-old, a Harvard-trained attorney? Yet this is exactly what Frank Abagnale (b. 1948) did for five years between his sixteenth and twenty-first birthdays.

STAR QUALITY
Baby-faced Leo DiCaprio was not a good choice to portray the mature-looking teenage Abagnale.

© Pictorial Press Ltd | Alamy

As has often been the case in these pages, much of our information about a shyster's life of crime comes from his or her own autobiography. For Abagnale, as for others, there is cause to doubt how much is actually true, how much is exaggeration, and how much is downright invention. He, like others of his kind, has woven deceit about himself like a coat that he wears proudly. He has more cause than most to talk up his youthful exploits, as he switched sides in the war on crime and now works as a consultant advising corporations and banks on how to avoid fraudsters and embezzlers like himself. The reader must decide how much is true or false, but what delicious irony, if Abagnale has pulled off yet another con on big business, the FBI and the banks – persuading them that he was a master criminal rather than a kid with big dreams and a fertile imagination.

Frank Abagnale, Jr. was born in Bronxville, New York, of an American father, also called Frank, and a French-Algerian mother. When his parents divorced in 1964, Frank Jr. remained with his father, while his three siblings went to live with his mother. He lived with Frank Sr. until his death in 1974. By then Abagnale was well advanced in his life of fraud, imposture and embezzlement. His first victim was his own dad. When Abagnale got his driver's licence and first car, he asked his dad for a credit card to pay for gas. Unwisely his father loaned him his own card as they shared the same Christian name, on the understanding that Frank, Jr. would be responsible for the bill.

Abagnale immediately worked out a scam to make some spending money for himself at his dad's expense. He would buy items with the card but do deals with the gas-station employee to keep the goods in exchange for fifty per cent of their value. In this way, in a few months, he had racked up a $2,500 credit-card bill that he kept secret from his father by hiding the bills. It was only when the company came to recover the debt that he owned up to the con. Even then his father was indulgent, because his tearaway son said that he needed the money to spend on girls. Thus began what was to be a five-year embezzling and fraud spree that was to take him to 26 countries and finally land him in jail in three.

With his family home broken up by divorce, the young Abagnale decided that what he wanted most out of life was excitement and money. He had one huge advantage for a young conman: he looked at least ten years older than he was. He forged his driver's licence, adding ten years to his age, and he was all set. With a fake ID, he opened his first bank account in New York, with $100 – the sum total of his worldly goods. The bank gave him a temporary chequebook, but when he inquired about deposit slips and was told he'd have to use the ones on the counter until his own printed slips came, he had a bright idea. Why not write his own account number in magnetic ink on the deposit slips, so that whenever a customer paid in a cheque the money would go into his own account? He netted $40,000 before the bank realised, and by then he was long gone.

His next scam was to pose as a Pan Am pilot, so that he could 'deadhead' – travel for free on other airlines' flights – from country to country,

## THE MAN OR THE MYTH?

staying in crew hotels and charging it all to the airline. He managed to obtain a real uniform from Pan Am's suppliers in New York – charged to the company's account – and faked a Pan Am ID card, by obtaining a sample from the 3M company that manufactured the real thing and sticking the Pan Am logo from a model aircraft kit onto the card. According to one estimate, Abagnale flew one million miles on 250 flights to 26 countries at Pan Am's expense between the ages of 16 and 18.

**TINKER, TAILOR, DOCTOR, ATTORNEY**

After almost being caught on a flight to New Orleans, Abagnale decided to retire from the airline business for a while and try his hand at medicine. He befriended a doctor who lived in his apartment block in Georgia and got a job as a hospital paediatrician supervising interns. Although he had zero medical training or knowledge, the job did not prove to be too challenging because he made sure that his supervisees did all the medical work. He remained in the job for about a year before deciding to go back to his old life in the air.

It was when Abagnale went back to his flying scam that he had a chance offer of a legal position in the office of the attorney general of the state of Louisiana. All he had to do to get the job was to fake a Harvard law transcript and pass the state's bar exam. The fake transcript was no problem, but he had to pass the exam, which he managed at his third attempt after cramming for eight weeks. Unfortunately, a fellow employee was a real Harvard law graduate, who began to become suspicious when Abagnale was evasive in his answers to questions about his time at their shared alma mater. Rather than be exposed, Abagnale resigned his position after eight months and went back to being a pilot.

When Abagnale turned 21, his luck finally ran out. An Air France stewardess he was dating recognised him from an Interpol wanted poster and denounced him to the French police. He was arrested, convicted, and served six months in a French prison. Upon his release, he was extradited to Sweden, where he served a further six months for forgery. Altogether, 12 European countries wanted to try Abagnale for various crimes. However, upon his release from jail in Sweden, he was deported back to the U.S. where he was arraigned for multiple counts of fraud and forgery. While awaiting trial, he managed to escape by posing as an undercover prisons inspector, and later as an FBI agent. His plan was to go to Brazil, which had no extradition treaty with the U.S., but he was caught in New York City before he could carry it out. He was sentenced to 12 years in federal prison.

Abagnale served five years of his term, until the government made him an offer he could not refuse: early release in exchange for unpaid help to catch other fraudsters and con-artists. The 26-year-old accepted and was released. But he still had to make a living. He tried his hand at various jobs but was fired when his employers discovered his criminal past. Finally he hit upon the idea that would make him his legitimate fortune. He offered his services to banks and businesses teaching them to avoid being the victims of fraudsters and embezzlers. He made enough money not only to pay back all those he had defrauded during his five-year crime spree but also to become a millionaire in his own right. Now a successful businessman, Abagnale is the founder and CEO of Abagnale & Associates, headquartered in Tulsa, Oklahoma, and is a trusted advisor to the FBI. Who says crime doesn't pay?

© Getty Images

**POACHER TURNED GAMEKEEPER**
Abagnale is now a successful businessman teaching corporations how not to get stung.

**DECEPTION**

Religious deceit

Military subterfuge

Financial fraud

Fake or counterfeit

Imposture or cross-dressing

Confidence trick

Scientific deception

# THE REAL-LIFE DA VINCI CODE: THE *DOSSIERS SECRETS*

**Main Culprits:** Pierre Plantard, Philippe de Chérisey and Gérard de Sède

**Motivation:** Delusions of grandeur; fame; financial gain

**Damage Done:** Misled the credulous; encouraged conspiracy theories and pseudo-history

*The first time that [Mary] Magdalene appears in the New Testament with any real significance is when she is described as being the first person to see Christ after the Resurrection – one reason she is revered as a saint in France and other places where churches are dedicated to her. One of the most persistent stories about the Holy Grail is that it was brought by Magdalene to France where, according to fourth-century legend, she landed at Marseilles. This is the French port city on the Mediterranean where the river Rhône, an established Phoenician trade route, reaches the sea.*

**From *Da Vinci Code Decoded* (2004) by M. Lunn**

The publishing sensation of 2004 was Dan Brown's (b. 1964) entirely fictitious adventure novel *The Da Vinci Code*. Neither Brown nor his publisher actually claimed that the people and events in the book were not made up. The thing that grabbed the media's and the public's imagination was that there might be a grain of truth behind his tale of an age-old conspiracy by the Roman Catholic Church to silence and obliterate a 'great secret' preserved by a secret society know as the Priory of Sion. After the success of the book and of the 2006 film, starring Tom Hanks, I am not giving anything away in revealing that the great secret that the priory is trying to protect is that Jesus Christ (c. 4 BCE–30 CE) was married to Mary Magdalene (fl. early 1st century CE), who bore him a child or children. Hence, the true heirs of Christ are not the successors of Saint Peter (c. 1 BCE–67 CE), the popes of Rome, but his living bloodline, which the Church had been trying to exterminate to preserve its own wealth and power.

The idea of Mary Magdalene as the only female apostle and the author of her own gospel is an ancient one that dates back to Antiquity. Although most scholars consider the *Gospel of Mary* to be apocryphal – that is, written much later after the events it claims to depict by someone other than Mary herself – she was an important figure for an esoteric Christian movement known as Gnosticism, which was opposed to the mainstream Church and its teachings. The Gnostics, like all other Christians the Church considered to be heretics, were hounded, persecuted, killed or forced into exile. In the traditions of the Greek Orthodox Church, after the death and resurrection of Jesus Christ, Mary Magdalene accompanied the Virgin Mary to the Greek city of Ephesus (now in western Turkey), where she died and was buried. Her body was taken to Constantinople, capital of the Byzantine Empire (now Istanbul), in 886, where it remains preserved as a precious relic.

**ENIGMA**
Several paintings, including this work by Poussin, are said to hide the secrets of the Priory of Sion.

Another much later tradition claims that she travelled to the Roman province of Gallia Narbonensis (now the Provence region in southern France), bringing with her the Holy Grail (the cup used by Christ at the last supper; see quote). During the Middle Ages two French abbeys claimed to have the remains of Mary Magdalene, though probably both were medieval fakes (see Fake Relics and Indulgences, pp. 41–7). The abbeys were wrecked and the relics destroyed during the French Revolution (1789), but one – the Church of La Sainte Beaume near Marseille – was restored in the nineteenth century. There is nothing in the French Catholic tradition about Mary, however, that claims she was ever married to Jesus or had children by him.

Dan Brown based his fictional story (and to what extent was decided by an expensive and unsuccessful legal action for plagiarism in 2006) on the work of Michael Baigent, Richard Leigh and Henry Lincoln, who published their non-fiction book, *Holy Blood, Holy Grail*, in 1982. While there are many similarities between Brown and Baigent *et al.* there are also significant differences. Brown involves the organisation Opus Dei, depicting it as the Catholic Church's hit squad, staffed by half-crazed monk-assassins. Baigent, Leigh and Lincoln based their theory about the surviving descendants of Jesus Christ and Mary Magdalene on documents they had discovered in France's equivalent of the Library of Congress or the British Library, the Bibliothèque Nationale de France in Paris in the 1970s while researching a historical series for the BBC. It is the origin and nature of these documents, entitled the *Dossiers Secrets d'Henri Lobineau* (*Secret Files of Henri Lobineau*) that we must investigate now, as they are the key to the whole mystery of the Jesus bloodline conspiracy theory made famous by *The Da Vinci Code*.

**HOLY GRAIL**     Now solidly republican, France was once a monarchy. The French beheaded one king in 1793, but that did not put an end to the crown. Even today there are sad relics of the *Ancien Régime*'s Bourbon dynasty, which returned briefly to power between 1815 and 1824; of the Orléanist dynasty – a side branch of the Bourbon house that ruled briefly during the mid-nineteenth century – and finally of the Bonapartist dynasty, heirs of the Emperor Napoleon I (1769–1821). In political terms, French monarchists represent a tiny political fringe (much like English republicans). Holding on to empty titles, long bereft of land, power, status or wealth, French royalists are trapped in a twilight world of extreme right-wing, ultra-conservative and ultra-Catholic politics, praying for the day when the people see sense and restore a king or emperor to the long-vacant throne of France.

During the many centuries of the French monarchy, prior to the Revolution of 1789, many dynasties had succeeded one another on the throne. One of the first to rule most of French territory, though France as a country did not yet exist, was the Merovingian dynasty, which reigned between the sixth and eight centuries. The *Dossiers Secrets* revealed an extraordinary secret, though not the one revealed in *Holy Blood, Holy Grail* or *The Da Vinci Code*. The 27 pages of the *Dossiers* are a mixed bag of documents, including Lobineau's *Genealogy of the Merovingian Kings and the Merovingian Origins of Several French and Foreign Families*; a partial history of the Priory of Sion and a list of its grand masters, which includes such luminaries as Leonardo da Vinci (1452–1519), Sir Isaac Newton (1643–1727), novelist Victor Hugo (1802–85) and artist Jean Cocteau (1889–1963); and a genealogy proving the direct descent of Pierre Plantard (1920–2000) from the last Merovingian king, Dagobert II (c. 650–79).

Was the line of the Merovingians, extinct for 1,300 years, about to be re-established? Were the Merovingians descendants of the Tribe of Benjamin who had fled from Israel to France? And had France – no, Europe – finally discovered an heir worthy of its throne? And finally, who was Pierre Plantard, heir apparent of the Merovingian dynasty?

Plantard was born in Paris in 1920. His parents were both in domestic service, and he himself trained as a draughtsman. As an adolescent he was drawn to that very heady French mix of royalist ultra-nationalism and ultra-Catholicism. During World War Two (1939–45), when the Germans ran France through a collaborationist regime in Vichy, Plantard tried to form several associations with strong nationalistic, anti-Semitic and anti-Masonic agendas. Instead of being pleased, the German authorities banned him from doing so. When he went ahead anyway, the Germans had him arrested and sent to prison for four months. In 1951, Plantard married and moved to Annemasse in southeastern France. In 1953 he served a further six months in jail for fraud. If Plantard was a king in waiting, destiny was taking time in revealing her hand.

In May 1956, Plantard decided to give destiny a nudge, and founded a local association called the Priory of Sion, which he described grandly as a 'Catholic Knighthood for the Promotion of an Independent

**CATHOLIC KNIGHT OF SION**

Traditionalist Union'; however, the aims of the Priory turned out to be quite modest, as it limited itself to campaigning for low-cost social housing in Annemasse. The name 'Sion' was not a reference to Israel or Jerusalem, but to the nearby Mount Sion. According to the French state, the Priory of Sion was dissolved in the fall of 1956 and has not been officially active since that date. But the creation of the Priory of Sion was only the first strand of a complex weave of invention, deceit and forgery that Plantard and his accomplices Philippe de Chérisey (1923–85) and Gérard de Sède (1921–2004) would create during the next decade.

In the early 1960s, Plantard met Noël Corbu (1912–68), a restaurant owner in the small village of Rennes-le-Château in the Languedoc region of southwestern France. Corbu was famous in France for his role in promoting the story of Father François Bérenger Saunière (1852–1917), the village priest of Rennes-le-Château, who Corbu claimed had discovered an ancient treasure and documents while renovating his church in 1891. The truth was a little more sordid. Saunière was actually defrauding his parishioners, charging for masses for the dead that he never actually said. However, the legend was much more interesting and better for Corbu's business, and the French media lapped up the hidden treasure story. Plantard decided to use the legend to his own advantage by manufacturing the mysterious documents that Saunière was said to have found with the treasure. They concerned, naturally, the completely imaginary medieval Priory of Sion, and evidence of Plantard's own links to Dagobert II.

> THE LEGEND WAS MUCH MORE INTERESTING AND BETTER FOR CORBU'S BUSINESS, AND THE FRENCH MEDIA LAPPED UP THE HIDDEN TREASURE STORY.

Along with Philippe de Chérisey, Plantard created the *Dossiers Secrets* and planted them in the French National Library in 1967. At the same time, another accomplice, author Gérard de Sède, wrote *L'Or de Rennes, ou La Vie insolite de Bérenger Saunière, curé de Rennes-le-Château* (*The Gold of Rennes, or The Strange Life of Bérenger Saunière, Priest of Rennes-le-Château*), re-titled in paperback as the much snappier *Le Trésor maudit de Rennes-le-Château* (*The Accursed Treasure of Rennes-le-Château*), which published accounts of the mysterious documents and their great secret. The book became a bestseller in France and was translated into English.

All that Plantard now needed was a likely mark who would 'discover' the originals and make all the connections that Plantard intended him to. The man who fortuitously walked into the frame was Henry Lincoln (b. 1930), a scriptwriter who had worked on the TV show *Doctor Who*, who had become intrigued by Rennes-le-Château after reading *Le Trésor maudit*. In the 1970s, he teamed up with American author Richard Leigh (b. 1943) and New Zealander Michael Baigent (b. 1948) to investigate the affair further, and found Plantard's faked *Dossiers* in the Bibliothèque Nationale. They published the bestselling *Holy Blood, Holy Grail* in 1982. It is to this book, rather than the *Dossiers*, that Dan Brown owes the idea that Jesus had married Mary Magdalene, whose descendants survived in France, protected by the Priory of Sion. However, Brown's novel is a fictional account of a pseudo-history, which is itself based on a set of forged documents.

**HOLY FAKER**
The grave of Father Bérenger Saunière, who inspired Plantard's fantasies of lost royal bloodlines.

Was there even a remote chance that Plantard really was a descendant of Dagobert II? Well, very likely, as long as Dagobert had children. Several mathematicians and statisticians have worked out that most humans of European descent (including North Americans) are descended from the Emperor Charlemagne (742–814), who lived almost a century after Dagobert and was the second ruler of the Carolingian dynasty that replaced the Merovingians. Therefore, in a very small way, we are all descended from ancient kings, emperors and saints.

**DECEPTION**

Religious deceit

Military subterfuge

Financial fraud

**Fake or counterfeit**

Imposture or cross-dressing

Confidence trick

Scientific deception

# I'M READY FOR MY CLOSE-UP: THE PATTERSON–GIMLIN FILM

**Main Culprits:** Roger Patterson and Robert Gimlin

**Motivation:** Fame and financial reward

**Damage Done:** Has made people believe in a non-existent animal

*Every Bigfoot buff remembers seeing the film for the first time. I was living in the Bay Area at the time and got to see it on television in an advertisement imploring me to get down to the local theatre and see the whole thing on the big screen. For some Bigfoot aficionados, seeing the film would literally change their lives [...] It is arguable that had this movie never been made, the legend of Bigfoot would have ended up on the junkheap of American folklore, remembered but no longer embraced as a worthwhile legend.*

**From *Bigfoot Exposed* (2004) by D. J. Daegling**

The inclusion of the Patterson–Gimlin film in these pages will please some readers and annoy others, because there is as yet no incontrovertible proof that the film is a hoax. Quite to the contrary, many have strived in print, video and now on the Internet, to make the case that the footage is entirely genuine and could not have been faked with the technology available in the late 1960s. The cine film shot by Roger Patterson (1926–72) and Robert Gimlin (b. 1931) on 20 October 1967, at Bluff Creek in the Six Rivers National Forest in northern California, gave the world its first clear sighting of the ape-like animal popularly known as 'Bigfoot'.

Bigfoot is a 'cryptid', that is, an unknown animal species whose existence has not been scientifically documented. The other cryptids featured in this book include the Feejee Mermaid (pp. 78–81) and the Loch Ness Monster (pp. 133–8). The former was beyond doubt a fake purchased and exhibited by the great showman P. T. Barnum; the latter – 'Nessie' – has proved to be extremely elusive, and all of the photographic and film evidence of its existence produced so far has been shown to be fabricated.

Bigfoot is also known as the Sasquatch – a name that is derived from a Native American word for 'hairy giant'. There are tales of 'wild' or 'hairy' men in the traditions of the Native North Americans of the West Coast of the U.S. and Canada, but these are not particularly unusual in many pre-industrial cultures. The wild men in question may refer to real animals, such as the orangutan of Borneo in Indonesia, which is known to the locals as the 'old man of the forest', or to mythological creatures, similar to our own fairies, gnomes and elves. Between the late nineteenth and mid-twentieth centuries there were a few uncorroborated sightings and reports of attacks by Sasquatch, but not enough to generate much interest.

© Bettmann | Corbis

**LOOKING AT ME?**
Bigfoot casually looks over 'her' shoulder at the cameraman before 'she' retreats into the forest.

When construction worker Jerry Crew reported finding sets of 40-cm (16 inch) footprints near Bluff Creek in northern California in 1958, Bigfoot got its name and was splashed all over the newspapers. Crew and a friend made plaster casts, which became the basis for a whole Bigfoot mythology that rivalled the ufology of men like Adamski (pp. 145–50). Fifty years later, after Crew's then boss Ray Wallace died, his family revealed that Wallace had manufactured the prints as a prank by tying carved wooden feet to his shoes. But by then it was much too late: two camps had emerged, the Bigfoot sceptics and the Bigfoot believers.

**MONKEYING AROUND**

The most sensational piece of evidence for Bigfoot's existence is the Patterson–Gimlin film of 1967, which is available in several versions on the Internet. It is said that the camera never lies, and the film does show something rather unusual. The scene is an area of open ground on the banks of Bluff Creek (already famous from the footprints of 1958). The ground is fairly open, being covered with rocks and dead trees, thus good filming country. According to Patterson and Gimlin's testimony, they rode up to the creek on horseback and spotted the creature walking along the far bank. Patterson immediately jumped off his horse, pulled the cine camera out of his saddlebag, and began to film.

The film lasts for less than a minute, and the first few seconds are so shaky that it's impossible to say what you are watching. However, this is only to be expected as the astounded Patterson struggled to get his camera set up and working. The film settles down and shows a heavily built ape-like creature, covered in dark brown fur, walking away from the camera. The creature looks a bit like a gorilla, with heavy brows and a flat face, its long arms swinging from side to side as it strides away. However, it clearly is not a gorilla because it is fully bipedal (walking upright on two legs) like a human. The great apes – gorillas, orangutans and chimpanzees – though they can stand on their hind legs, usually use all four limbs for locomotion. The creature casually looks back towards the camera and then disappears into the forest.

Two things are striking about the creature in the film. The first is that it is apparently female, to judge by a large pair of fur-covered breasts. Again this makes it different from the great apes, whose breasts are not covered in fur. The second is that the creature does not seem fazed by the presence of two men on horseback. For an animal renowned for being so shy, and said to be so aggressive that it attacks humans, it is not running away or attacking. It walks away from the creek towards the undergrowth without any apparent rush or concern. At one point it looks over its shoulder at the cameraman.

Let us for a moment consider that the creature in the film is a true cryptid. What could it be? Our cousins, the great apes, evolved in Africa and Asia, and none are found in the Americas, where the largest primates are small monkeys found in Central and South America. Nor are there any extinct great apes in the North American fossil record. In any event, Bigfoot is a bit of an anatomical puzzle, having the fur, cranial characteristics and muscular bulk of a gorilla but an extremely upright human-like gait. Gorillas are anatomically very different from us and cannot walk in the manner of the creature in the film. Another problem is that all known apes evolved and currently live in the balmy climate of the tropics rather than in the cold of the northwestern U.S. and Canada.

**A HOMINID FAR FROM HOME**

Another theory is that Bigfoot is an early hominid (a human ancestor; see Piltdown Man, (pp. 85–90), which has somehow managed to hang on in the vast wildernesses of North America. The problems with this hypothesis are similar to those with Nessie being a dinosaur. Humanity's first bipedal ancestors appeared in Africa about 4 million years BP. It took them several million years to reach Asia and Europe. Humans did not arrive in the Americas until much later – at the earliest 50,000 years BP, but the more widely accepted date is around 12,000 years BP. As with the great apes, there are no hominids in the North American fossil record. Additionally, one of any creature is not much good, so there must be a sizeable population of Bigfoot, otherwise the species would have long ago become extinct. A large population of animals up to eight feet tall is difficult to hide, and even more difficult to feed adequately in the inhospitable wilderness of northwestern America.

Let us imagine that Bigfoot is something quite unique in the animal kingdom – neither great ape nor hominid – maybe a giant sloth. It would have existed in the Northwest for millions of years, and there would be more evidence that a few footprints, sightings and a shaky film – most of which date from 1958 or later. Paleontologists routinely dig up the fossilised skeletons of dinosaurs that lived over 65 million years BP, but they have been unable to find so much as a single bone, skull or tooth, recent or fossilised, of a giant creature that is supposed to walk through the forests of the Pacific coast. Although the area is indeed a vast wilderness, it is far from being untracked, as the sightings and Patterson–Gimlin film clearly demonstrate. Interestingly, since the late 1950s Bigfoot has been seen far away from home, in the Great Lakes area, Florida and Texas.

Turning to the film itself, many pages of scholarly opinion have been devoted to its analysis. Believers point out that the 'man in a gorilla-suit' jibe cannot be true because no one has ever been able to produce the suit or to recreate it. They say that you can see the muscles moving under

the skin and that a normal-sized human could not reproduce the gait of an animal over 2.1 m (seven feet) tall. Sceptics counter that it could be an extremely well-made suit thin enough to show the wearer's muscular movement, and that the problem of the gait is impossible to resolve because we do not have any accurate way of judging the creature's size, other than Patterson's testimony, or know the speed the film was shot at. Played at different speeds, the gait of the animal can be made to look more or less human. To my untutored eye, and taking in account the evidence given above about the lack of physical evidence for Bigfoot, I tend to agree with the man-in-an-ape-suit hypothesis.

**PRIME SUSPECT**
In many cases of Bigfoot sightings, a misidentified bear is probably the most likely explanation.

It is true that the hoaxers of 1967 did not have access to CGI technology and the sophisticated prosthetics, animatronics and make-up that are now routinely used in films. However, it is an interesting coincidence that just before Patterson shot the film, John Chambers (1923–2001), who produced Mr. Spock's ears for the original *Star Trek*, had created a set of Oscar-winning ape suits for the first *Planet of the Apes* movie released in 1968. The film was shot in Colorado and southern California between May and August 1967. Until his death, Chambers denied any involvement in the Patterson–Gimlin film, but it is not inconceivable that it was a man dressed in one of his extraordinarily lifelike costumes who took a stroll in Bluff Creek in October 1967.

# THE SEXUAL EVOLUTIONIST: DR. CHARLOTTE BACH

**DECEPTION**

Religious deceit

Military subterfuge

Financial fraud

Fake or counterfeit

**Imposture or cross-dressing**

Confidence trick

Scientific deception

**Main Culprit:** Karoly Hajdu

**Motivation:** Fame and recognition

**Damage Done:** Led to his early death from an undiagnosed cancer

*When he is a man he is, unlike the homosexual, masculine with all his manly virtues and shortcomings. When he is a woman he is the woman of his ideals, free of the grime of everyday life.*

**Excerpt from *Hypnosis* (1961) by Michael Karoly, a.k.a. Charlotte Bach**

The nature of human sexuality is a question that has fascinated and baffled some of the greatest minds in history. Sigmund Freud (1856–1939) placed it at the centre of his theory of psychoanalysis; Alfred Kinsey (1894–1956) spent a lifetime studying and recording its intricacies; and many contemporary researchers continue to theorise the relationship between biological sex, social gender and sexual orientation. As we have seen in the cases of the Chevalier/Chevalière d'Éon (pp. 63–7) and of Stanisława Walasiewicz (pp. 121–3), the determination of a person's sex and gender is not always straightforward. Although it is only fairly recently that a person's biological sex can be re-assigned (at least in terms of appearance if not function), to change social gender, a person need only change his or her clothes, voice and mannerisms.

According to Charles Darwin (1809–82) sexual selection played a central role in evolution. He argued that the competition between animals and humans for mates was what drove evolution forward. This theory is not universally endorsed, and several alternatives have been put forward. One of the most controversial of these anti-Darwinian theories was advanced by Dr. Charlotte Bach (1920–81), a Hungarian émigré living in the United Kingdom. But Charlotte was not everything she seemed and turned out to be the living embodiment of the theory that she advocated.

IT WAS ONLY AFTER HER DEATH IN 1981 THAT THE TRUTH ABOUT BACH WAS FINALLY REVEALED..

It was only after her death in 1981 that the truth about Bach was finally revealed. She had no academic qualifications, and she was not biologically female. Bach was born in 1920 in the town of Kipest, near the Hungarian capital of Budapest, and was christened as a boy under the name of Karoly Hajdu. His father was a tailor by profession, who opened a shop in Budapest when Karoly was three years old. Karoly was a bright schoolboy but something of an oddball even as a child. He had no friends his own age other than his siblings. Although he had dropped out of school early, when he received his draft papers in 1941 – when Hungary had joined World War Two (1939–45) on the German side – he managed to get a student exemption. Meanwhile, his father's tailoring business was prospering and attracting a high-class clientele.

Like others in this book who realised that an accident of birth can make the difference between social status, fame, wealth and power, or poverty and obscurity, he decided to re-invent himself. A forged birth certificate and expensive-looking visiting cards transformed Karoly from a humble mister into a baron. During the war, the fascist Hungarian government deported hundreds of thousands of Jews, sending them to their deaths in Nazi extermination camps. All the while, Karoly was making good money without apparently working for it. He was suspected of looting abandoned houses in Budapest's large Jewish ghetto. He left Hungary, like many of his fellow-countrymen and women, when the Moscow-backed communist government took over after the war. His destination was Britain, where he arrived in 1948.

In Britain, Karoly became the impeccably dressed Baron Carl Hajdu. He held down several jobs before moving to London where he married and opened a lettings agency. During the anti-communist Hungarian uprising of 1956, Hajdu collected money for Hungarian freedom fighters, but when the money vanished, he was convicted of fraud and declared bankrupt. Unabashed, Hajdu re-invented himself again, this time as the hypnotherapist Michel Karoly. His good looks and suave manner soon attracted a well-to-do clientele, and he became an 'agony uncle' for a leading British magazine. He prospered until the sudden death of his wife and stepson in 1965. He had a breakdown, was again declared bankrupt, and served a short term in prison.

Karoly had in turn been Carl Hajdu and Michel Karoly, but on his release from jail he effected his most far-reaching transformation: from male to female. Karoly had had transvestite episodes throughout his life, but in 1968, unencumbered with a wife and family, he decided that he would henceforth live as a woman. He chose the persona of Dr. Charlotte Bach. The transformation was a difficult one to pull off. She was tall for a woman at 1.8m (5'11"), and had a masculine appearance and a deep voice. However, she played her new role with such confidence that everyone she met thought that she was a woman, albeit a very masculine one, whom many thought to be a lesbian.

**HOMO MUTANS, HOMO LUMINENS**

Charlotte awarded herself the title of doctor, claiming to have been a lecturer at one of Budapest's leading universities before the communist takeover. She also told her friends that she was a widow who had lost both husband and son in 1965 – accurate apart from the sexes of the people concerned. In 1971, she produced a 521-page manuscript entitled *Homo Mutans, Homo Luminens* (*Man the Changer, Man the Light-bringer*), outlining a revolutionary theory of evolution that she called 'human ethology'.

The theory's main proposition is that humans, being divided into male and female, experience an intense and destabilising separation anxiety. This creates a drive in both men and women to become a member of the opposite sex – a union that must perpetually escape them as long as they are trapped in one sexual and gender identity. Individuals deal with this dilemma in different ways: some develop a drive to dominate the environment and their fellow humans; others challenge established practices and values to create new ways of being human.

**DEVIANTS**
Gay Lib campaigners of the 1970s enthusiastically adopted the Bach theories of evolution through deviation.

These behavioural deviations can be expressed either negatively or positively. For example, homosexuality, though it is non-reproductive, can contribute to reproductive behaviour. Anticipating gay marriage and adoption, Bach foresaw that gays and lesbians could have their own children, or, if childless, could play their part as teachers and carers of the children of others. The conclusion of *Homo Mutans* is that the resolution of the universal bisexual tension through sexual deviation from the heterosexual norm is the mainspring of evolution and a key source of human creativity and cultural development.

Although her writing style was ungrammatical and often difficult to follow, her ideas attracted considerable interest among both academics and laymen. During the 1970s she gave talks at her home in north London, and she was invited to lecture at several universities, including Cambridge and Sussex. The members of the nascent British Gay Liberation movement also picked up on human ethology, as they found that her ideas supported their own struggle for acceptance by mainstream society.

In the last ten years of her life, Charlotte Bach attained an intellectual respectability verging on cult status. The author Colin Wilson (b. 1931) was one of her admirers, saying that Bach's work was worthy of a Nobel Prize and as significant as Einstein's Theory of Relativity.

# GHOSTING HUGHES: CLIFFORD IRVING

**DECEPTION**

Religious deceit

Military subterfuge

Financial fraud

**Fake or counterfeit**

Imposture or cross-dressing

Confidence trick

Scientific deception

**Main Culprit:** Clifford Irving

**Motivation:** Fame and financial gain

**Damage Done:** Embarrassed McGraw-Hill; earned its authors a prison term

*This must go down in history. I only wish I were still in the movie business, because I don't remember any script as wild or as stretching the imagination as this yarn has turned out to be. I don't know what's in [the book]. I don't know [the author].*

**Excerpt from Howard Hughes' televised broadcast denying the authenticity of Irving's autobiography**

We have seen that financial gain is not the only motive for the deceptions featured in this book. Sometimes the person concerned was making a point – that he or she was as good as a past master or at least good enough to deceive the experts. Take the cases of the William Ireland (pp. 58–62) and Marius Casadesus (pp. 129–32). The motive behind this latest case of literary forgery was not purely money, though a considerable sum in cash did change hands, but it was also a gigantic hoax on the publishing world and on one of the twentieth century's most enigmatic of billionaires, the eccentric Howard Hughes (1905–76). The perpetrator of the hoax was the American writer Clifford Irving (b. 1930), a man whom we have already met as the author of the biography of art forger Elmyr de Hory (pp. 151–5).

Industrialist, engineer, film director, aviator and philanthropist, Howard Hughes was the embodiment of the American dream. He was born in Texas, the son of a successful businessman and inventor, who had made a fortune in manufacturing equipment for the oil industry. Like his father, Hughes was a gifted engineer. Aged 11, he built a radio transmitter – said to be the first in Houston, Texas – as well as another Texas first,

a 'motorised bicycle'. At the age of 14 he was already taking flying lessons, anticipating his love of all things aeronautical in years to come. He was orphaned while still a minor, losing his mother in 1922 and his father in 1925. Although he had not reached his twenty-first birthday – then the age of civil majority – he obtained control of his father's business at the age of 19. He immediately dropped out of college, got married, and moved to Hollywood to try and make it in the film business. Unlike other Hollywood hopefuls, however, Hughes had the advantage of a considerable fortune to back up his talent and ambitions.

**VICTIM**
Howard Hughes in better days, before he became the eccentric recluse who lived naked in his Las Vegas penthouse.

Hughes turned out to be a gifted film director and producer. He made a string of hit movies between the late 1920s and early 1940s, including the Oscar-winning comedy *Two Arabian Nights* (1927), and the Western *The Outlaw* (1943), which launched the career of actor Jane Russell (b. 1921). He divorced his first wife in 1929, and henceforth associated with some of the most glamorous actors of the day, including Bette Davis (1908–89), Ava Gardner (1922–90) and Katherine Hepburn

(1907–2003). However, his lifelong passion remained designing, building and flying airplanes. He famously built what was then the world's largest powered aircraft, *The Spruce Goose*, which only flew once before being mothballed; set several flying records; and bought a controlling stake in TWA, which he transformed into one of the world's leading airlines.

Hughes seemed to be the man who had everything – wealth, power, fame; the most beautiful and glamorous women at his beck and call; and excitement from his many aviation achievements – but at the same time he was a deeply disturbed individual, whose mental eccentricities became more and more pronounced as he grew older. Hughes suffered from OCD (obsessive-compulsive disorder), which when combined with huge amounts of power and money made for a very dangerous combination. He became reclusive and obsessive about his health, spent long periods of time naked, and refused to shave or cut his hair and nails. He moved anonymously from hotel suite to hotel suite, and famously bought the Desert Inn in Las Vegas, Nevada, which became the nerve centre of his financial empire. By 1972, Hughes had disappeared from public life for over a decade. At that moment, Clifford Irving approached publisher McGraw-Hill with the extraordinary news that the reclusive Hughes had approached him to ghost his autobiography.

Irving was born in New York, the son of a magazine cartoon artist. He graduated from Cornell, where he set his first novel, *On a Darkling Plain* (1956). He published his second, *The Losers* (1958), while he was working as a copy-editor for the *New York Times*. Although neither book was a bestseller, they were very favorably reviewed. He published his third novel, *The Valley*, in 1960. Having established his literary reputation, he travelled around the world and married and divorced several times. He seemed to be destined to be a moderately successful, critically respected author of the bohemian 1960s, sharing his time between the U.S. and Europe. It was when he was living on the Mediterranean island of Ibiza during the late 1960s that he met forger Elmyr de Hory and wrote his biography, *Fake!* (1969), which was later made into a documentary film by Orson Welles.

It is possible that Irving's encounter with de Hory gave him the idea of forging the autobiography of the reclusive Howard Hughes.

**TRUE LIES, FALSE TRUTHS**

He and fellow author Richard Suskind (d. 1999) decided to fake the book, believing that Hughes was too ill or camera-shy to denounce the autobiography as a forgery. Suskind did the bulk of the research, while Irving exercised his considerable talents as a forger and confidence trickster to sell the idea to the rather staid New York publishing house, McGraw-Hill. He needed proof that Hughes had commissioned him to write an autobiography, so he began by forging a letter from Hughes, which he faked by imitating published samples of Hughes' handwriting. Irving took the precaution of having Hughes request that the project remain a secret until close to the publication date.

McGraw-Hill, unable to believe its luck, because a no-holds-barred autobiography of the reclusive Hughes was sure to be the publishing sensation of the decade, agreed to pay Irving $100,000 and Hughes $665,000 – even at 1970 prices, it was a bargain. The publisher paid by cheque, which Irving's wife deposited in a Swiss bank account under the false name of 'H. R. Hughes'. The forgers set to work. Suskind obtained all the published material on Hughes, as well as the private files of Time-Life, and the unpublished memoirs of Hughes' former business manager Noah Dietrich (1889–1982), which Irving obtained by deception. At the same time, to keep up the pretence, Irving travelled to remote, exotic locations for supposed 'interviews' with Hughes.

**TO KEEP UP THE PRETENCE, IRVING TRAVELLED TO REMOTE, EXOTIC LOCATIONS FOR SUPPOSED 'INTERVIEWS' WITH HUGHES.**

Irving and Suskind delivered the Hughes autobiography at the end of 1971. Irving had been careful to include further forged handwritten notes by Hughes with the manuscript to convince the publisher and the experts it had employed to confirm the authenticity of the material. Satisfied, McGraw-Hill decided to rush the book for publication, announcing the title for its spring 1972 list, and selling the serialisation rights to Time-Life's *Life* magazine. Now that McGraw-Hill and Life had gone public, it was crunch time for Irving and Suskind. Would Hughes come out of seclusion to challenge the book, or would he, as they hoped, stay quiet for fear of the storm of intrusive publicity it would trigger?

At first, all seemed to be going to plan. Acquaintances and staffers of the billionaire declared that the autobiography must be a fake but without a categorical denial from Hughes himself, nothing could be proved. The controversy raged in the media, with opinions for and against. McGraw-Hill and Time-Life had a handwriting expert check out Hughes' letters and notes, and he declared them to be genuine. Irving even submitted to a lie-detector test, which he managed to pass. Meanwhile, the great man remained silent through the dying months of 1971.

By January, however, Hughes finally lost patience with the Irving circus. He contacted seven journalists who had known him before his retirement from the world and organised for them to be televised taking a conference call from him in the Bahamas. During the broadcast Hughes denounced Irving (see quote), but Irving countered that the man in the broadcast was an impostor. Outraged, Hughes sued Irving, McGraw-Hill and Time-Life. Irving continued to deny everything, but Hughes' money had a very long reach. The Swiss authorities investigated a deposit of $750,000 under the name of 'H(elga) R. Hughes', identifying Irving's wife as the mysterious depositor. Irving confessed at the end of January. He and Suskind were convicted of fraud. Irving served 17 months in jail, and repaid the advance to McGraw-Hill; Suskind, as the junior partner, got six months. After his release, Irving picked up his writing career and published several bestsellers. He told the story behind the Hughes autobiography in *The Hoax* (1981), which was made into a film of the same name in 2007, starring Richard Gere as Irving.

© Getty Images

As for Hughes, he had only four unhappy years left to live. He died, appropriately maybe, onboard an aircraft in April 1976. He weighed a mere 41 kg (90 pounds), and his long toe and fingernails, hair and beard made him unrecognisable from the picture of the dashing aviator and film director of the 1930s and 40s. The man who had it all died of kidney failure aggravated by an addiction to painkilling drugs and malnutrition.

**HOAXERS**
Irving (left) and Suskind hoped that the maverick Hughes was too ill or reclusive to denounce the forgery.

**DECEPTION**

Religious deceit

Military subterfuge

Financial fraud

**Fake or counterfeit**

Imposture or cross-dressing

Confidence trick

Scientific deception

# CEREAL KILLERS: CROP CIRCLES

**Main Culprits:** Doug Bower and Dave Chorley

**Motivation:** Fame and fun

**Damage Done:** Made millions believe in UFOs

*One summer's evening in 1978 after several pints in the Percy Hobbs [pub] Doug Bower and Dave Chorley were taking the air on a bridle path on the Longwood Estate, near Cheesefoot Head. They were talking about UFOs. Bower (who used to live in Melbourne, Australia) recalled a case in Queensland, where a UFO had reportedly ascended from a swirled nest of marsh-grass. 'What do you think would happen if we put a nest over there?' Bower joked to Chorley, pointing to a nearby wheatfield. 'People would think a flying saucer had landed.'*

**Jim Schnabel quoted on Circlemakers.org**

Certain beliefs are infectious. We have seen earlier that one sighting can trigger a nationwide outbreak. Immediately after the Loch Ness Monster (pp. 133–8) was first spotted, after centuries of obscurity, Nessie was popping up in the loch morning, noon and night to pose for photos and film. At least Nessie had the decency to stay in situ in Scotland, not migrate across the country like her American cryptid cousin, Bigfoot (pp. 190–4), who has been seen far from his/her original home in the cold, wooded Northwest all the way to the tropical swamps of the Southeast. Similarly, once the first postwar flying saucer (see George Adamski, pp. 145–50) had been spotted in American skies in 1947, people were beating downs the doors of newspaper offices to report UFO sightings, and later close encounters and flights with their alien occupants. A great many of these sightings were conscious hoaxes, and the remainder can be explained as misidentifications of natural phenomena, birds, planes or other man-made objects.

The subject of this article – crop circles – however, is slightly different, because to believers they represent the physical evidence of UFOs or other paranormal phenomena that seem to be so difficult to document in any other way. To give a brief explanation to the uninitiated, a crop circle is a circle – though usually now a complex pattern of circles and other geometric shapes – that is found in mature fields of cereals such as corn, rye and barley in the summer months before harvest. The phenomenon was first observed in the UK in the 1970s, but in the past three decades crop circles have been reported all over the world. The first crop circles were fairly small and simple affairs but they rapidly became more complex and larger, sometimes occupying entire fields and with so many elements that the casual observer cannot imagine how they have been made without any telltale tracks or other signs of human involvement.

Let us look at the different hypotheses that circle believers have put forward. The least paranormal explanation is that they are caused by some kind of rare and as yet unobserved natural phenomenon – ball lightning, localised tornados, hail, freak winds, a sudden drop in atmospheric pressure – which could explain why crops are flattened in a circular pattern. If crop circles were restricted to simple circle shapes that explanation might hold water. Nature does create many regular shapes,

**LEY LINES, FAIRY RINGS AND UFO NESTS**

including spirals, ovals and circles, but some of the highly complex patterns that have been created would require a level of coincidence similar to that of Hamlet being written by a bunch of monkeys hitting computer keyboards at random – something theoretically possible if you had several billion years and several billion monkeys to spare.

Another perfectly natural phenomenon, despite its name, that has been put forward as an explanation is the 'fairy ring', which is a circular growth of fungi found in forest clearings. Fairy rings, however, are not known to occur in cereal crops. More fancifully, fairies, goblins, elves, ghosts, demons and spirits have also been identified as the possible creators of crop circles. The fairy folk are known to be mischievous, often verging on the downright destructive. However, since the beginning of the twenty-first century, very few people above the age of four will readily admit that they believe in elves or fairies. More respectable than fairies are the New Age beliefs in the mysterious earth currents known as ley lines first described by Alfred Watkins (1855–1935) in 1921. Leys criss-cross the British countryside, linking natural features and ancient megalithic sites. Watkins believed that leys were geodetic energy conduits linking sites of power. However, the most rigorous scientific investigations have failed to reveal any evidence of the existence of leys or the energies they are supposed to transmit. The most popular explanation put forward by circle believers, however, is that they are evidence of UFO activity – either as the physical evidence of landing sites, or patterns created by the UFOs' occupants remotely for reasons best known to themselves.

**DO-IT-YOURSELF CIRCLES**

Circles continued to appear through the 1980s, with a particular concentration in the south of England, in the counties of Hampshire and Wiltshire, which are both known for their ancient sites, including the prehistoric site of Stonehenge and the evocative ruins of Glastonbury Abbey, which is closely associated with the Arthurian legend. In 1991, Doug Bower and Dave Chorley, two practical jokers from Southampton, Hampshire, admitted that they had been responsible for the outbreak of crop circles in the locality (see quote). They explained that they created their first circle with nothing more sophisticated than planks, rope, hats and bits of wire.

At first the pair created simple circles that mimicked supposed UFO landing sites known as 'UFO nests'. But when the British media began to speculate that the circles were caused by natural phenomena, they decided to execute much more complex patterns that contained straight lines that could not be explained away so simply. These new circles attracted considerable media interest, and journalists and believers flocked to the area in the hope of seeing a UFO in the act of circle creation. So far, these hopes have been disappointed.

Websites such as Circlemakers (circlemakers.org) give instructions on how to go about making your own crop circles. To make a simple circle, position a collaborator at the centre point of the circle with one end of the string, hold the other end, and flatten the stalks of grain with a plank. Chorley and Bower claimed that they could create a 12 m (40 feet) circle in about a quarter of an hour. Naturally with more people, more rope, measuring tapes, sighting devices, and more planks, you can go to town with the number of circles or the patterns you can create. A complex pattern requires forward planning and sighting devices, but ultimately all you are doing is scaling up from a paper design onto the blank canvas of a cornfield.

Circles of great complexity continue to appear worldwide, though the southern UK remains a crop-circle hotspot in the late summer. Famous circles include the Cambridge (UK) 'Mandelbrot circle' of 1991 and the South African 'BMW circle' of 1993. All so far have proved to be hoaxes – with the perpetrators filming themselves to catch out circle believers who have confidently announced that this time, the circle has to be the real thing. Despite these repeated disappointments, believers continue to argue that a few circles are too complex, or that there is no way that humans could have created them without being spotted or leaving evidence. Given human ingenuity, we can discount the former, and as for the latter, all you need is that most paranormal of instruments, the household broom, to hide your tracks.

**COMPLEXITY**
From simple designs, crop circles evolved into ever more complex patterns with no conceivable natural explanation.

© Creative Commons | Hansueli Krapf

Let us say, for the sake of argument, that a few circles are genuine mysteries – just as not all UFOs are weather balloons, clouds or flocks of birds. Let us imagine that we are aliens. We have travelled hundreds if not thousands of light years across the galaxy for a spot of interstellar tourism and come across a planet inhabited by sentient (if slightly loopy) life forms. Needless to say, we have awesome technology, meaning that we are able to remain undetected by all usual means such as radar and satellite tracking (unless the government is hushing up our visit, of course). But nevertheless we want to leave the earthlings a calling card, or merely want to somehow record our passing like the vandals who carve their initials on national monuments and trees. So what do we do? We find a cereal field and create an interesting pattern before heading back to Zeta Reticuli. There is one thing that we know about visiting aliens, which is that they must have summer holidays like us, because they always seem to visit in the late summer and early autumn. Perhaps Mars is a better winter destination for E.T.

**THEY MUST HAVE SUMMER HOLIDAYS LIKE US, BECAUSE THEY ALWAYS SEEM TO VISIT IN THE LATE SUMMER AND EARLY AUTUMN.**

Like UFO, Bigfoot and Nessie believers, circle faithful have a strong need to believe. They analyse the minutiae of sightings and evidence, getting bogged down in arguments about details without looking at the bigger picture, which is why aliens + spaceships + super technology = crop circles in cereal fields? The answer is, unless our alien visitors have a very strange sense of humour, or use cereal crops on their own home worlds as a sort of answerphone message: 'Came to your planet, you were out, we left you this interesting geometric pattern in a field in Hampshire', then crop circles are invariably clever human hoaxes.

# LUCK OF THE DEVIL: NICK PERRY

**DECEPTION**

Religious deceit

Military subterfuge

Financial fraud

Fake or counterfeit

Imposture or cross-dressing

**Confidence trick**

Scientific deception

**Main Culprits:** Nick Perry, Edward Plevel, Peter and Jack Maragos, Joseph Bock and Fred Luman

**Motivation:** Financial gain

**Damage Done:** Defrauded Pennsylvania Lottery players and beneficiaries

*The most popular Pennsylvania Lottery game was and is the Daily Number. Introduced March 1, 1977, it was the first of the Lottery's numbers games where players selected their own three-digit number. In addition, it was the first time players learned whether or not they were winners through a live, televised drawing of the Daily Number, broadcast six nights a week at 7 pm.*

**From the History page of the official Pennsylvania lottery website, which is strangely quiet about the 'Triple Six Fix'**

© iStockphoto

A lottery to raise money for the state or a good cause is not a new idea. There were lotteries in ancient China and Rome. The first early-modern lottery dates from fifteenth-century Europe, and the first one in the Americas from the early seventeenth. Lotteries thrived in the United States through to the late nineteenth century, but then scandals and mismanagement brought the whole institution into disrepute, leading to a complete ban in 1900. The first modern lottery in the U.S. was started by the state of New Hampshire in 1964. At the time of writing there are lotteries in 42 states, in DC, and several U.S. territories, as well as several interstate lotteries. The lottery that concerns us here is the lottery of the Commonwealth of Pennsylvania that began in 1972.

We should all know that the probabilities of winning a lottery jackpot are many millions to one. When our numbers fail to come up once again, we can comfort ourselves with the thought that the proceeds of the lottery go to good causes. In the case of the Penn State lottery, the beneficiaries were the senior citizens of the state. The lottery operated several games, but in 1980, the most popular was the 'Daily Number' game. Players picked their own three-digit number and could purchase a ticket costing from 50¢ to $5. If they matched the number exactly, the payout was 500 to 1 (so up to $25,000). If they matched fewer numbers or had the numbers in the wrong order, they would scoop between 50 and 160 to 1.

**NUMBERS GAME**
John Travolta as Nick Perry in the movie version of the 666 lottery fraud, *Lucky Numbers*

Not everybody was happy with the odds offered by the Pennsylvania Lottery, however. Nick Perry (1916–2003) and his accomplices decided to give Lady Luck a helping hand by 'fixing' the televised Daily Number draw for the evening of 24 April 1980. The scam was a clever one, and had the conspirators been a little less greedy, they might have got away with it.

You would think that fixing a televised lottery draw would be nigh on impossible. The first people you'd have to fool would be the millions of eagle-eyed viewers in the state who tuned in to watch the Daily Number broadcast daily at 6.58 pm; then there were the people working in the studio – the technicians, production staff and gofers – and the Pennsylvania senior who started the draw; and finally the state official who was always present to ensure fair play. The machine and balls were kept under lock and key when not in use. The whole system should have been tamper-proof, shouldn't it? There were just too many people around to involve them all in a conspiracy.

Nick Perry was a native of Pittsburgh of American-Greek extraction. His real name was Nicholas Pericles Katsafanas. He went into broadcasting after serving in the U.S. Navy during World War Two (1939–45). He joined Pittsburgh's WTAE-TV in 1958, starting as an announcer and later becoming a news and sports presenter. In 1977, he became the host of the daily live broadcast of the Pennsylvania Lottery draw, held in the studios of the TV station. As the host of the draw show, Perry was in the ideal position to work out a scam, and three years into his tenure, he came up with what should have been a foolproof plan.

To rig a lottery in which players have to pick six numbers from 1 to 49 would be very difficult without anyone noticing, so Perry chose the Daily Number, which only requires three numbers to come up. The balls used in lottery draws are numbered ping-pong balls. Perry worked out that if the balls were weighted, they would fly up as normal but be just a little too heavy to be drawn into the vacuum tube that pulled the winning numbers out of the machines. In order to ensure that a single-number combination such as 999 would be picked, the balls from 0 to 8 would have to be weighted, but Perry thought this would be too risky, so he opted to tamper with eight out of the ten balls, leaving the 4 and 6 balls untouched. This reduced the number of possible winning combinations to the eight combinations of four and six: 444, 446, 464, 466, 644, 646, 664, and the 'number of the beast', 666.

Perry needed several accomplices to put his plan into motion. He first subverted Joseph Bock, who was WTAE-TV's art director, and got him to make a duplicate set of balls for the 24 April draw. Bock weighted eight of the balls by injecting them with a small amount of latex paint and then applied the numbers, exactly duplicating the original set. Next Perry needed unhindered access to the drawing machine to do the switch. His second accomplice was Pennsylvania Lottery official Edward Plevel, who agreed to leave the machine unattended at key stages during the evening. WTAE-TV staffer Fred Luman was brought in to switch the balls both before and after the draw. Bock was to burn

**SCREWBALLS**

the balls immediately after they had served their criminal purpose. Finally, Perry needed someone unconnected with the station or the lottery to buy lottery tickets. He gave this task to his business associates, the Maragos brothers, who went around the state the day of the draw betting heavily on the eight possible numbers.

The fixed draw went exactly to plan. With Plevel turning a blind eye, Luman switched the balls. Perry announced the draw as usual, and it was made by Pennsylvania senior Violet Lowery, who was totally unaware that she was taking part in a fraud watched by around six million viewers. Luman switched the balls back, and Bock destroyed the duplicate set. Now all that Perry and his crew had to do was to collect their winnings, estimated to be around $1.8 million. However, the Maragos brothers had been greedy and careless. They told many of their friends and relations to bet on the eight numbers, and the unusual betting pattern alerted the authorities that something was up. Worse, they made a pay-phone call to the TV station while buying a large number of tickets from a bar. The call was traced to the studio's announcer's booth, implicating Perry in the fix.

THE UNUSUAL BETTING PATTERN ALERTED THE AUTHORITIES THAT SOMETHING WAS UP.

Luman and Bock pleaded guilty in exchange for lighter sentences, and the Maragos brothers turned state's evidence to avoid imprisonment. The whole conspiracy was exposed, although until his death Perry denied any involvement in the affair. Plevel went to jail for two years, while Perry was sentenced to seven years for criminal conspiracy, criminal mischief, theft by deception, rigging a publicly exhibited contest, and perjury.

# WHEN MAGGIE PHONED RONNIE: THATCHERGATE

**DECEPTION**

Religious deceit

Military subterfuge

Financial fraud

**Fake or counterfeit**

Imposture or cross-dressing

Confidence trick

Scientific deception

**Main Culprits:** Crass

**Motivation:** Political hoax

**Damage Done:** Embarrassed the media and the U.S. intelligence community who blamed the KGB

*Ronald Reagan: 'Oh, God, it's not right! You caused the Sheffield to have been hit. Those missiles we followed on screens. You must have too, and not let them know. What do you hope to gain?'*

**Excerpt from the Thatchergate tape**

Cast your mind back almost three decades to the heady days of the early 1980s: punk rock, unrestrained free-market capitalism and nuclear Armageddon were all on the agenda, and the whole show was run by the most famous political double act of the century: the 40th president of the Union (1981–89), Ronald Reagan (1911–2004), and Britain's first and only female prime minister (1979–90), Margaret Thatcher (b. 1925). The two leaders – the 'Iron Lady' and the affable Hollywood actor turned politician – were on the best of terms and met and conversed often.

In the days before the Internet, Skype and mobile phones, people had to rely on fixed telephones, which were often subject to 'crossed lines' – a 'leak' of part or all of a conversation from one line to another. In 1982, Dutch journalists received an anonymous tape purporting to be a recording of part of a conversation between President Reagan and Prime Minister Thatcher. The call was garbled, incomplete and difficult to follow because of the high levels of interference and extraneous noise, but the voices were instantly recognisable. The period was dominated by two major events: the Falklands War (April–June 1982) and the Soviet–American spat over Intermediate Nuclear Forces (INF), and the taped exchange dealt with both in a rather startling fashion.

**BATTLESHIPS AND BOMBS**

The conversation begins with a discussion of events during the Falklands War. The Falkland Islands (Islas Malvinas in Spanish) is a barren archipelago deep in the South Atlantic, about as far away from anywhere as you can get, and populated largely by sheep. The nearest mainland – Argentina – is 480 km (300 miles) to the west. By an accident of history, the Falklands-Malvinas have been British since the early nineteenth century but also claimed by Argentina. In April 1982, the right-wing dictatorship of General Galtieri (1926–2003) launched an invasion of the islands, believing that the British government was too far away and too hard-up to intervene. Margaret Thatcher, however, saw it as the ideal opportunity to make political capital during tough times at home. She sent a British taskforce to regain control of the islands.

Although the U.S., a close ally of both Argentina and Britain, was trying to broker a deal through negotiation, all hopes of peace evaporated when a British submarine sank the Argentine warship the *General Belgrano* with the loss of over 300 lives. Two days later, an Argentine missile hit the British warship HMS *Sheffield*, with the loss of 24 lives. In the tape, Reagan refers to both these incidents that took place in the early days of the war, implying that Thatcher had deliberately targeted the *Belgrano* in order to scupper the American peace efforts. Thatcher is heard to say, 'Argentina was the invader! Force has been used. It's been used now, punishing them as quickly as possible.' Reagan then accuses Thatcher of allowing the *Sheffield* to be hit to ensure that there would be an armed conflict between the two countries.

The conversation then moves on to U.S. nuclear policy in the event of a Soviet-led invasion of Europe. The early 1980s were a period of heightened tension between the U.S. and NATO on one side and the Soviet Union and Warsaw Pact countries on the other. The fall of the Berlin Wall and the end of Communism were still a decade away. The Strategic Arms Limitation treaties (SALT I and II) had been only partially effective in reducing the nuclear arsenals of the U.S. and Soviet Union. At this point in the tape, Reagan says chillingly, 'In conflict, we will launch missiles on allies for effective limitation of the Soviet Union.' This meant that the U.S. would target European countries to deter a Soviet attack. The last few garbled phrases suggest that the president might even consider bombing London if necessary.

**MAGGIE AND RON**
Thatcher and Reagan were such close friends that they met and spoke on the phone frequently.

Explosive stuff, had the tape proved to be genuine. However, the Dutch journalists to whom it was sent were immediately sceptical. A subsequent examination of the tape revealed that it was not the recording of a conversation, but a complete fabrication created from edited portions of speeches by both leaders that had been spliced together. The U.S. State Department immediately pointed the finger at the Soviet intelligence service, the KGB, which was well known for producing fake documents. A manufactured tape would have been a first for the technologically fairly basic KGB, but the U.S. and UK press also ran with the Soviet fake explanation.

In 1984, the British Sunday newspaper, *The Observer*, which then had a reputation for investigative journalism, revealed that the Thatchergate tape was not a dastardly Soviet plot but had been put together by members of the rock band Crass in a farmhouse in the small English town of Epping, Essex, just outside London. The band was formed in 1977, describing itself as 'anarcho-punk', with a strong feminist, anti-racist, anti-war, anti-consumerist and anti-globalisation agenda. Crass didn't expect the kind of reaction the tapes elicited from the U.S. government and the media. Interviewed later, one of the band members said: 'Feedback from that was more than we thought it would be. We just really didn't think people would be taken in by it. It just goes to show what you can do.' Another member added in justification: 'We believe that although the tape is a hoax what is said in it is in effect true. We were amazed that the tape had been attributed to the KGB.' The band disbanded in 1984.

THE BAND DESCRIBED ITSELF AS 'ANARCHO-PUNK', WITH A STRONG FEMINIST, ANTI-RACIST, ANTI-WAR, ANTI-CONSUMERIST AND ANTI-GLOBALISATION AGENDA.

# 'TO DO TODAY: INVADE POLAND': THE HITLER DIARIES

**DECEPTION**

Religious deceit

Military subterfuge

Financial fraud

**Fake or counterfeit**

Imposture or cross-dressing

Confidence trick

Scientific deception

**Main Culprits:** Konrad Kujau and Gerd Heidemann

**Motivation:** Financial gain

**Damage Done:** Embarrassed the media and senior historians who believed the diaries to be genuine

Though word of the story had spread for several days, the blood-red banner headline was startling. Proclaimed West Germany's raffish picture magazine Stern: HITLER'S DIARIES DISCOVERED. To trumpet its acquisition of 62 volumes dated from 1932 to 1945, the entire span of Hitler's Third Reich, Stern summoned more than 200 print and television reporters from around the world to its art deco headquarters in Hamburg. There, at a self-congratulatory three-hour press conference, Editor-in-Chief Peter Koch announced: 'I am 100% convinced that Hitler wrote every single word in those books.'

**Excerpt from 'Hitler's Diaries: Real or Fake?' Time, 9 May 1983**

There is something vaguely depressing about the interest some people have in collecting the mementos of psychotic criminals, serial killers and mass murderers. An area of this type of trade that has flourished in the past sixty years is Nazi memorabilia – insignia, uniforms, documents and weapons.

In Germany, the collecting of Nazi memorabilia is illegal, adding the spice of criminality to this rather bizarre pastime. Underground networks of dealers cater for the trade, and wherever the merchandise is clandestine, there is a ready-made opportunity for the forger to hoodwink customers with fake goods. The surprising thing about the affair of the *Hitler Diaries*, whose publication was proudly announced to the world by the editor of Germany's *Stern* magazine in 1983 (see quote) is that no one had thought of doing it earlier.

Germany's Chancellor, Adolf Hitler, who in 1934 awarded himself the title of *Führer* (Leader), was not noted for his literary endeavours. He wrote *Mein Kampf* (*My Struggle*) in 1925. Even that fervent admirer of Hitler, the Italian dictator Benito Mussolini (1883–1945), described the

book as 'a boring tome that I have never been able to read,' filled with 'little more than commonplace clichés.' Hitler was a master of propaganda and self-aggrandisement, but he owed this to his talents as a demagogue and not to the merits of his prose or the incisiveness of his intellect. There are many surviving film and sound archives of the dictator, carefully crafted by his Minister of Propaganda, Joseph Goebbels (1897–1945).

In the dying days of the war, with the Soviet Red Army just hours away from capturing him, Hitler cheated the executioner by shooting himself in the head while biting into a cyanide capsule. SS officers burned his body, along with that of his wife, Eva. Berlin surrendered two days later,

**FÜHRER**
Hitler was not a noted author; even fellow dictator Mussolini thought his prose was execrable.

and the Russians removed Hitler's remains and buried them in secret. Whatever documents were left unburned in Hitler's bunker fell into Russian hands. There is no record in the available Russian archives of any personal papers left by the German dictator.

Still, there is nothing to say that Hitler did not keep a diary to record the significant events of his political and military career: 'Burned down the Chancellery and blamed it on the Jews and communists'; 'Marched into Paris'; 'Ordered the "final solution" to the Jewish "problem"'; 'Invaded the Soviet Union – it'll all be over by Christmas.'

## REWRITING HISTORY

In 1981, *Stern* journalist Gerd Heidemann (b. 1931) told his employers that he had obtained a cache of Nazi documents, including several volumes of Hitler's diaries covering the period 1932 to 1945. Heidemann claimed that the material had been smuggled out of communist East Germany by a Dr. Fischer. The whereabouts of the documents between 1945 and 1981 was never made clear, but Heidemann said they had been rescued from a crashed aircraft fleeing the Russian advance on Berlin in April 1945, and kept secret from the world and the East German authorities for almost forty years. For the next 18 months, *Stern* paid Heidemann DM9 million (about $6 million at the time) for sixty-one diary volumes, each bearing the monogram 'AH', and additional material supposedly taken out of Hitler's bunker.

Like Yale University, the owners of the Vinland map (see pp. 168–72), *Stern* had the problem of authenticating the documents while at the same time keeping them secret in order to maintain their exclusive. The magazine made the same mistake of not submitting the ink, paper and binding of the diaries to forensic tests to ascertain if they were genuine. Had they done so they could have saved themselves a great deal of money and embarrassment. In the event, they showed samples of the diaries to handwriting experts and historians, who certified the diaries as genuine. This was just what Heidemann and his accomplices were hoping for. With the material authenticated, they could drip-feed the magazine with more and more forgeries and collect the money, which would be spent or hidden away and never recovered.

The most senior historian to have sight of the diaries was Sir Hugh Trevor-Roper (1914–2003), Master of Peterhouse College, Cambridge. Trevor-Roper was also a director of the London *Times* which, along with *Newsweek* in the U.S., was considering buying serialisation rights to the diaries. He flew to Switzerland to view the documents, and wrote in the *Times* the following day that he was convinced that 'the documents are authentic; that the history of their wanderings since 1945 is true; and that the standard accounts of Hitler's writing habits, of his personality and, even, perhaps, of some public events, may in consequence have to be revised.' Trevor-Roper was not only an expert in the history of the Third Reich but he had also been sent by the British government to investigate the circumstances of Hitler's death in November 1945, to counter Soviet propaganda that the Führer had survived and was living in hiding in the West under American protection.

**DENOUNCER**
Holocaust denier and Hitler fan Irving stood up at the press conference to denounce the diaries as fakes.

The April press conference held in Hamburg by *Stern* to announce the discovery of the diaries did not go according to plan. The controversial British writer and Nazi sympathiser David Irving (b. 1938), who was convicted of holocaust denial in Austria in 2006, attended the press conference, bringing with him forged Nazi documents that he said came from the same source. He denounced the diaries and Trevor-Roper, shouting: 'I know the collection from which these diaries come. It is an old collection, full of forgeries. I have some here!' He was forcibly ejected from the hall, but his interruption was actually irrelevant because Trevor-Roper had also had second thoughts and was using the press conference to qualify his endorsement of the diaries.

## FAKING HITLER

The West German National Archives and British forensic and handwriting specialists now subjected the diaries to a proper examination. They were immediately revealed for what they were: very poor forgeries. The paper, ink and binding were all of postwar manufacture; the handwriting, though it superficially resembled Hitler's, was a poor imitation of the genuine article; the diaries contained many historical inaccuracies and anachronisms; finally, the monogram on the cheap faux-leather cover of the diaries was not 'AH' but 'FH', but in Gothic capitals, the letters 'A' and 'F' look very similar.

Heidemann had been the front man who had sold the diaries, but he was not their creator. Our would-be Hitler was the petty crook, dealer in Nazi memorabilia and forger, Konrad Kujau (1938–2000). Born a year before the outbreak of war, Kujau was a young child when Hitler committed suicide. He grew up in East Germany, from which he was forced to flee in 1957 to evade arrest by the police after being charged with theft.

He settled in Stuttgart and was soon in trouble with the West German police, serving short sentences for theft and forgery. In the 1970s, he got involved in the illegal trade in Nazi memorabilia between East and West Germany, often forging documents to give the objects he was selling a false provenance and to increase their value. Realising that there was money to be made in Nazi forgeries, he painted a few fake Hitlers (the Führer was a notably mediocre painter), and passed off a handwritten version of *Mein Kampf* as Hitler's original manuscript.

As early as 1978 Kujau had come up with the diary scam, and he had sold a volume of 'Hitler's diary' to a German collector. Heidemann learned of the diary and contacted Kujau. The forger produced 61 volumes for Heidemann, selling them to the journalist for the relatively cheap price of DM2.5 million ($1.2 million). Although Heidemann tried to claim that he was Kujau's innocent dupe, he was sentenced to five years for fraud. Kujau was sentenced to four and a half years for forgery. The editors of *Stern*, *The Times* and *Newsweek* all resigned, and Trevor-Roper's reputation as a historian was fatally compromised.

REALISING THAT THERE WAS MONEY TO BE MADE IN NAZI FORGERIES, HE PAINTED A FEW FAKE HITLERS.

**DECEPTION**

Religious deceit

Military subterfuge

Financial fraud

Fake or counterfeit

Imposture or cross-dressing

Confidence trick

**Scientific deception**

# COLD COMFORT: PONS AND FLEISCHMANN

**Main Culprits:** Stanley Pons and Martin Fleischmann

**Motivation:** Fame

**Damage Done:** Promoted pseudo-science; put back research in cold fusion for decades

*Given that each gallon of water contains only 127 milligrams of deuterium, there is yet more potential cold fusion energy in one cubic mile of seawater than the energy from all the known oil reserves on Earth. The oceans of the world contain 20 trillion metric tons of heavy water – enough to last 5.7 billion years at the present rate of the world's energy consumption. Motorists can look forward to their cold fusion cars getting 55 million miles per gallon of heavy water!*

**From Carbon Dating, Cold Fusion, and a Curve Ball (2004) by D. Moon**

In this decade of oil price hikes and accelerating global warming, the dream of limitless supplies of clean, cheap energy is the holy grail of the physical sciences. Ever since Albert Einstein's (1879–1955) famous $E=mc^2$, we know that we can get the most energy from the tiniest components of matter: atoms and their component particles. Even a quantity of ordinary matter contains huge amounts of pent-up energy – so much so that, to take an example at random, a ham sandwich (hold the mayo and the pickle) could take out a small city, if you were able to release the energy stored in it. Fortunately for the planet and the human race, most matter is so stable that the contents of your fridge are not likely to go critical any time soon and obliterate the eastern seaboard. There are elements in nature that are suitably unstable – such as uranium – but they are incredibly rare, exist in minute quantities, and need to be processed intensively before they can be used as fuel for nuclear reactors or materials for nuclear weapons.

Since World War Two (1939–45), we have been able to use the huge potential of nuclear fission – the splitting of atoms either in A-bombs or in nuclear reactors – to produce energy. Unfortunately, fission also creates huge quantities of waste that remains radioactive for thousands of years. Another solution to the energy problem is nuclear *fusion*. Instead of splitting an atom to release the energy it contains, you force the nuclei of two atoms to fuse together. The fusion of light atomic nuclei, such as hydrogen (H), releases an enormous amount of energy. Even better, hydrogen is the most common element in the universe and there is a considerable amount on earth in the form of water ($H_2O$). The sun, along with all other stars, is a gigantic fusion reactor,

© Time & Life Pictures | Getty Images

**DYNAMIC DUO**
The main victim of Pons and Fleischmann's scientific fiasco was cold fusion research itself.

and this gives you an idea of the problems involved in creating and containing a 'hot' or 'thermonuclear' fusion reaction. A star is not only massively large compared to the earth, it is also massively hot (in the range of millions of degrees), and generates huge internal pressures that contain the fusion reaction.

So far we have been successful in producing thermonuclear fusion in H-bombs (not exactly a boon to humanity) and for fractions of a second in experimental fusion reactors, in which superhot plasma is contained by an immensely powerful magnetic field – a process that requires a huge amount of energy in itself. There is an alternative to hot fusion, however, which is known as 'cold' fusion, because it can occur at considerably lower temperatures than in the heart of stars or H-bombs – theoretically at room temperature.

One type of cold fusion – muon-catalysed fusion – has been known since the 1950s and can be produced fairly reliably with the right equipment. To get the reaction started, you bombard a frozen block containing the three isotopes of hydrogen, protium, deuterium and tritium, with a stream of particles known as muons, which trigger the fusion reaction. Problem solved, you might think. We build a ton of these muon-catalysed-fusion reactors and forget about oil hikes, carbon footprints and global warming. Unfortunately, muon-catalysed fusion depends on muons, particles that are too unstable and erratic to sustain a reaction that can be used as a reliable power source. Back to square one. Until 1989, that is, when two electrochemists working at the University of Utah, Martin Fleischmann (b. 1927) and Stanley Pons (b. 1943), announced the breakthrough that humanity had been waiting for: the realisation of a reliable cold fusion process based on a palladium–deuterium–heavy water system.

**GETTING INTO HOT WATER**

Fleischmann was born in Karlovy Vary (now in the Czech Republic) and Pons in Valdese, North Carolina. Both men have impeccable academic qualifications. Fleischmann is a graduate of Imperial College, London, and Pons of the University of Southampton. It was at Southampton that the two men first met, and they continued their academic association at the University of Utah. In the early 1980s they conducted a series of experiments that led them to believe that they had discovered a way to produce nuclear fusion at room temperature.

Their experiment consisted of creating an electrolytic cell, which is a standard piece of chemistry kit used to break down chemical compounds by passing an electrical current through a solution. The cell consists of a solution (electrolyte), a positive electrode (anode) and a negative electrode (cathode), in a container of some kind. Most of us have seen the electrolysis of water in secondary school chemistry – that is, the breakdown of water ($H_2O$) into oxygen and hydrogen gas when a current is passed through water in a beaker.

Pons and Fleischmann's electrolytic cell was fundamentally the same as one used in the electrolysis of water, apart from the materials used. The experiment was conducted in a calorimeter – an insulated container used to measure the heat produced by a chemical reaction. The liquid in the calorimeter was 'heavy' water, thus called because it contains high levels of deuterium (2H), a naturally occurring isotope of hydrogen (see quote); the cathode was made of palladium (Pd), a rare silver-coloured precious metal similar to platinum. When they passed an electrical current through the cell, most of the time the power input and output of the cell remained constant (meaning that no energy was being created by an electrochemical process) and the water was stable at 30°C. On occasion, however, the temperature of the water would shoot up to 50°C although there had been no increase in the power input. Although the effect would last only two days and could not be repeated in the cell, the increase in temperature was a significant gain in heat. The pair concluded that they had discovered a new form of cold fusion that might have a commercial application, unlike muon-catalysed fusion.

A discovery of this magnitude could not be kept secret for long. The pair needed federal funding to conduct further experiments, and a grant application required peer review by other researchers in the field. Pons and Fleischmann made their experiments and results known to a team working on muon-catalysed fusion at Brigham Young University, and the two groups promised to publish their results simultaneously in the leading American scientific periodical, *Nature*. So far, Pons and Fleischmann were following the scientific book: involving other researchers and waiting to make their findings public until another team could confirm them. However, in March 1989, when both groups were ready to publish their joint findings, Pons and Fleischmann broke with academic precedent and ethical practice and went to press early in the *Journal of Electroanalytical Chemistry*, seriously putting the Brigham Young team's nose out of joint. In their defence, it must be said that they had been pressured by the University of Utah, which was worried about establishing a prior claim to research that was likely to be the most commercially valuable in modern times.

THE PRESS PICKED UP ON THE ANNOUNCEMENT AND THE MEDIA CIRCUS GOT UNDERWAY. THE TWO MEN BECAME INSTANT SCIENTIFIC CELEBRITIES AND WERE HAILED AS THE SAVIOURS OF HUMANKIND.

The press picked up on the announcement and the media circus got underway. The two men became instant scientific celebrities and were hailed as the saviours of humankind. Nobel Prizes were in the offing. All that needed to happen was for a number of respected institutions to recreate their experiments and confirm their results. Universities worldwide immediately set to work. Two teams, one at Georgia Tech and another at Stanford, reported early success, but Caltech and the CERN laboratories in Europe reported repeated failures. By the summer of 1989 articles critical of the pair's work were appearing in the scientific press, and by November the U.S. Department of Energy issued a report that put the validity of Pons and Fleischmann's work in doubt, questioned the value of cold fusion as a viable source of energy, and rejected their funding application.

There is no evidence or suggestion that Pons and Fleischmann ever falsified their experimental results or made deliberate fraudulent claims. They continue to stand by their results. However, their peers accused them of being sloppy and inaccurate in their experimental work, as well as unethical in the way they had made the initial announcement. They left Utah soon after, but were invited to continue their research at a lab funded by Japan's Toyota Corp. in France, until Toyota closed the project down in 1998. Several isolated groups continue research in cold fusion but the Pons and Fleischmann fiasco has meant that most mainstream scientists, along with the national funding bodies that they advise, will not take the subject seriously. As a result, the billions of research dollars that could go to cold fusion now go exclusively to hot fusion. Pons and Fleischmann may not have set out to deceive like many in this book, but, in the long run, the results of their mistakes could be far costlier for humanity than the depredations of any number of financial fraudsters and confidence tricksters.

# COME AND SEE WHAT'S ON THE SLAB: ALIEN AUTOPSY

**DECEPTION**

Religious deceit

Military subterfuge

Financial fraud

Fake or counterfeit

Imposture or cross-dressing

Confidence trick

Scientific deception

**Main Culprit:** Ray Santilli

**Motivation:** Fame

**Damage Done:** Fooled the credulous into believing in UFOs and the Roswell conspiracy theory

When the ratings for Alien Autopsy began to slip after three years, Fox announced that it had hired its own experts to examine the film. Using high-tech 'NASA-type video enhancements', they revealed the shocking truth: the film was a fake. Was Fox chagrined at having been duped? Not at all. Fox boasted of having exposed 'one of the biggest hoaxes of all time'. A highly promoted special was aired that described how the autopsy film had been faked. Fox had managed to make a profit from the Roswell incident coming and going.

**From *Voodoo Science: The Road from Foolishness to Fraud* (2000) by R. L. Park**

It would be impossible to understand the impact of the showing of the alien autopsy footage on 28 August 1995, without knowing something of the 'Roswell UFO incident' that occurred half a world away and fifty years before. Roswell is now so deeply ingrained into the American psyche, that to one side, it confirms the duplicity of the U.S. federal government, and the existence of a worldwide conspiracy to prevent the average person from finding out that we have been visited by UFOs, and now routinely meet and converse with them; and to the other, that a section of the American public will swallow the most absurd rubbish as long as it packaged in the right way.

The location for the strange events of July 1947 was the small town of Roswell (pop. 45,293 in 2000), Chaves County, New Mexico.

Roswell is about 320 km (200 miles) from the nearest major population centres, which include Albuquerque (199 miles), El Paso (203 miles) and Santa Fe (192 miles). The area is desert-dry, and residents make their living from ranching and oil. You can imagine that not a lot goes on in downtown Roswell of an evening. From 1941 to 1967, the city was home to the USAF's largest Strategic Air Command base, Walker Air Force Base, better known to us as Roswell Army Air Field, which is 5 km (3 miles) south of Roswell proper: an ideal location for a major military installation, far away from prying eyes, and the distractions that a big city would offer to its military personnel. The base was home to some fairly heavyweight and highly sensitive hardware during the Cold War, including long-range bombers and Atlas strategic missiles.

**DEBRIS**
Crashed flying saucer or weather balloon? The USAF produced remains to counter UFO claims.

Contrary to its depiction in the movie *Independence Day* (1996), the base was decommissioned in 1967 and is now a civilian air facility known as the Roswell International Air Center (RIAC). In addition to the commercial and municipal airports, RIAC hosts several installations on its spacious grounds, including fireworks, plastics, bus and candy factories; a university campus; the New Mexico Rehabilitation Center; and a testing station for Boeing (or that's what they want you to believe).

© AFP | Getty Images

Now we need to travel back in time 50 years to a very different United States that had just emerged from one war and was about to enter into the ideological deep freeze known as the Cold War – a period noted for its military paranoia and secrecy. The U.S. had deployed its first A-bombs on Japan (August 1945) and knew that the Soviet Union was developing nuclear weapons of its own. The xenophobic atmosphere of an undeclared foreign threat was transmuted into the plots of sci-fi B-movies about alien invaders. Many of these were set in unassuming small towns in the Southeast, and featured a clean-cut, square-jawed hero, and his high-pitched, accident-prone, but very curvaceous female companion, who together succeeded in alerting the sceptical authorities and saved the planet in 90 minutes and for a budget of less than $100,000.

On 9 July 1947, Walker Air Force Base issued a statement saying that its personnel had recovered debris from a crashed 'flying disc' (the term 'flying saucer' had not yet been coined for UFOs) from the vicinity of Roswell. The press responded with banner headlines, but the excitement was short-lived. The Air Force immediately retracted the statement, and said that what they had found was the debris of a high-altitude weather balloon. At a press conference, the debris was shown to the press, confirming its terrestrial origins. The case was closed and quickly forgotten, and the tabloids moved on to new and more interesting sightings, such as the close encounter claims of George Adamski (pp. 145–50).

The Roswell incident remained dormant for three decades, until resurrected in 1978 by nuclear physicist turned professional 'ufologist' Stanton Friedman (b. 1934). Friedman believes that we receive regular visits from an alien civilisation whose home is in the planetary systems orbiting the stars Zeta Reticuli 1 and 2, which are 39 light years away from our own sun. He is certain that the government of the United States has conspired since the 1940s to keep this knowledge secret from the general public. He revisited the case and interviewed witnesses to the Roswell incident. The media, including that organ of scientific truth, the *National Enquirer*, got into the act, and the story 'just done growed and growed' like Topsy. Books and TV specials appeared through the 1980s and 90s, each giving slightly different versions of the story,

**THE ALIENS HAVE (CRASH) LANDED**

but all contributing to making Roswell the UFO capital of the world. Finally in 1989, a witness came forward claiming that autopsies on the bodies of dead aliens recovered from the crashed flying saucer had been carried out at Roswell.

## CSI ROSWELL

In August 1995, a British TV station announced that it had obtained footage of the alien autopsy performed soon after the crash at the Walker Air Base in 1947. The broadcast garnered one of the largest worldwide audiences ever recorded. Before describing the contents of the film, there are several general points worth noting about how the film (available on various websites) was shot. First, the film is shot in black and white. Colour film had been available since before the Second World War, and though much more expensive, you'd think that such an important event as the first recorded autopsy of an extraterrestrial visitor might merit full Technicolor.

Second, the footage seems to be shot with a single handheld camera, operated by a cameraman who has either had one drink too many or has never operated a camera before, such is the jerkiness of the film as it switches from one view of the alien body to another. As with the previous point about colour, you'd imagine that an important autopsy might merit more than one camera (just on the grounds that one might malfunction and the film might be lost or damaged), and that the large cine cameras used in the late 1940s would be mounted on fixed tripods to get the optimum views of the procedure. There is not only constant movement of the camera, but the close-ups are extremely blurred. There are also many whiteouts and blackouts during the film. Third is the absence of a soundtrack, though we are well into the age of the 'talkies'.

In short the whole of the footage has a very amateurish look, as though shot on a home cine camera on low-quality film stock by an inexperienced cameraman. Not at all what one would expect for one of the most important autopsies ever carried out on U.S. soil. Next we turn to the 16 min 51 sec film itself. The setting certainly looks the part. The autopsy is held in a room that appears to be a medical facility of the late 1940s, with a large wall-mounted clock that comes into shot from time to time, indicating to the viewer how much time is elapsing. The room is kitted out with medical equipment and trays of instruments.

An old-style microphone hangs from the ceiling over the table to record the medical examiner's findings, and another room can be glimpsed through a glass panel.

The visible 'cast' consists of three persons. Two men in white biohazard suits conduct the autopsy itself, and a third in a surgeon's mask, hat and gown stands behind the glass window of the other room. Again you wonder: only three people present at this incredibly significant occasion, and a setting that was probably primitive even by 1940s standards. You'd expect the top brass of the base and a crowd of Washington bigwigs to be behind the glass window observing, and probably more than two medical personnel in the room itself. You could explain the small number of people and the primitive conditions by a need to proceed speedily with the autopsy. However, they did have refrigeration in 1947, and I have to ask why conduct the procedure in Roswell, when you could do it in total secrecy at a much better equipped and staffed government lab in Washington?

Then there is the alien body itself. It is not unlike the extraterrestrials popularised by such films as *Close Encounters of the Third Kind* (1977) and *E.T.* (1982). Although shot in black and white, it seems to be a 'grey' – a child-sized alien with a swollen abdomen, no apparent sexual organs, and large black eyes without pupils, irises or eyelids. One leg has a deep wound that exposes the bones and tissue beneath the skin. The alien is very humanoid in appearance, but has six toes and fingers instead of five. Once we have been given a good view of the corpse, the autopsy begins. The ME takes tissue samples from the leg wound (blurred close-up). He then uses a scalpel to slice along the neck and down the abdomen to expose the internal organs (also blurred). He proceeds to empty the body cavity of its contents with all the care of a butcher 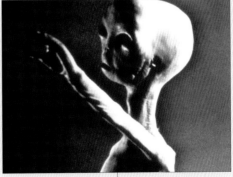 gutting a chicken. He removes the black membranes over the eyes, revealing a white membrane underneath, then sets to work on the skull, peeling back the skin and then sawing it open so that they can remove the brain, which he places on a tray. The footage is extremely poorly shot and extremely dull.

**PHONE HOME**
A 'grey' from *Close Encounters of the Third Kind* – a likely inspiration for Santilli's alien creation.

© Photos 12 | Alamy

**ROSWELL,
NEW MEXICO,
LONDON**

The film appeared, by another strange coincidence, at the same time as the U.S. government released the results of an internal investigation into the Roswell incident. The government published two reports, the first in 1995, and the second in 1997. The first concluded that the material recovered at Roswell in 1947 was from a top-secret government program known as 'Project Mogul'. Mogul consisted of high-altitude balloons that carried microphones to detect the sounds of Russian nuclear tests. The project was quickly shelved when other, more reliable detection methods were found. The second report explained stories of recovered alien bodies as memories of human military casualties, 'crash-test' dummies used in USAF experiments, and hoaxes (but they would say that, wouldn't they?).

The truth, however, came out in 2006. Fox exposed the film as a fraud (see quote), but its creator, Ray Santilli (b. 1957), still maintains that he obtained a badly degraded copy of a genuine autopsy film, and that just a few of the frames were salvageable. Santilli was born in London of immigrant Italian parents. He left school to join a rock band, and in 1982 he founded AMP Entertainment, which represented many of the best-known rock musicians of the British musical scene of the 1980s. He claimed to have acquired the alien autopsy footage in 1992. Instead of releasing the few surviving frames, Santilli decided to recreate the film, inserting the few genuine frames (these have never been identified). The footage was filmed with actors in an empty North London apartment kitted out to look like a 1940s medical facility. A sculptor created the alien body, which was filled with sheep's brains covered in jelly, chicken entrails, and other animal parts to simulate the alien's organs, bones and muscles.

Despite the two U.S. government reports and Santilli's confession, the Roswell UFO incident continues to be the centrepiece of an elaborate conspiracy theory about a government cover-up. However, what the Roswell believers have to explain is why, in a world when the U.S. no longer has a monopoly on advanced space science, all governments on earth – be they capitalist, socialist, communist, atheist, Christian, Hindu or Islamic – have agreed to keep the existence of aliens secret; and why a race of super-intelligent beings, possibly from Zeta Reticuli, has agreed to keep its visits secret.

# THE LOST BOY:
# FRÉDÉRIC BOURDIN

**DECEPTION**

Religious deceit

Military subterfuge

Financial fraud

Fake or counterfeit

**Imposture or cross-dressing**

Confidence trick

Scientific deception

**Main Culprit:** Frédéric Bourdin

**Motivation:** A twisted search for security and love

**Damage Done:** Gave false hope to the families who had lost children

[Bourdin] hitchhiked to Paris, where, scared and hungry, he invented his first fake character: he approached a police officer and told him that he was a lost British teen named Jimmy Sale. 'I dreamed they would send me to England, where I always imagined life was more beautiful,' he recalls.

**From 'The Chameleon' by D. Grann, *The New Yorker*,
11 August 2008**

One of the themes of this book is the nature of identity. Our identities are made up of several components: there are physical characteristics such as age, physiological sex and appearance; and social characteristics, such as gender, nationality, education, religion, social class and profession. Most of us take it for granted that our identities are fixed, and that they form the changeless core of our inner selves. However, having read the past entries, you should be aware that what we consider to be the most essential human characteristics can be changed: sex, sexual orientation and gender do not have to match; names, social class and nationality are like garments to be put on and off at will; and educational and professional qualifications are often optional extras. Even age can be faked, as in the case of Frank Abagnale (pp. 179–83), who as a teenager, pretended to be a man in his late twenties.

**DISCRIMINATION**
The son of a mixed French-Algerian union, Bourdin was at a disadvantage from birth in racially divided France.

As to why people want to be someone other than they were born and raised, motives vary. It could be for kicks; to escape the limitations imposed by society on their gender, ethnic origin, nationality or social class; as a result of mental illness; or to obtain power, fame and, of course, money. But the motives for this final case of imposture are perhaps the most poignant – even more so than that of poor deluded Anna Anderson, a.k.a. Anastasia (see pp. 102–6), who, after so many years of pretence, probably came to believe that she was the deceased Romanov grand duchess. Frédéric Bourdin (b. 1974) did not claim to be a lost prince or an airline pilot; he did not create fake identities for money, fame or social advancement. One character, which he played over and over again until the age of 31, was that of a lost and lonely, orphaned and abused adolescent boy.

**FOREVER YOUNG**

Looking at a picture of Bourdin taken in 2005, it is hard to imagine how he could have passed himself off as a teenager. Naturally, he employed as many cosmetic tricks as he could get away with, but most of all he dressed and acted the part to perfection – he walked the teenage walk and talked the teenage talk. Even the doctor who examined him when he was 30, certified that he was an adolescent of 14. Often, it seems, we see what we want to believe – so a flock of birds can be a flying saucer, a log floating on a Scottish loch, a long-extinct reptile, and a balding 30-year-old man, a disturbed teenage boy.

Bourdin's true-life story is as least as tragic as that of his many invented identities. He is the illegitimate child of a French factory worker and an Algerian immigrant known to him as Kaci but whom he has never met. Bourdin's parents split up when his mother discovered that the father of her unborn child was already married. France has a large population of North African origin, from her former colonies of Algeria and Tunisia. Although there are many second- and third-generation French of North African origin, for the most part they form an underprivileged group, disbarred from full participation by the majority white, Christian population. This led to serious riots in the Paris suburbs in 2005 and 2007. As an illegitimate child of mixed heritage, the young Bourdin was always to have difficulty fitting in with his peers.

AS AN ILLEGITIMATE CHILD OF MIXED HERITAGE, THE YOUNG BOURDIN WAS ALWAYS TO HAVE DIFFICULTY FITTING IN WITH HIS PEERS.

At the age of two he was taken into care by social services, which considered his mother to be unfit. He was entrusted to the care of his grandparents, who lived in a small village near the French port of Nantes. Although he was a bright and engaging child, he also showed early signs of mental instability and antisocial behaviour. At the age of 12, after a series of minor thefts, he was sent to the first of the many children's homes in which he would spend the rest of his adolescence. Aged 16, he ran away to Paris, and invented his first false identity – that of missing British teenager Jimmy Sale – in the hope of being sent to England (see quote). Although he did not manage to fool the authorities this time, because he could speak only a few words of English, the experience set the pattern that he would follow for the next fifteen years in as many countries across the globe.

During his career Bourdin assumed at least 39 identities, three of which were those of real missing teens. In 1997, when he was 23, he claimed to be Nicholas Barclay, the teenage son of an American family from San Antonio, Texas, who had gone missing in 1994. Although he did not resemble the missing boy, and had different-coloured eyes, he managed to convince the Barclays that he was their son. He lived with them for three months until he was unmasked by a DNA test. He was sentenced to six years in jail and deported to France on his release.

Back in France, he claimed to be another missing teen, Leo Balley, only to be exposed by another DNA test. In 2004, he was in Spain pretending to be Ruben Sánchez Espinoza, the son of a mother killed in the Madrid train bombings. Once again he was identified as an impostor and returned to France.

His last, and considering his age, his most daring imposture, took place between May and June 2005. He once again adopted the identity of a Spanish orphan, this time the 15-year-old Francisco Hernández-Fernández who had been found penniless and traumatised on the French side of the Spanish border. The authorities housed him in shelter for young adults in the town of Pau and enrolled him at a local high school, where he managed to fool both pupils and staff for several weeks. He was only discovered when one of his teachers recognised him from a TV documentary about his career as a serial impostor. He was taken into custody and investigated by the police, who suspected that he was a paedophile, and by psychiatrists, who thought that he might be mentally ill. However, he was cleared on both counts. Even then the authorities were not sure what to do with him, because his imposture was not covered by any criminal statute. In the end he was given a six-month suspended sentence for using a fake ID in the name of Leo Balley.

**SERIAL PRETENDER**

David Grann, who interviewed Bourdin for *The New Yorker* in 2008, revealed a sad individual whose only motive for a life of deception was a search for the love and affection that he had never experienced as a child. In 2007 Bourdin married and has since fathered a daughter. He resides in the vicinity of Pau with his family. As to whether the 'chameleon', as he was nicknamed by the French press, is completely cured of his addiction to serial imposture, only time will tell. Perhaps we haven't heard the last of Frédéric Bourdin, who once said of himself, 'I am a manipulator [....] My job is to manipulate.'

# SEND IN THE CLONES: HWANG WOO-SUK

**DECEPTION**

Religious deceit

Military subterfuge

Financial fraud

Fake or counterfeit

Imposture or cross-dressing

Confidence trick

Scientific deception

**Main Culprit:** Hwang Woo-suk

**Motivation:** Fame

**Damage Done:** Embarrassed the Korean government and academic establishment; put back genuine research into the cloning of stem cells

*I produced several cloned cows and also transgenic cloned pigs. At the time I thought that if our technology could be married with medical technology this could be a good way to develop treatment for people with diseases such as diabetes, spinal cord injury or Parkinson's. So we talked with medical colleagues. Last year we published our human cloning work and this year we made stem cells for individual patients.*

*We are doing more studies. I want to find out safety and efficacy using our stem cell lines into animal models.*

**From a BBC interview with Hwang Woo-suk in 2005 at the height of his fame**

Science is not a glamorous business. For every Stephen Hawking (b. 1942) or Carl Sagan (1934–96), there are thousands of researchers working in obscurity, with little hope of recognition outside the very narrow confines of their field. The discoveries that move science forward, such as the theory of evolution or the theory of relativity, only occur once in a century, and then have to be verified and elaborated by decades of experiments. But the glory (and the Nobel Prize) goes to the initial discoverer.

In previous entries in this book we have seen scientific deceptions both consciously planned (see Piltdown Man, pp. 85–90) and brought

about by incompetence (Pons and Fleischmann, pp. 222–6). In the former case, the deception was not discovered for forty years because the standards of scientific proof were not as rigorous as they are today; in the latter, the fact that no other researcher in the world could conclusively repeat Pons and Fleischmann's experiments quickly proved that their work was either fraudulent or deeply flawed. With the case of cold fusion in mind, it is surprising that Korean veterinarian and biotechnologist Hwang Woo-suk (b. 1953) managed to get away with his deception for so many years.

**KOREA'S SHAME**
Once lauded as a national hero in South Korea, Hwang now lives in disgrace and obscurity.

Hwang was protected by two things: the first was that the fields he worked in, cloning and stem cell research, are so hemmed in with ethical and legal restrictions in the U.S. and Europe; and the second was the protection and support of the South Korean government and big business, its academic community, and people who were naturally proud of their homegrown biotech genius. Stem-cell therapies are widely believed to be the answer to everything from premature baldness to spinal-cord injuries, heart disease and cancer. The man who would succeed in mass-producing stem cells for therapeutic work would be well on his way to earning a Nobel Prize for medicine and a place in the science hall of fame.

Hwang was born in Chungnam Province in western South Korea in the closing year of the Korean War (1950–3). He grew up in a small village with five siblings, losing his father when he was only five years old. Although he had to work on the family farm throughout his schooling, he matriculated from Daejeon High School and won a place at the prestigious Seoul National University, where he pursued studies in veterinary medicine. He practised as a veterinarian for a short time before returning to Seoul to complete his PhD in theriogenology – the study and practice of animal reproduction. In a BBC interview in 2005, he said, 'My dream when I was at school was the same as it is now. I had the same dream to become a scientist. So I trained as a vet. My first major was cow research.'

He reported his first breakthrough in February 1999 with the cloning of a dairy cow called Yeongrong-i. This came three years after a British team had hit the headlines by cloning the first large mammal, Dolly the sheep (1996–2003). In April 1999, he announced the successful cloning of a second cow. However, in neither instance did he publish his research notes and data for peer review. His other unsubstantiated cloning claims included work on pigs, dogs, and the promise to bring back extinct mammoths and Siberian tigers. Hwang had already attracted considerable media attention in South Korea for his animal work, but what shot him to international fame was the claims he made for his successes in human cloning and stem-cell research in 2004 and 2005.

Research into human cloning and stem cells is extremely controversial, especially in the U.S. where there is such a strong pro-life lobby. Although the two fields raise different ethical issues, they are also closely related in research terms. Cloning is the reproduction of an animal or human through the implantation of their DNA into an egg whose original DNA has been removed. This has been done for a range of animals but not yet in humans. The ethical problem is not just that the success rate is very low in cloning animals – 1 in 277 at the time of Dolly the sheep – but also the whole issue of whether it is right to recreate an already living person.

Stem cells are the body's cellular building blocks and repair toolkit rolled into one. Embryonic stem cells can transform themselves into all

**FROM FARM BOY TO ONE OF THE 'PEOPLE WHO MATTERED 2004'**

the types of cells needed to construct a human body – skin, bone and muscle, nerve and blood cells. And therein lies their incredible value. In theory, they could be used to regenerate damaged organs and nerve fibres, and heal wounds and the damage caused by cancer and coronary heart disease. Stem cells are also found in adults, but these have much more limited capabilities. Recent breakthroughs have reduced the need for embryonic stem cells; however, these were not available when Hwang first announced his discoveries. In the late 1990s and early 2000s, the really valuable cells for research and therapeutic purposes

Dolly the Sheep

**HELLO DOLLY**
Many mammals, including mice and sheep, have been cloned successfully since Hwang's faked claims.

had to come from human blastocysts (a very early developmental stage of the embryo), which could in theory have gone on to develop into human beings – hence the violent opposition of pro-lifers. Even for people who do not oppose abortion, the idea of creating human embryos to harvest their stem cells smacks of Frankenstein science.

In 2004 Hwang announced that he had created an embryonic stem-cell line through cloning from a single human donor. He made this claim in the March issue of *Science* magazine, one of the leading peer-reviewed scientific journals in the world. If the claim had been genuine, it would have been an extraordinary first, opening the way for therapeutic applications. A year later, he reported even greater success in the cloning of 11 stem-cell lines from several different donors. This was the breakthrough the medical world had been waiting for. It meant that custom-made stem cells could be created for patients that would avoid the problems associated with the rejection of tissue from donors that are well known in organ transplantation. Hwang was hailed as a national hero – the 'Pride of Korea'.

In November 2005, however, Gerald Schatten (b. 1949), a senior American stem-cell researcher at the University of Pittsburgh and a collaborator of Hwang's, who had been included as one of the co-authors of the 2005 *Science* paper, asked the journal to withdraw his name, on the grounds that he had doubts about how Hwang had obtained his donor eggs. A Korean TV current-affairs show revealed that eggs had been obtained for money and by coercion from Hwang's female researchers in breach of ethical rules. Hwang admitted his team's wrongdoing and offered to resign as the person ultimately responsible, but he claimed that his subordinates had broken the ethical protocols without his knowledge. The Korean people rallied behind their scientific star, and his lab was deluged with offers of egg donations.

The game, however, was almost up for Hwang. The University of Seoul's investigation into his work concluded that 9 of his 11 stem-cell lines had been faked and serious doubts existed about the remaining two. *Science* immediately retracted the 2004 and 2005 papers. In January 2006, Hwang held another press conference, apologising once again but blaming his subordinates for falsifying the results. In March, the university dismissed him from all his academic posts, and in May, he and two of his collaborators were indicted on charges of fraud, embezzlement of research funds, and breaches of Korea's bioethics law. Investigations revealed that Hwang had been embezzling billions of won (millions of dollars) in research funds to buy eggs from donors and bribe executives whose companies then sponsored his research. In October 2009, a Seoul court found Hwang guilty and sentenced him to a two-year suspended sentence.

In a final bizarre twist to the story of Hwang's fabricated stem cells, subsequent reviews of his work have concluded that not all his claims were faked. He did succeed in cloning an Afghan hound called Snappy, and it is possible that several of his stem-cell lines were produced by a process known as parthenogenesis – the development of an embryo from an unfertilised egg, which is a common form of reproduction in plants and invertebrates, and is found in a few reptiles, birds and fish. If this were correct, it would be a major scientific breakthrough in its own right. Hwang continues research in animal cloning at a small local institute.

IN MARCH, THE UNIVERSITY DISMISSED HWANG FROM ALL HIS ACADEMIC POSTS, AND IN MAY, HE AND TWO OF HIS COLLABORATORS WERE INDICTED ON CHARGES OF FRAUD.

**DECEPTION**

Religious deceit

Military subterfuge

Financial fraud

Fake or counterfeit

Imposture or cross-dressing

Confidence trick

Scientific deception

# PENNIES FROM HEAVEN: KAZUTSUGI NAMI

**Main Culprit:** Kazutsugi Nami

**Motivation:** Financial gain

**Damage Done:** Defrauded and ruined thousands of investors

*[Nami's] most recent venture lured investors with the promise of 36 per cent annual interest. The scale of the money accumulated was not clear but, according to L&G's administrators, 50,000 people entrusted the company with a total of 226 billion yen (£1.75 billion).*

**Excerpt from 'Japanese businessman Kazutsugi Nami arrested for £1bn fraud', Timesonline.com, 6 February 2009**

There is something particularly Japanese about the 'Enten' scam of 2004–7, and not just because it took place in the 'Land of the Rising Sun'. Although Japan is still the world's second-largest economy after the U.S., it has been in recession since the bursting of the Japanese asset bubble in 1990, which anticipated the rest of the world's credit crunch of 2007–9. The Japanese have been hit by a double whammy: just as they were starting to get out of their own recession, the world economy ground to a halt as credit dried up, and American and European consumers stopped buying Japanese cars, MP3 players and computers. Traditionally a high-savings economy, Japan has a rock-bottom interest rate of 0.1 per cent, and negative growth and inflation, meaning that savers cannot hope to make money on their savings through the usual means: the stock market, bonds and bank deposits. It is an ideal atmosphere for the get-rich-quick merchants, shysters and fraudsters to exploit the fears and hopes of unsophisticated investors and savers.

Our penultimate fraudster, Japanese entrepreneur Kazutsugi Nami (b. 1933), had a clever take on the pyramid scheme and a counterfeit currency rolled into one. Your average counterfeiter manufactures fake bills of well-known currencies – dollars, pounds or euros – and tries to pass them off as the real thing. Of course, most fakes are easy to spot, and the poor counterfeiter is soon caught. A much better scheme is to attempt to forge 'real' bank bills as Alves Reis did in Portugal (pp. 107–11). However, even with the genuine article, you risk being caught out by the banks, who employ much stricter security measures. Nami had an even better idea: to create the *enten*, a virtual electronic currency. He chose the name with some care. The Japanese character *en* means yen, which is Japan's currency; *ten* is the character for 'Heaven' – and this is where it gets particularly Japanese.

© AFP | Getty Images

**CULT LEADER**
Nami's scam combined economic fraud with a particularly Japanese brand of religious hokum.

Since the late nineteenth century, when Japan opened itself to the West, the country has been home to many 'New Religions' – cultish amalgams of Buddhist, native Shinto and foreign religious traditions, which offer health, wealth and happiness to their devotees, though often this means the health, wealth and happiness of the cult's leader. Although the *enten* scam was a purely financial fraud, it did have religious overtones. Nami claimed to have received a 'divine mandate to eliminate world poverty', and in an interview with the Japanese media, he confidently predicted, 'Because of the financial crisis, countries will adopt the *enten* in three years' time. I will start shining and become world famous. I will certainly move the world.' His investors often appeared more like cult followers, implicitly accepting Nami's outrageous assurances, and defending him even after the scheme had been declared bankrupt.

**A CAREER IN FRAUD**

Seventy-six-year-old Nami is no stranger to bankruptcy, fraud and prison. He is a serial offender with convictions dating back to the 1970s when he set up several companies operating as pyramid schemes (for an explanation of pyramid and Ponzi schemes, see Charles Ponzi, pp. 96–101). In 1973 he set up Nozakku Co., which sold stones that Nami claimed could transform tap water into mineral water. The authorities repeatedly shut his operations down, and finally sent him to jail in 1978. After his release from prison, he set up a new company, the Tokyo-based Ladies and Gentlemen (L&G) Co., which started off selling futons (Japanese-style bedding) and health food in 1987. It was through this unlikely vehicle that Nami chose to start his latest investment scam. In 2001, he began to collect funds from investors who were sure the company was sound because it had been in business for well over a decade.

In 2004, Nami devised the electronic currency he called the *enten* and issued it to investors who could pay ¥100,000 ($1,000) to join the scheme. He assured his marks that the *enten* would become legal tender in a post-recession world order. He reeled investors in with promises of 36 per cent annual returns, many hundreds of times higher than the official interest rate offered by the Japanese government and banks. He held enten fairs to promote the scheme and attracted 37,000 small investors, many of whom entrusted him with all their life savings. The scheme was a Ponzi scheme, which paid off investors with money collected from the deposits of others. There was no conceivable other way Nami could offer such high returns.

By early 2007, the scheme was in deep trouble and could no longer afford to pay its dividends in yen. Instead Nami paid his investors in *enten*, which could be redeemed for online goods marketed by L&G and other Nami affiliates. However, sensing the end was nigh, thousands of investors tried to withdraw their money, resulting in the near bankruptcy of the scheme. In October, Japan's financial authorities raided L&G's offices and shut its operations down, and declared it bankrupt in November. In all Nami is said to have collected ¥126 billion ($1.26 billion) from investors between 2001 and 2007, and a further ¥118 million ($1.8 million) between July and December 2007, when the scheme was all but bust.

The ponderous workings of the Japanese legal system, which make a sick sloth look positively sprightly, finally caught up with Nami in early 2009. The police tracked him to a restaurant where he was enjoying an early breakfast at 5.30 am on 4 February. Quizzed by a huge posse of press and TV reporters, Nami refused to admit his guilt and hit back at the authorities: 'It was not a fraud,' he said. 'The police have destroyed my businesses [...] I am a victim of the police investigation.' He added, 'Time will tell if I'm a conman or a swindler. I'm leading 50,000 people. Can they charge a company this big with fraud?'

THE PONDEROUS WORKINGS OF THE JAPANESE LEGAL SYSTEM, WHICH MAKE A SICK SLOTH LOOK POSITIVELY SPRIGHTLY, FINALLY CAUGHT UP WITH NAMI IN EARLY 2009.

In truth, Japan's recent history is littered with countless financial scandals, bubbles and frauds – a fact that can be partly attributed to the nature of Japanese society. As a long-time resident of Japan during the years of its asset bubble, I can testify that Japan remains an incredibly trusting society. Members of the older generation, who shun credit cards, routinely carry large amounts of cash with them. However, even if they are unlucky enough to lose their wallets or purses, more often than not these are handed in to the police, who return them to their rightful owners. In this trusting environment a shark like Nami can thrive. Despite multiple convictions and bankruptcies, he was able to set up yet another pyramid scam. This kind of thing, you'd think, could never happen in the investment-savvy, well-regulated financial worlds of the U.S. and Europe. But you'd be dead wrong. Our last entry, appropriately enough, describes the biggest fraud in financial history, when one man took private and institutional investors for a cool $65 billion.

**DECEPTION**

Religious deceit

Military subterfuge

**Financial fraud**

Fake or counterfeit

Imposture or cross-dressing

Confidence trick

Scientific deception

# THE $65BN PONZI SCHEME: BERNARD MADOFF

**Main Culprit:** Bernard Madoff

**Motivation:** Financial gain

**Damage Done:** Defrauded and ruined thousands of private and institutional investors; ruined several educational bodies and charities that had invested with him or that he funded

*Investors would write cheques or sometimes wire their money directly into his JP Morgan Chase bank account [...] This account was where Madoff would do the 'cash in, cash out' transactions for investors of the bogus hedge fund. This was nothing like a real hedge fund, where investors fill out paperwork to ensure they are accredited, or wealthy enough to invest, and actually receive shares in a limited partnership. Most Madoff victims didn't know the difference, however, or if they did, they were coming in through an outside third party, such as a feeder fund. Feeder funds were an important source of investment for Madoff, but so were family and friends – many of whom were working on commission when they urged others to put money with Madoff.*

**From 'How Bernard Madoff Escaped Detection' by
E. Arvedlund, FT.com, 4 September 2009**

Our final deceiver has certainly earned his place in this book as the highest-earning fraudster of modern times. Bernard Madoff (b. 1938) made off with a cool $65 billion. In his day, Charles Ponzi (1882–1949) netted quite a sum with his short-lived 'Ponzi scheme' – enough for the scam to be named after him (pp. 96–101), but Ponzi's paltry millions pale into insignificance when compared to Madoff's take, which he amassed over three decades. His criminal achievement is so breathtaking that I'd recommend renaming Ponzi schemes 'Madoff schemes', so that his name can be associated with the crime (until, that is, the next clever crook bests his record).

**PREDATOR**
The genial Madoff preyed on his co-religionists, specifically targeting Jewish individuals, institutions and charities.

Madoff is not only notable for the total amount he managed to scam, but also for the length of time he managed to get away with his fraudulent dealings, which may have begun as early as the 1980s. During this time, Madoff was a Wall Street market-maker and former chairman of NASDAQ (National Association of Securities Dealers Automated Quotations). Not only did he managed to hoodwink individual investors, he scammed major international financial institutions, and survived several investigation by the Securities and Exchange Commission (SEC), the body charged with overseeing the probity of financial institutions.

Until his arrest in 2008, Madoff could have been a poster boy for the American dream: successful businessman, self-made millionaire, devoted husband and father, philanthropist, pillar of the community. The son of a plumber-turned-stockbroker, Madoff was born and raised in Queens, New York City. He went to college, majoring in Political Science, and attended law school for one year before ditching it in favour of business. In 1959, he married his school sweetheart, Ruth. The couple lived in Roslyn and later Montauk, New York. At the time of his arrest, he listed his primary residence as a condo on New York's Upper East Side. This was only part of his declared property portfolio that included a house in Palm Beach, Florida, and another in France.

**SELF-MADE MADOFF**

Madoff did not come from old money: the newlyweds scrimped and saved $5,000 to set up Bernard L. Madoff Investment Securities LLC in 1960. The firm began as a 'penny stock' trader – dealing with stocks worth under $5 that could be bought over the counter. Madoff could not compete directly with the big boys on the New York Stock Exchange (NYSE), so he experimented with the then new computer technology to quote stock prices and fulfill orders for the retail brokers who dealt with small investors.

Madoff prospered and became a leading member of the National Association of Securities Dealers (NASD), the private body that oversaw the stock market, which had an advisory role with the SEC. When the NASD founded NASDAQ in 1971, the new exchange used the computer technology that Madoff's firm had pioneered. In 2008, Madoff Investment Securities was the largest market-maker on NASDAQ and the sixth-largest on the NYSE. Madoff himself served several terms as chairman of NASDAQ. Unlike other Ponzi scams, Madoff's scheme did not promise unrealistic returns of 20 per cent plus. He offered his investors a steady ten per cent on their money, which as long as the market was rising would not raise suspicions. He ran a double set of books, the public one fabricated to satisfy his investors, auditors and the SEC, and a private one that kept his Ponzi scheme afloat.

Madoff got away with it for so long because he wasn't just a Wall Street insider, he was a founding member of the U.S. free-market capitalist system. Doubting his honesty would probably be the same as accusing George Washington of being in the pay of the British or Abraham Lincoln of being a secret pro-slaver. During the 1970s and '80s the U.S. prospered, and Madoff prospered with it. He was a family man: wife Ruth, sons Andrew and Mark, brother Peter and niece Shana all worked for the firm and earned handsome paycheques and bonuses. True to that other great American tradition of the wealthy giving back through charitable donations and endowments, Madoff was a generous philanthropist and political donor. He was a trustee of and financial adviser to several charitable, cultural and educational bodies; he donated $6 million to lymphoma research; and he endowed the Madoff Family Foundation, which he ran with wife Ruth, with $19 million of what turned out to be other people's money. The foundation funded a range of cultural, health and educational projects, many of them in the Jewish community.

DOUBTING HIS HONESTY WOULD PROBABLY BE THE SAME AS ACCUSING GEORGE WASHINGTON OF BEING IN THE PAY OF THE BRITISH OR ABRAHAM LINCOLN OF BEING A SECRET PRO-SLAVER.

Madoff did not manage to fool everyone. In 1999 and again in 2005 and 2007, financial analyst Harry Markopolos reported Madoff to the SEC, but he was so well respected and so well connected that the authorities failed to investigate the complaints. What did for Madoff was the credit crunch. A Ponzi scheme depends on a steady volume of new investors to put funds in with which the scheme can pay off existing investors. While the good times rolled, investors got their money. As long as times were good, more money flowed in than out, and investigators estimate that half of the scheme's investors profited. But with the financial crisis, when investors needed to withdraw money, Madoff could not plug the growing black hole at the centre of the scheme.

Having realised the game was up in December 2008, Madoff decided to come clean, and here comes the strangest part of the story. Remember that his closest business associates were his sons, niece, wife and brother. He admitted to his sons that his business had been a Ponzi scheme all along and was now going bust. They in turn reported their father to the authorities, and the rest, as they say, is in the court transcripts. But this leaves many unanswered questions, not least about the degree of complicity among Madoff's closest business associates. In an article on the breaking scandal, *Forbes* magazine posed a question that it's safe to assume was on the lips of many an outside observer: 'What his four family members in Ascot knew is a puzzle that everyone wants answered, but one thing is certain: it's virtually impossible to have returns like Madoff reported, and it should have been a major warning signal.'

**MADOFF COMES CLEAN**

Madoff was arrested and indicted for securities fraud on 11 December. His lawyer asked for bail and a twelve-year sentence, which he argued would match his client's natural lifespan, but the court rejected both petitions. In June 2009, the court ordered Madoff to pay back $170 billion and sentenced him to the maximum term of 150 years in prison. At the time of writing, legal actions are still continuing against Madoff family members to recover monies that they earned from the scheme.

The main victims of the scam were not the big institutional investors, who only have themselves to blame and can absorb the loss (or get the taxpayer to do so), but individual investors and non-profit-making organisations. Madoff was particularly good at targeting fellow Jews whom he met socially in Palm Beach and Long Island, and he took advantage of the less stringent regulations governing the investments of charitable foundations to escape detection. When Madoff Investment Securities went under it took down with it many Jewish charities working in the U.S. and overseas. Extraordinarily, Madoff not only betrayed the financial system he helped to create, he also exploited his co-religionists in the most cynical way possible, and then literally snatched the bread from the mouths of widows and orphans. Despite his ready admission of guilt, he has refused to reveal who else was involved in the scam. In possibly the only noble, but still perverse, act of his life, he had become the fall guy for his accomplices.

**WALL STREET**
The Madoff affair epitomised the gulf that had opened up between Wall Street and Main Street since the 1980s.

The really interesting thing about Madoff is not that he got away with it for such a long time, the amount he scammed, or the fact that the regulators trusted him to such an extent that they refused to investigate his business dealings, but why he did it at all. He was a successful businessman, with the trust of the business community, the regulators, and his investors, who could have made several sizeable fortunes honestly. Even during the worst recession to hit the world since 1929, Wall Street seems to be managing to make handsome profits and pay its executives large salaries and bonuses. Why throw everything away – reputation, family, the trust of his own community? Maybe he realised that the system was so flawed and so easy to exploit that he did it just because he could; maybe he was driven by some deep-seated drive to self-destruction or by the thrill of seeing how long he could avoid getting caught.

With the puzzle that is Bernard Madoff, we come to the end of this survey of deception through the ages. We have seen different types of deceits: in Antiquity and the Middle Ages, when religion was at the centre of everyday life, religious frauds were common; when gender roles and social classes were rigidly differentiated in the early modern period, we saw many cases of imposture and cross-dressing. The modern period has seen deceptions that take advantage of new technologies – photography, film and video – to create convincing counterfeits.

And with their escapist tendencies, modern-day humans have tried to convince themselves of the existence of fairies, monsters and aliens.

As finance has become the driving force in the evolution of human affairs, however, so financial scams have taken centre stage. Financial frauds have been so frequent in the past fifty years that this whole book could have been devoted to them. Does this mean that dishonesty is built into Western capitalism? When happiness is equated with power, wealth and fame, it's not so surprising that some people decide to take shortcuts to obtain them. But the lesson that anyone should take away from these pages, is that, possibly with the exception of Mr. Madoff, who got away with his Ponzi scheme for thirty years, and Mr. Abagnale, who made a business of unmasking fraudsters, very few of our scammers, impostors and confidence tricksters have benefited from their extraordinary schemes. The sad truth is that if they had applied their intelligence, talents and charm to legitimate pursuits, they probably would have led much more contented lives.

# FURTHER READING

There are many good general reference works available in printed form or online covering many of the entries featured in this book. Still one of the most authoritative is the *Encyclopaedia Britannica*, available for free at most large public and school libraries, and online at britannica.com as a subscription service. Another reference source that is increasingly used by authors and journalists is the ubiquitous Wikipedia (en.wikipedia.org). The content of Wikipedia, however, is user-generated, and is not independently verified. As a result there are inaccurate or biased articles included in the Wiki database. Nevertheless, it provides a good starting point to find references on most topics.

Specialist websites that I have found useful for this book include the *Catholic Encyclopaedia* (newadvent.org/cathen) and the Museum of Hoaxes (museumofhoaxes.com). All website addresses were correct at the time of writing, but it is the nature of the Internet that URLs change. If a website is no longer active or has moved, please conduct a search on the topic in a search engine such as google.com. The most recent entries are not yet covered in books, but a great deal of material is available from websites such as the BBC, CNN, major English-language newspapers and the online archives of magazines such as *The Economist, Newsweek, Vanity Fair* and *The New Yorker.*

The books and articles listed below fall into two categories: in certain instances, they provide detailed accounts of the topics covered in the entries; in others they give the reader a general background on the period, person or topic. I have tried to include both whenever these were available. Several of the books included are strongly biased either for or against the topic under discussion. Whenever such a book is included, I have also included a balancing work supporting the opposite point of view.

I have also included materials about entries in other media, including videos of hoax films (most of these are available at Internet sites such as youtube.com) and also film and TV dramatisations of the events described in the entries, though often these do not necessarily stick faithfully to the facts, and take Hollywood liberties with storylines and characters.

## Ancient Oracles

Curnow, T. (2004) *The Oracles of the Ancient World,* London: Duckworth

Broad, W. J. (2007) *The Oracle: Ancient Delphi and the Science Behind Its Lost Secrets*, New York: Penguin Press

## Odysseus

Homer (2003) *The Iliad,* trans. by P. Jones, London: Penguin Books

Homer (2006) *The Odyssey,* trans. by R. Fagles, London: Penguin Books

Strauss, B. (2006) *The Trojan War: A New History*, New York: Simon & Schuster

## Nero

Shotter, D. (2008) *Nero Caesar Augustus,* Harlow: Pearson

Suetonius trans. by Graves, R. (2007) *The Twelve Caesars,* London: Penguin Books

Griffin, M. T. (1985) *Nero: The End of a Dynasty*, New Haven, CT: Yale University Press, 1985

## *The Donation of Constantine*

Bowersock, G. W. (2008) *On the Donation of Constantine,* Cambridge, MA: Harvard University Press

Chamberlin, E. R. (2003) *The Bad Popes,* London: The History Press

Becher, M. (2003) *Charlemagne*, trans. by D. S. Bachrach, New Haven, CT: Yale University Press

## Pope Joan

Cross, D. Woolfolk (2009) *Pope Joan,* New York: Three Rivers Press

*Pope Joan* (2009) motion picture, dir. Sonke Wortmann

## Hua Mulan

Kingston, M. H. (1981) *The Woman Warrior,* London: Picador

*Mulan* (1998) Animated film, Disney Animated Pictures

## Lambert Simnel and Perkin Warbeck

Hicks, M. (2003) *Richard III,* London: The History Press

Bucholz, R. O. (2009) *Early Modern England, 1485–1714,* Oxford: Wiley–Blackwell

William Shakespeare's Wars of the Roses cycle of history plays (1590s): *Richard II, Henry IV (Parts 1 & 2), Henry V, Henry VI (Parts 1, 2 & 3), Richard III*

## Fake Relics and Indulgences

Chaucer, G. (2005) 'The Pardoner's Tale' in *The Canterbury Tales,* London: Penguin Books

Swanson, R. N. (2007) *Indulgences in Late Medieval England,* Cambridge: Cambridge University Press

Vauchez, A. (1997) *Sainthood in the Later Middle Ages,* Cambridge: Cambridge University Press

http://www.catholic-ew.org.uk/ccb/catholic_church/relics_of_st_therese_of_lisieux/what_are_relics

## The False Dimitrys

Hosking, G. (2002) *Russia and the Russians,* London: Penguin Books

Perrie, M. (2002) *Pretenders and Popular Monarchism in Early Modern Russia,* Cambridge: Cambridge University Press

## 'Count' Cagliostro

Faulks, P. (2008) *The Masonic Magician: The Life and Death of Count Cagliostro and His Egyptian Rite,* London: Watkins Publishing

McCalman, I. (2004) *The Seven Ordeals of Count Cagliostro,* London: Arrow Books

## William Ireland

Ireland, W. H. (2001 [1805]) *The Confessions of William Henry Ireland,* Elibron Classics

Pierce, P. (2004) *The Great Shakespeare Fraud: The Strange, True Story of William-Henry Ireland,* Stroud: Sutton Publishing

## Chevalier and Chevalière d'Éon

D'Éon de Beaumont, C. (2001) *The Maiden of Tonnerre: The Vicissitudes of the Chevalier and the Chevalière d'Éon,* trans. by R. Champagne, N. Ekstein, and G. Kates, Baltimore: Johns Hopkins University Press

Grzesiak, N. (2000) *Le Chevalier d'Éon,* Paris: Acropole

## Caraboo of Javasu

Raison, J. and Goldie, M. (1994) *The Servant Girl Princess Caraboo,* Moreton-in-the-Marsh: Windrush Press

Wells, J. (1994) *Princess Caraboo: Her True Story,* London: Pan Macmillan

## Hong Xiuquan

Reilly, T. H. (2004) *The Taiping Heavenly Kingdom: Rebellion and the Blasphemy of Empire,* Seattle: University of Washington Press

Spence, J. D. (1996) *God's Chinese Son,* New York: Norton

## Feejee Mermaid

Barnum, P. T. (2005) *The Colossal P.T. Barnum Reader: Nothing Else Like It in the Universe,* ed. By J. W. Cook, Champaign, IL: University of Illinois Press

## *Ompax spatuloides* and the Furry Trout

G. P. Whitley, G. P. (2009) 'Laporte, François Louis Nompar de Caumont (1810–1880)' in the *Australian Dictionary of Biography,* online edition

## Piltdown Man

Weiner, J. S. and Stringer, C. (2003 [1955]) *The Piltdown Forgery,* Oxford: Oxford University Press

Spencer, F. (1990) *Piltdown: A Scientific Forgery,* Oxford: Oxford University Press

## The Cottingley Fairies

Conan Doyle, A. (2006 [1922]) *The Coming of the Fairies,* London: Hodder & Stoughton

http://www.cottingley.net/fairies.shtml

Randi, J. (1982), *Flim-Flam!,* Amherst, NY: Prometheus Books

## Charles Ponzi

Zuckoff, M. (2006) *Ponzi's Scheme: The True Story of a Financial Legend,* New York: Random House

Dunn, D. (2004) *Ponzi: The Incredible True Story of the King of Financial Cons,* New York: Broadway

### Anna Anderson

Welch, F. (2007) *A Romanov Fantasy: Life at the Court of Anna Anderson,* New York: Norton

Massie, R. K. (1995) *The Romanovs: The Final Chapter*, New York: Random House

### Artur Alves Reis

Teigh Bloom, M. (1966) *The Man Who Stole Portugal,* London: Secker & Warburg

Wigan, H. (2004) 'The Effects of the Portuguese Bank Note Crisis', Working Paper No 82/04, London School of Economics

### The Zinoviev Letter

Bennett, G. (2006) *Churchill's Man of Mystery: Desmond Morton and the World of Intelligence,* London: Taylor & Francis.

The National Archives (2009) 'The Zinoviev Letter', (http://yourarchives.nationalarchives.gov.uk)

### Victor Lustig

Johnson, J. F. and Miller, F. (1961) *The Man Who Sold the Eiffel Tower,* New York: Doubleday

Velinger, J. (2003) 'Victor Lustig, the man who (could have) sold the world', Radio Prague online (http://www.radio.cz/en)

### Stanisława Walasiewicz

Tibballs, G. (2003) *Great Sporting Scandals,* London: Robson Books

### Lysenkoism

Joravsky, D. (1970) *The Lysenko Affair,* Cambridge, MA: Harvard University Press

Soyfer, V. N. (1994) *Lysenko and the Tragedy of Soviet Science*, New Brunswick: Rutgers University Press

### Marius Casadesus

http://www.casadesus.com

Eisen, C. (2006) *The Cambridge Mozart Encyclopedia*, Cambridge: Cambridge University Press

### Loch Ness Monster Hoaxes

Bauer, H. H. (1986) *The Enigma of Loch Ness,* Champaign, IL: University of Illinois Press

Martin, D. and Boyd, A. (1999) *Nessie: The Surgeon's Photograph Exposed*, Books for Dillons only (on-demand publishing)

### Operation Fortitude

Howard, M. E. and Hinsley, F. H. (1990) *British Intelligence in the Second World War: Volume 5, Strategic Deception*, Cambridge: Cambridge University Press

Axelrod, A. (2006) *Patton: A Biography*, Basingstoke: Palgrave Macmillan

### George Adamski

Solomon, Professor (1998) *How to Make the Most of a Flying Saucer Experience,* Baltimore: Top Hat Press

www.adamskifoundation.com, the official site of the George Adamski Foundation, which upholds Adamski's claims about UFOs and his alien encounters

### Elmyr de Hory

*F for Fake* (1974) movie directed by Orson Welles

Irving, C. (1969) *Fake! The Story of Elmyr de Hory the Greatest Art Forger of Our Time,* New York: McGraw-Hill

### The Brassiere Brigade

McIver, S. B. (1995) *Murder in the Tropics*, Sarasota, FL: Pineapple Press

### 'Black Admiral' Portrait

Baard, E. (2006) 'A Painting's Secret', *The New Yorker Magazine Archive Website*

### Cyril Hoskin

Rampa, Lobsang T. (1956) *The Third Eye,* London: Secker & Warburg

www.lobsangrampa.net, a website that still presents Hoskin's fake biography

## Vinland Map

Seaver, K. A. (2004) *Maps, Myths and Men: The Story of the Vinland Map,* Stanford, CA: Stanford University Press

Skelton, R. A. *et al.* (1965) *The Vinland Map and the Tartar Relation,* New Haven, CT: Yale University Press

## Spaghetti Harvest

www.museumofhoaxes.com has an excellent database of April Fool's Day hoaxes

www.youtube.com for the original broadcast of the Swiss Spaghetti Harvest, 1957

## Frank W. Abagnale, Jr.

Abagnale, F. W. (1980) *Catch Me If You Can,* New York: Grosset & Dunlap

www.abagnale.com

## The *Dossiers Secrets*

Baigent, M., Leigh, R., and Lincoln, H. (2005) *Holy Blood, Holy Grail,* New York: Delacorte Press

Brown, D. (2004) *The Da Vinci Code,* New York: Doubleday

Olson, C. E. (2004) *The Da Vinci Hoax,* San Francisco: Ignatius Press

## The Patterson–Gimlin Film

Daegling, D. J. (2004) *Bigfoot Exposed: An Anthropologist Examines America's Enduring Legend,* Walnut Creek, CA: Altamira Press

Patterson, R. and Murphy, C. L. (2005) *The Bigfoot Film Controversy,* Blaine, WA: Hancock House

## Dr. Charlotte Bach

Bach, C. (1973) 'Homo Mutans, Homo Luminens: An Introduction to Human Ethology', unpub. MSS, London School of Economics

Wheen, F. (2002) *Who Was Dr Charlotte Bach?* London: Short Books

www.charlottebach.org

## Clifford Irving

Irving, C. (2007) *The Hoax,* New York: Hyperion

Irving, C. (2008) *Howard Hughes: The Autobiography,* London: John Blake Publishing

*The Hoax* (2006) movie directed by Lasse Hallström

## Crop Circles

Schnabel, J. (2002) *Round in Circles,* New York: Prometheus

www.circlemakers.org

Irving, R. and Lundberg, J. (2006) *The Field Guide: The Art, History and Philosophy of Crop Circle Making,* London: Strange Attractor

Pringle, L. (2004) *Crop Circles,* Norwich: Jarrold Publishing

## Nick Perry

*Lucky Numbers* (2000) movie directed by Nora Ephron

www.tubecityonline.com/history/perry.html

## Thatchergate

www.southern.com/southern/label/CRC/1238.html has a copy of the transcript and the press coverage of the Thatchergate affair

Beckett, C. (2006) *Margaret Thatcher,* London: Haus Publishing Ltd

## The Hitler Diaries

Harris, R. (1987) *Selling Hitler,* New York: Penguin Books

Henry, W. A., Lee, G. and Ludtke, M. (1983) 'Hitler's Diaries: Real or Fake?' *Time,* 9 May 1983

## Pons and Fleischmann

Fleischmann, M., Pons, S., Anderson, M. W., Li, L. J., Hawkins, M. (1990) 'Calorimetry of the Palladium–Deuterium–Heavy Water System', *Journal of Electroanalytical Chemistry,* 287: 293–348

Simon, B. (2002) *Undead Science: Science Studies and the Afterlife of Cold Fusion,* New Brunswick, NJ: Rutgers University Press

## Alien Autopsy

*Alien Autopsy* (2006) movie directed by Jonny Campbell. Spoof about the Alien Autopsy hoax

Footage of the Alien Autopsy hoax can be seen on alienvideo. net and youtube.com

### Frédéric Bourdin

Grann, D. (2008) 'The Chameleon', *The New Yorker,* 11 August

http://news.bbc.co.uk/1/hi/world/europe/4087370.stm, 'France holds "Chameleon" impostor'


### Hwang Woo-suk

BBC News 'S Korea cloning research was fake' at newsbbc.co.uk, 23 December 2005

BBC News 'Profile: Hwang Woo-suk' at newsbbc.co.uk, 26 October 2009

BBC News 'S Korea clone scientist convicted' at newsbbc.co.uk, 26 October 2009


### Kazutsugi Nami

BBC News 'Chairman arrested in Japan "scam"' at newsbbc.co.uk, 5 February 2009

*Japan Times* online 'L&G execs arrested over investor fraud', Friday, 6 February 2009


### Bernard Madoff

Arvedlund, E. (2009) 'How Bernard Madoff Escaped Detection' at FT.com

Arvedlund, E. (2009) *Madoff: The Man Who Stole $65 Billion,* London: Penguin

BBC News 'Unravelling the Madoff Hustle' at newsbbc.co.uk, 26 June 2009

BBC News 'Fraudster Madoff Gets 150 years' at newsbbc.co.uk, 29 June 2009

www.guardian.co.uk/business/bernard-madoff for stories on the Madoff affair

www.vanityfair.com has an excellent Madoff archive